UNBOUND

A STORY OF SNOW AND SELF-DISCOVERY

STEPH JAGGER

HARPER WAVE

UNBOUND. Copyright © 2017 by Stephanie Jagger. All rights reserved. Printed in the United States of America. No part of this book may be used or reproduced in any manner whatsoever without written permission except in the case of brief quotations embodied in critical articles and reviews. For information, address HarperCollins Publishers, 195 Broadway, New York, NY 10007.

HarperCollins books may be purchased for educational, business, or sales promotional use. For information, please email the Special Markets Department at SPsales@harpercollins.com.

Republished with permission of Princeton University Press, from *The King and the Corpse* by Heinrich Zimmer © 1993; permission conveyed through Copyright Clearance Center, Inc.

FIRST EDITION

Designed by Bonni Leon-Berman

Library of Congress Cataloging-in-Publication Data has been applied for.

ISBN 978-0-06-241810-4

17 18 19 20 21   RRD   10 9 8 7 6 5 4 3 2 1

To my father, who taught me how to ski,
and to my husband, who taught me how to fly.

Contents

THE SEEDS of all our thoughtlessly accomplished deeds have quietly accumulated in a dark and hidden treasury—the subsoil, so to speak, of our life of consciousness. And it is as though a thread of destiny that we had long been spinning had slowly entangled us without our knowing, and now, by some accident, were suddenly jerked taut. We discover that we are trapped in an inescapable net into which we have thoughtlessly delivered ourselves. We are implicated in an adventure of unknown proportions. And even if we meet it with self-confidence and the best of faith, it will inevitably prove to be something very different, very much more complicated, dangerous, and difficult, than we expect. Since we permitted it to escape us in its entirety, it cannot but astonish us now in its details.

—**HEINRICH ZIMMER**, *THE KING AND THE CORPSE*

INTRODUCTION: The First Crack

I WAS ON ALL FOURS in a gravel parking lot, cowering like a wounded dog. My knees were planted firmly in the dirt, my tail was tucked, and little bits of rock and sharp scree dug into the palms of my hands. Scattered around me was all of my gear, lying facedown where I'd flung it. My skis and poles were huddled together like shell-shocked soldiers, and my backpack lay still, totally lifeless. My helmet was to my right. It rolled gently from side to side, mocking me from the cheap seats. This had not been part of the plan.

My breath began to hitch. Two or three sharp inhales before everything inside me came pouring out in a wet, choppy howl. The sound ripped through the air with force, tearing it right down the middle.

I was three months into a year-long adventure, a ski-based Blizzard of Oz I'd dreamed up in an effort to prove, once and for all, that I was worth my salt and then some. So imagine my surprise when I found myself here—not on top of a mountain but at the bottom, in the parking lot, wailing at the world in anger and frustration.

Tears slipped down my cheeks, and thin strands of drool ran over my lips and chin. I watched a whole river of snot as it dripped from my face to the small patch of gravel in front of me, and I saw the earth do the work it was made to do—soak everything up. For better or worse, it absorbed it all. A few wisps of my hair blew around in the wind, sticking to my cheeks and lips for a brief moment before taking off once again. I wondered if the threads of my discomfort would do the same, if the humiliation of not being able to man up on that particular day could be soaked up or blown away. I hoped it would.

Everything around me was shrapnel, chewed up and spit out just like I'd been that day. Thick splinters of rock and fragmented stone had been cast off the mountains and crushed into a fine chalky powder, ground down by tire chains and the tread of four-wheel drives. This was a place for the rugged. This was Arthur's Pass, in the Southern Alps of New Zealand, and there I was on my hands and knees, a stance that, unless you're an MMA fighter in the midst of a ground and pound, does not suggest rugged.

And if I wanted anything in life, it was to be that: the unflinching, capable-of-withstanding kind of rugged. I wanted to be seen as the person who marched into the arena, and I wanted to be known as the one who remained on my feet, or in this case, on my skis. I wanted proof I could go it alone, proof that I was man enough, strong enough, and finally good enough. Hence the very goal I had created for myself—five continents, 4 million vertical feet of skiing, chasing winter around the world with what most people were calling "a huge set of balls." But alas, there I was, three months in, staring straight down at the dirt. This had not been part of the plan.

"Get up," I told myself. "Get up." The scorn was thick on my tongue.

I may have been naive going into all of this, but not naive enough to think I could get through ten months of solo globetrotting without a few lousy days in the mix. This wasn't my first time at the rodeo. I'd traveled to far-flung places, I'd been to foreign countries before. I had a decent grasp of what form and flavor of shit might come flying my way. On top of that, I'd spent a fair bit of time thinking about the demands of this particular trip. I knew there would be missed flights and frustrated cabdrivers. I knew I would stay in hotel rooms whose bedspreads could light up an episode of *CSI: Miami*. I understood what would be required of my body—I was sure to lose toenails and gain thigh. I knew the skin on my nose and cheeks would chap, dry, and peel off. My clothes would stink. I would stink.

I also knew I would lose things. Little bits of my gear were sure to be strewn and scattered all over the world. Sunglasses would be the first to go, they always are, but guidebooks, plug converters, and underwear, the pairs I would hand-wash in hotel sinks and leave hanging in dank little washrooms, they would go too.

I was good with all that. In some strange way, I looked forward to it. Every grand adventure is better with a few war stories, a badge or two of honor for the victor. But perhaps that's what I was most naive about. All of the above were mere mishaps, trite challenges, and situations in which I could easily prove my bravado and maintain a sense of control. It was the latter that hadn't occurred to me: the possibility that I might lose exactly that—control—especially in the way I was losing it now. It was a conundrum that even the strongest piece of duct tape couldn't solve, and let me tell you, I packed a fair bit of duct tape in the event of conundrums.

There were two other cars in the parking lot, and unless they were hiding, terrified of interrupting a woman in the throes of an adult temper tantrum, there were no people. No humans to see me or hear me, thank God. This was not an example of "playing it cool," which, on a side note, is something my best friend Alix believes is my greatest strength. I dreaded being caught like this, in a place where my emotions had pushed me down and pinned me to the ground; if I was going to flail about in a pool of self-humiliation, I much preferred to do it alone.

Get. Up.

I wiped my nose with the back of my hand and reached for the dinged-up trailer hitch of my rental car. I pulled myself to standing and fished the car keys out of my pocket. I lifted the back gate of the car and slouched down on the bumper. My calves trembled as I unbuckled my ski boots and pulled each of them off. I looked down at the worn buckles, little bits of paint and enamel missing from the edges. I watched as the boots slipped out of my hand and I heard them hit the ground, crunching against the gravel, little rocks scraping at their outer shells.

I took a breath and shook my head.

"Get your shit together, Jagger," I said.

There would be no emotional coup today. I wouldn't allow it. Instead, I did what I always did. I did what strong people do. I whipped up a speech—a scolding, disguised as a pep talk. Something to cut me down to size and get me back on track.

I'm three months in, I'm already behind, and I feel like I'm splintering in two. That can't happen. This trip isn't about cracking open. This isn't about getting to know my worst and my weakest. This is about my best and my bravest. Get up.

The lecture worked like a charm. But what I didn't know at the time was that becoming one's best and being one's bravest involves cracking open. It means shattering most, if not all, of ourselves. If I had known that, if I had any inkling this journey was going to involve my ego and a sledgehammer, I would have stayed just where I was. Because who chooses to walk into a mess like that? Who brings in a wrecking ball when the load-bearing walls are still, you know, bearing loads? No one. We wait until we're broken, we wait until our lives are a crumbling mess, before we examine ourselves, before we look in the mirror. No one ups and changes a close-to-perfect life.

The late afternoon sun cut through the air, revealing layers of dust that hung from the sky in thick slabs. Spring was encroaching. I could smell it, warm wood expanding in the heat. On the edge of the parking lot, giant beech trees stood at attention, wearing moss-colored jackets. I looked down at all of my gear strewn about on the ground. The answer was simple: I would clean it all up and move on. I would sleep it off and start skiing again in the morning. Somewhere different. Somewhere that wasn't a shit show. I would keep going, and I would ignore the crack that had started to run straight down my load-bearing beam.

I gathered everything up, threw it in the back of the car, and climbed in. I sat for a few minutes and looked out at the mountains. Arthur's Pass is one of the highest vertebrae of the South Island's mountainous spine, a rocky divide between east and west. Far below the surface there are two tectonic plates, whose sole purpose seems to be forcing themselves upon one another, pushing and twisting in order to form a craggy artery that, quite literally, splits the South Island in two. The Maori once used this very place as a hunting route, a path from the calm shores and rolling plains of the east to the unruly hem of the Tasman Sea in the west, from one side of a place to another.

Perhaps I shouldn't have been surprised to find myself there. Perhaps it was the perfect place for the first fracture to form in my carefully built facade. It was, after all, a place where glaciers and deeply gorged rivers have worked for eons to expose the marrow, a place where land is literally being carved from the bone. If it hadn't been for the blindfold my ego had firmly wrapped around my face, perhaps I would have seen it all coming.

I started the engine, pulled out of the lot, and made my way onto a small dirt road. This whole skiing-around-the-world thing—it was as going to be a hell of a lot harder than I originally thought.

PART ONE

THE TIP OF THE ICEBERG

She puts on her armor, mounts her modern-day
steed, leaves loved ones behind, and goes in search
of the golden treasure.

—MAUREEN MURDOCK, *THE HEROINE'S JOURNEY*

1

A BLUE TIN SIGN AND
A BOX OF RIBBONS

ALTHOUGH CONSIDERED a major north-south artery, Highway 99 is better described as a small Canadian throughway. It winds north from the US border before vanishing into the depths of British Columbia. Drive halfway up the curvy two-laner, and you'll find yourself in Whistler, a resort town tucked into the Coast mountain range.

Naturally, Whistler's a bit of a showboat. A series of glaciers sit sparkling at her crown, and a national park runs down her back like a thick sheet of hair. It would be easy to mistake her as a love child, the result of some torrid affair between a place like Chamonix and a rugged Canadian lumberjack. She has a rough kind of beauty, but there's also a refinement, the kind that lets you know she won't be staying the night. Oh, who's kidding who? Enough Aussies live there now that you can count on her staying the night.

Many people recognize Whistler by name, but not many know

she boasts two gargantuan mountains, Whistler and Blackcomb. She is beyond compare, a giant snowy behemoth, and a place of true Canadian glory. In fact, the only thing that could be more Canadian or more majestic would be Celine Dion and Justin Bieber coming together for a three-night commitment at one of the casinos near Niagara Falls, which, upon the arrival of "Biebon," would suddenly turn into a cascade of tawny maple syrup.

In 1989 my parents purchased a cabin in Whistler. I was eight years old, and lucky as shit. The cabin was a two-hour drive from our house in Vancouver, and we went there most weekends. It was a habit I kept through to adulthood, the mountains calling me north each winter through my early twenties.

Every Friday I would leave work, walk the few blocks from my apartment to the bus terminal, and hop on the express bound for Whistler. Once there, I loaded onto a local bus that dropped me off on a road just above my parents' cabin. I used to stand on the road and watch the bus drive away, its lights getting dimmer and dimmer until finally I was left in the dark, nothing but my own breath hanging in the air, and a gazillion stars up above me. I'd stand in the stillness, questions about what came next in my life on pause, expectations frozen, if only for a few minutes.

I savored that moment on the road, when there was nothing around but me. It was solace, a temporary reprieve from my fixation on what came after this and then after that, from my single-minded focus on ticking the boxes of life's to-do list.

One Friday in February of 2009, the scene was no different. I escaped up to Whistler and lingered outside as the bus pulled away. A small amount of boredom had crept into my life of late. I was content, happy with everything I had and everything I'd done, but it still wasn't enough. My life had begun to feel like a collection of kindling, and I wanted big blocks of wood, and giant sparks to go with them.

My entire life to date had been spent doing one thing and one thing only—chasing after goals in dogged pursuit of accomplishment. At twenty-five, after years of darting from one goal to the next in a blur of box-ticking and brisk achievement, I'd already checked off many of the biggest boxes: I'd sailed through multiple academic requirements, and my passport was covered in stamps. I'd run in multiple marathons and a handful of triathlons. I had a good job in sales and marketing, I'd bought a big-city condo with money of my own, filled it with all the right things, and with the cash left over, I'd made my first investments. My life was a laser-focused blaze of efficiency and execution designed around being able to answer the question "What's next?"—one that I spat out on a regular occasion and worked hard to answer with in-your-face boldness. It was a truly obsessive quest.

That night, I couldn't shake a niggling sense of dissatisfaction, the idea that I was missing something, that what was next was something more, bigger, better, and different from what I had now. I tilted my head to the sky. A rush of air moved across my face, and goose bumps rose up on my skin. I felt huge flakes of snow land on my cheeks and eyelashes, and watched as thousands of lace doilies fell from the sky. The stars were in hiding, and my predictions from earlier that afternoon had been right—the sheets of rain in Vancouver had traveled north and turned into snow. A lot of it.

Thick confetti slammed into the mountains all night long, and when I woke up the next morning, I could barely believe my eyes. Everything in sight was covered in a deep, downy layer of snow, and in a rare trifecta of perfection, especially for Whistler, it was also sunny and bone-bitingly cold. I drank my coffee, made a plan to meet a few friends, and watched as tiny snow crystals floated through the air like fairy dust. I knew we were in for an epic day of skiing.

With blue skies cracking open above us and a knee-deep carpet of snow under our skis, we opted for the Whistler side of the resort. More specifically, we hit up an area of the mountain dominated by two fast-moving chairlifts, Symphony and Harmony. From the lift we could see three massive bowls of untouched powder beneath us, each filled to the brim.

All morning, and well into the afternoon, we skied those bowls until we hit their gutters, arriving at the bottom of each run completely and utterly spent. Once there, we loaded back onto the lifts and did it again. We skied hard all day long—harder than hard. My legs were throbbing, lactic acid spread from my quads to my calves, and then finally down into my feet and my tiny little toes. It was a euphoric mix—I was fully awake but completely exhausted. I wanted the feeling to last.

Each chairlift ride was a blessing, ten minutes of badly needed rest and recovery. I collapsed onto one of them in the late afternoon and leaned back. My feet dangled below me, and my head came to a rest on the back of the chair. I looked up into the sky and inhaled deeply, releasing the air as my cheeks turned up in a smile.

And then, right there, perhaps because of all that fairy dust, I was struck with a grand idea, a bolt straight out of the shining blue sky. It was the answer to "What's next?" and the perfect box for me to strike a giant check through. Or perhaps, more accurately, it was exactly what was needed to fan all the flames.

I immediately announced my idea.

"I'm gonna do this," I said with confidence. "I'm going to quit my job and ski around the world." I felt a shiver move up my right arm.

Silence hung heavy in the air. Other than some light panting, leftover breath from our last run, there was no response.

A few moments passed, and the silence was replaced with a light snickering sound. Then chuckles. Then full snorting.

"Good one, Jagger," said one of the guys. "Now that's what I call a fucking pipe dream!"

"Yeah! What's stopping you?" added my friend Scott before crumpling forward in laughter.

Eventually they all chimed in, each taking turns to shoot down what was a truly absurd and, apparently, comical idea.

"Don't you think you're a little young to retire?" one of them said.

"You're a good skier, Jagger. But you're not *that* good."

"Sounds nice, but remember that little thing you've got called a mortgage?"

It was enough to snuff out the small flame, and it didn't take long for my own voice to chime in.

They're right. I laughed, shaking my head from side to side. *What the fuck am I thinking? I've done big goals, but that's a little much.*

As we approached the top of the lift, a blue tin sign caught my eye:

RAISE RESTRAINING DEVICE

Another shiver. This one started at the base of my spine and moved up through my body, causing my shoulders to shudder.

I'd seen the sign before, thousands of times. It's posted at the top of every lift in the resort—but this time something was different, something about it made me pause. I looked back at it one more time:

RAISE RESTRAINING DEVICE

What's holding me back? I asked myself. What's my restraining device? My job? My mortgage? I can figure out what to do with those things.

The match was lit. All I had to do now was drop it.

A series of questions instantly spun through my head: How long would this take? How much would it cost? What about plane tickets? I think I'm going to do this. Am I actually going to do this?

I was onto something, and I knew it. These kinds of bolts from the blue weren't new to me. "What's next?" was a question that lived on the tip of my tongue. I knew how to recognize answers as they came flying toward me, and I knew what to do with them the moment they arrived.

I got home that afternoon and Googled "round the world flights." Seventeen months later, I was at the boarding gate. I was going to follow winter around the world, and I was going to try to ski 4 million vertical feet in the time I was gone.[1]

Chasing winter around the globe with some pie-in-the-sky goal attached to the end made perfect sense to me. This was just the latest in a lifetime pursuit of blue ribbons, evidence of which can be found inside a white banker's box, one that sits in the guest room of my childhood home.

.˙●.

MY PARENTS HAVE LIVED in the same house for thirty-three years. I was a blond, adorably fat two-year-old when we moved in. The house is on a gorgeous tree-lined street in Vancouver. Cherry, birch, and maple trees bend from one side of the street to the other, creating a beautiful tunnel of leaves and flickering light. There are only a handful of evergreens in the neighborhood, and

---

1   Just in case you were wondering, the measurement of vertical feet looks at the vertical elevation drop from the top of a mountain to the bottom. This is different from total distance skied, which, to get all *Bill Nye the Science Guy* on you, depends on the steepness of the slope.

two of them sit on my parents' front lawn. If this were a fairy tale, and some might argue it is, those two trees would be the gate, the entrance into the world in which I grew up.

The guest room is by far my favorite room in the house. I love the light yellow paint on the walls and the cream-colored sheets my mom makes the bed with. I love the big windows that look out over the backyard, and the bright, clean light that pours in and tells me I'm home. I love the small white desk and the photo of my dad that sits on top of it. But out of everything in that room, the closet takes the cake. Every time I go back for a visit, I walk upstairs and head straight to that closet, because in my mind it's our family museum.

The closet is brimming with objects. First, there is a fine collection of hats: cowboy hats from my family's brief stint in the Wild West, a top hat from a costume party, and a large, wide-brimmed sun hat. There's also a rack full of dresses. Some are ladies in waiting, sitting patiently, wondering when their era is set to return. The others, like my sister's aubergine-colored prom dress, simply serve as a beautiful reminder of some great occasion in the past. On the floor, there are a handful of dusty and dated shoes, well worn from whatever decade they walked into and out of. And on a rack above the shoes is the banker's box. It's been sitting in that closet for seventeen years.

Most people would call it a memory chest, albeit a bit of a flimsy one, but to me it's a box full of proof. Inside, there's some faded memorabilia from my childhood, a scattering of small trinkets and tchotchkes, bundles of gossipy letters, and a handful of photos from the days of Fuji film. Mostly, though, the box is home to one thing: prize ribbons, a lot of them. And that's where the proof part comes in.

Given the sheer volume of ribbons, it would be easy to assume I was a competitive child, that my little elementary ego lived and died on the results of semiannual egg-and-spoon races. But assumptions can be tricky; they don't always tell the truth. What the box of ribbons really tells me is that somewhere deep inside myself, I thought that if I just kept showing up and crossing finish lines, there was a chance I would finally be seen. That one day, fingers crossed, I would become the person I'd always wanted to become, the one I was supposed to be, bound to be—another exemplary Jagger. That's what the whole box was about after all—proving that I could be just as good as the others, that I was one of them, that I could both fit in and stand out.

Next to the banker's box is a collection of something else—a small, disorganized stack of newspaper clippings and magazine articles beginning to yellow, curling ever so slightly at the corners. The stories in the clippings are about a woman who broke a world record. Each article chronicles her journey of skiing more vertical feet in one year than any other person. Each article provides a written account of her doing the extraordinary, achieving what many would call an impossible dream. That woman is me. I suppose an argument could be made that this achievement was yet another ribbon, final proof that I became the kind of Jagger people expected, but that would be mostly in name. What I really did was become someone else entirely.

2

GROWING UP GOAT AND A RED PILLBOX HAT

I RECENTLY read a fable called *The Roar of Awakening*. I wept when I read it because the story, like any good story, rolled to the center of things. Or, at the very least, it rolled to the center of *my* things.

It was about a baby tiger cub who had been adopted by a herd of goats. Like all animals, goats have a particular way of succeeding, expectations about what it means to be an exemplary goat. And because our baby cub believed he was a goat, he worked hard to be the best little billy possible. He ate like a goat, and talked like a goat, and spent his days doing all sorts of goaty things.

One day, an older tiger came upon the herd, and spotted the cub nibbling away on some grass.

"What on earth are you doing?" he roared. He grabbed the cub by the scruff of the neck and dragged him to a nearby pond. "Look!" he said, pointing down at the reflection. "You're not a goat. You're a tiger!"

The young tiger stared at the water and grew uneasy. He looked just like the older tiger. But I'm a goat, he thought to himself. I'm a goat.

Exasperated, the older tiger pulled the youngster back to the field. He killed one of the goats, tore off a piece of its flesh, and forced it into the mouth of the young cub. The older tiger watched as the youngster hesitantly gnawed on the meat. The cub slowly chewed, and then he chewed some more. Eventually, and much to his surprise, he licked his chops and growled in satisfaction. He stretched his front paws, and then, feeling his true nature for the very first time, he felt a strange noise bursting forth from his throat. It was the triumphant roar of a tiger.

I was raised by a herd of goats. I think a lot of us are. We're all surrounded by expectations. They might be different, but they're expectations nonetheless, inherited ways of doing and being, scripts for how and what we're supposed to accomplish, for who we're supposed to become.

I've been told that my script was pretty easy, and I have to agree. I had it good. My little goat herd was kind, and life within it was comfortable. As Paul Simon put it, I was born at the right time, and, I would add, to the right people, in the right neighborhood, with the right opportunities for goaty success.

My potential was clear and the path straightforward. What I was bound to do and who I was bound to become was obvious. I would eat from a well-manicured lawn, I would bleat in a moderate but conservative-leaning tone, and I would build a life that looked similar to the one my parents had built. It was set to include some great things, like a house, a marriage, and a gaggle of children who would spend their days bouncing up and down on a bright orange Sundance trampoline. There was an expectation of achievement and a built-in sense of abundance to match. Most people would call that a win-win.

Although the rules around this life weren't openly discussed, I am certain of their existence. They were woven into every thread of my family's DNA. I learned about this on the day I was born.

It was December, and the year was 1980. My three older siblings were brought to the hospital to meet the newest addition to the family, a healthy eight-pounder named Steph. My eldest brother Charlie expressed the keenest interest. He stepped in really close to get a good view, his hands resting on the edge of my pink baby blanket. After a short while he turned to face my parents and sighed. "She has *a lot* of rules to learn," he said with consternation.

I've heard my mother tell this story dozens of times, and each time she is beaming with pride. She would never play favorites, but my hunch has always been that she loves Charlie the most. Charlie who knows the rules. Charlie who *follows* the rules. Charlie whose brain is made of mostly pragmatic gray matter.

The other bits and bobs about my life, the school I went to, the games of kick-the-can we played in the lane, the conversations at our dinner table each night, were idyllic. It was the best of times. And if worst of times happened, I don't have a recollection of them. I was as happy as can be, living the kind of life that most people would beg, borrow, and steal for. I donned my woolly little goat cap with pride. I ate from the sweetest, greenest grass. I was exactly like the tiger cub.

Looking back there were some signs, small clues along the way that suggested I might not be the Jagger I thought I was. The first was the fact that, as hard as I tried, I could not curl my tongue. Every Jagger I knew could curl their tongue . . . and whistle. I couldn't whistle either.

It must be the cleft of my palate, I told myself in earnest, *or perhaps the roof of my mouth.*

Some evidence, though, was much harder to deny, like the words spoken by my own mother.

"Where did you come from?" she'd say, a mix of bewilderment and concern moving through her eyes.

She asked me this question a lot. It was a regular response to something I'd said or done.

She asked it when she found me sitting in my bedroom reading a copy of *Not Without My Daughter*. I was nine, and apparently quite curious about what could go wrong in Iran.

She asked it again when I told her I'd booked a ticket and would be traveling on my own through Equatorial Africa.

"Five months," I said. "I'll be gone for five months."

She must have asked the question a thousand times over, but it didn't matter. I didn't pause. Not once did I stop to reflect, to ask myself, *Right . . . where* do *I come from?* I never did this, because unfortunately I do have something in common with goats—I'm headstrong, I'm willful, and I'm stubborn as fuck.

Oh, and while I'm putting my cards on the table, I should also mention that I'm a Capricorn, so from an astrological perspective, I'm actually 100 percent goat. But I digress.

I ignored the evidence. I raced through life, sights set on ribbons, heart set on proving I was as good a goat as any. The clefts, the comments, and the proverbial questions, they were just things that got in my way—so, *whoosh*, under the carpet they went. Tiny little things swept right under the rug.

Perhaps that's what made it so difficult to walk into the forest and never look back. Because when you add it all up—the idyllic life in the perfect herd, the tenacious little girl dead set on fitting in, and the rug so thick it could cover up a slaughtered cow—well, it just makes sense to stay put. To play it safe. To shoot for the targets in front of me, the ones I was expected to hit. What crazy kid (that's a goat pun, by the way) would walk away from a life like this? What woman born into a win-win has the audacity to ask for something more? I sure as hell didn't know any.

MY MOTHER GREW UP in the home of an accountant, and my father under the roof of an engineer. Both of their lives were framed in good sense, with black-and-white matting placed perfectly around the edges. But of course there is always more to a picture than what has been set and mounted for us to see.

They met in the tenth grade. My father was hooked the moment he spotted her, a dark-haired Shirley MacLaine in her heyday walking through the hallways of Magee Secondary School. Between the freckles and the amply filled sweater set, any young man with a grain of common sense would have been. On their first date, they went to the Queen Elizabeth Theatre to see the Chad Mitchell Trio. My mom wore a gray dress, with red shoes and a matching pillbox hat. My parents have been inseparable ever since.

My granny used to tell stories of how cheeky my mother had been as a child. "Oh, she was naughty. Always getting into trouble," she would say before relaying her favorite stories about my mom's ill behavior. The time my mother convinced her younger sister to stick candy-shaped hearts so far up her nose that medical dislodging was required. Or the time my mom came downstairs and announced she was ready for church, her hair brushed out à la Billie "Buckwheat" Thomas. I've always loved thinking of my mother as a young woman walking up to the boundaries of life so she could stick her tongue out in the face of it all before making a farting noise and walking away. Maybe that's because I've never really met that woman, never really known that girl. Where did she come from? Where did she go?

My mother is still cheeky, but never in a way that could be interpreted as naughty or troublesome or anywhere close to breaking the rules. She was eighteen years old when she learned the difference, which, as it turned out, was a rather large one. Cheeky rarely has any actual consequences, and if there is one thing my mother knows well, it's consequences.

My parents found out they were pregnant in the fall of 1965. They were eighteen years old, just out of high school, and their options were limited. Parental consent was required if they wanted to marry, and although they loved each other, I don't think either of them wished to be married—not yet, not that early. Although abortion was an option, it wasn't yet legal. A medical procedure that took place in a basement or on someone's kitchen table, I'm sure it was deemed too risky in the hearts and minds of my young parents. So they went with the only other option remaining: my mother went to a camp for unwed girls. She gave her firstborn up for adoption, and promptly blocked the whole thing from her memory. From that point on, my mother kept her toes a safe distance from the line, and lived life well within the rules set out by . . . well, by just about anyone.

My parents got married a few years after their first child was born, and for more than two decades they kept his birth a secret. Perhaps my siblings saw it differently, but what I saw growing up was a woman who interpreted life as risk and consequence, as a contract written definitively in black-and-white terms. Although she was optimistic in general, her focus almost always narrowed in on what could go wrong, and she never looked for silver linings. That was, and still is, my father's job.

This isn't to say my mom isn't joyful or fun—she is, very much so. It's just that before she gets to the fun and enjoyment part of life, she spends a considerable amount of time losing sleep over things. Worry is her signature emotion. She wears it like other women her age wear Chanel No. 5. It has taken time, but I've come to understand her worry as a sign of her love. The more she frets about something or someone, the more she cares. And if this worry gives her a nosebleed, which it does on occasion, I interpret it as a sign of her complete and utter devotion. Although alarming in many ways, the sight of a white tissue in my mother's hand, balled up and spotted with bright red blood, is also comforting to me.

My mother wasn't my only female role model. There were other women in my life just beyond the space she occupied, but they all played a similar role. Regardless of the era in which they grew up, it seemed they were all reading from fairly traditional scripts. They knew their way around sewing machines and Cuisinarts, and they knew how to make the kind of loot bags that pleased a crowd. They packed lunches and shuttled kids to soccer games, piano lessons, and play dates. They brushed the teeth of toddlers and tucked them into bed. They made an art out of things like folding fitted sheets, something I've never come close to understanding how to do. These women were loyal, and they created the kinds of homes you wanted to run back to, the kinds of homes you *do* run back to. I can still smell the freshly baked scones, I can still hear their laugher from the kitchen as I bounce up and down on the bright green Radio Flyer inchworm. They loved and they worried.

All of this shaped my idea of what it meant to be a woman. But at the same time, the message of my generation was to dream big. We were the little girls who were told we could go on to do anything and become anyone we wanted. I found this to be confusing when I looked at the women around me, when I looked at my mother. Were they dreaming big? Were they doing anything and becoming anyone they wanted? It didn't seem so. How was it possible for them to be holding so much love in one hand, while the other seemed so full of restraint?

My mother still has the red pillbox hat from her first date with my father. She keeps it on the top shelf of her bedroom closet, away from the panoply of hats in the guest room. That's how I knew it was special. The other hats were hats. This hat was a crown.

When I was a little girl, I used to drag a chair through my

parents' room and over to her side of the closet. If I stood on my tippy-toes, I could just reach the top shelf. I would carefully unwrap the tissue paper, place it on the bedspread, and walk over to the mirror, hat in hand. I stood in front of that mirror many times, red pillbox hat on my head. It never quite fit. We were meant to wear different hats, she and I.

So what does a girl do when she realizes that her mother's hat doesn't fit on her head?

I consulted the book of unspoken rules and went straight to the section on rams. If I couldn't be my mother, I would have to be my father—or at a very minimum, I would have to pull off a masterful imitation. And when you're about to base your life on an imitation, it better be good. You're going to have to overcompensate, overaccomplish, and overcompete. You're going to have to spend your life in a quest for prize ribbons; otherwise, everyone will know you're a fraud.

I grew up in Canada, so you're probably thinking I went with the Rocky Mountain ram. But no, I chose the Markhor, because, well, have you ever seen one? They're the most majestic male goat on the planet. Their horns spiral into the air, three or four times the size of Angelina's horns in the movie *Maleficent*. If I was going to be a ram, and I was, I would have to go all the way. And the Markhor was all the way and then some.

So that's what I did. I outrammed the rams. I rammed all over the place. I pushed aside the example my mother had offered, the one she served on the table with love, and I turned a blind eye to my sister—she'd been first in line for the red pillbox hat anyways, and to be honest, it looked perfect on her. I picked out a set of sturdy blinders, put them on, and marched forward. I began measuring myself against my brothers' successes. I vied hard for my father's attention. I developed a masculine ideal, and I put my sweet little nose to the grindstone in order to meet it. I buried everything female deep down inside, and I sank my teeth into anything and everything that would help me be seen as a ram.

I worked hard to become everything I thought my father was. I made a checklist and then started ticking each and every one of the boxes. I took my ski instructor's course when I was sixteen years old, just like he did. I went to university, something not many women in my family had done. I made good money, and I used my horns to push my way up the corporate ladder. I owned my own place. I became a shoe connoisseur and a weekend warrior on skis. I listened to the Rolling Stones, I drank wine, and I traveled to France. I crafted a beautiful replica of my father's life and called it my own. I accomplished. A lot.

I was desperate to prove I was one of the guys because proving that would mean no one would find out that I didn't want the marriage and the kids and the bright orange Sundance trampoline. I wasn't interested in scones and packed lunches. We weren't a religious family, but I can tell you with confidence that not wanting all of this was as close as I could get to committing a cardinal sin. And for most people, sins are best kept secret.

The hardest part of this, though—the part I tried my best to ignore—was that somewhere deep inside myself, I knew I didn't have what it took to become one of the women. I wasn't the type of person who could pair grace with fistfuls of restraint. I wasn't the type of person who could pair anything with restraint.

So I spent my life looking for the next big thing, the next race, the next ribbon, the next way I could prove I had worth somewhere else, somewhere other than the sewing machine. But no matter how much I did or how much I had, it was never enough. Perhaps that's why the blue tin sign at the top of Whistler spoke to me in the way that it did that day. It was the perfect bait to lure me in. A trip around the world? Skiing 4 million feet? That was definitive evidence that I was one of the guys. That was inarguable.

What I didn't know at the time was how much the Universe likes to dress up divine intervention as a fancy piece of blue-ribbon bait. It would be a while before I figured that part out, before I understood that what lures us into adventure is often the opposite of what will get us safely to the other side of it.

3

SHIT, SEÑORA, AND A MAN WHO SINGS TO RAW FISH

I DON'T remember arriving at the airport or checking in to my flight. I assume I heaved my giant ski bag onto a weigh scale at some point, but I can't recall doing it. I have a hazy memory of my sister filling the role of private chauffeur, providing breathing room between me and the arsenal of questions my mother's nervous energy was spewing in my direction.

I don't remember what I was wearing or what I ate for breakfast. I think there was orange juice involved because I have a blurry memory of spilling a little on the kitchen floor, just in front of the fridge. Had I used a blue J-cloth to wipe it up? There was always a blue J-cloth in my mother's kitchen.

I don't remember any of the conversations at the airport, but I do remember the moment my niece climbed into my arms. Time stopped when she wrapped herself around me, and for that brief moment we were the only two people in the world.

Each of her four-year-old limbs folded around me, and she held on as if it was the last time she was ever going to lay eyes on me, a wise woman in a sinewy thirty-five-pound body. It was hard to tell whether she was giving me a blessing or begging me not to go. I suppose it could have been either. The two of us stood there straddling the line between before and after, and it felt as though a small bridge appeared, an exit ramp. I wondered what would happen if I took this exit, if I left the life I'd been living, albeit temporarily. I worried that the road back—the one that could safely bring me home—would cease to exist. I'm not sure how my niece knew this, but I swear she did.

I don't remember when the hug stopped, nor do I remember actually going through airport security, or boarding the plane. I have a vague recollection of a layover in the Dallas airport, but landing in Santiago, Chile, and checking into my hotel are a blank. The only thing I recall with clarity is the mushroom pizza I had for dinner, because I fucking love mushroom pizza.

And then I woke up the next morning. It was July 15, 2010.

Someone was knocking very loudly on the door of my hotel room. I rolled over and searched the bedside table for the watch I'd left there the night before. The room was pitch-black. I pressed the button on the side of my watch, and the small screen lit up. I squinted: 6:53 a.m.

Shit.

I had slept right through my six o'clock alarm.

I threw back the covers, swung my legs off the bed, and opened the door of my room. Standing in front of me was a small Chilean man. He was young, maybe twenty years old, and his dark brown eyes had a hint of panic in them.

"El coche. Su coche está aquí," he said.

"Cinco minuto," I said, holding up my hand to ensure I was in fact communicating the number five. "Give me five minutes."

I gestured toward my ski bag, which he promptly grabbed. He rolled it out the door and started up the small spiral staircase. I was grateful to be spared the labor.

I turned to face the room, and my eyes immediately went to the pile of clothes resting on the back of a chair. Blue jeans, a white cotton T-shirt, a pair of pink underwear, and a neon yellow sports bra. I peeled off my pajamas and stuffed them into my suitcase, then threw on all the clothes I'd worn the day before. I brushed my teeth, swiped a stick of deodorant under each armpit, and tossed my toiletry bag into my suitcase.

While I put on my watch, I ran through a mental checklist.

Laptop, camera, wallet . . . passport.

I grabbed the remaining bags and made my way up the stairs.

A large white van was parked in front of the hotel. My ski bag had already been loaded into the back, and the driver signaled that he would take care of the rest. The door to the passenger side was wide open, and I saw three men sitting inside, all of whom were grinning kindly at me. One of the men pointed to the front seat, which was apparently all mine. I opened the door and climbed in.

"Hi. I'm Ricardo," said one of the guys in the back of the van. "I speak English. Don't worry, we will stop and get some breakfast." A five o'clock shadow made Ricardo look a bit older than he was, but his rosy cheeks and eager eyes gave away his youth. He was twenty, twenty-five at the most.

"This is Hugo," he said, the *h* remaining silent, as he pointed to the man with the biggest smile of the bunch. Hugo had a round face that was full of energy. His eyes were huge, he had a thin mustache, and he wore a black beanie that appeared to be covering a smooth bowling-ball head.

"He's from Buenos Aires," added Ricardo.

"Hola, Hugo," I said, making sure to leave my *h*'s behind.

"This is Alonso," Ricardo continued. "He works at Portillo. I think he is the aerobics instructor." He turned to look at the man in the back of the van. "Aeróbicos, sí?" he asked.

"Uno, dos, tres, cuatro!" said Alonso before clapping his hands in the air. "Sí!"

Alonso was quite tanned, and even though it was winter he was wearing a brightly colored tracksuit, one that had a bit of a shimmer to it. A scarf was tied loosely around his neck, alongside a medium-size gold chain. He was going to freeze his ass off once we got to the mountains.

"And our driver," said Ricardo, pointing to the man who was climbing into the front of the car. "His name is Nico."

Nico nodded at me kindly, gestured for Ricardo to close the side door, and then turned to start the van.

"Vamanos," I said, and although it wasn't a joke, every man in the car burst into laughter before tearing into an exchange of boisterous-sounding Spanish. It became quickly apparent that the Spanish spoken in Santiago was *a lot* faster than the Spanish of the Vancouver School Board's level-two class, which I'd taken in preparation.

About twenty minutes into our trip, Nico pulled into a gas station that had a mini-mart attached. I went in and bought a giant coffee and grabbed a mysterious-looking yogurty drink from one of the fridges. Since I had yet to wrap my mind around the Chilean peso, I paid for my items by holding out a fistful of coins and letting the cashier pluck the change from my hand. This was something I had previously vowed never to do while traveling, but I knew I was going to have to let go of some of my rules if I wanted to survive the next ten months.

The cashier rolled her eyes at me, so, using pig Latin, I told her she wasn't better than me. This filled me with pride. I figured my fluency in pig Latin meant I was just a few steps closer to mastering its linguistic cousin, Spanish.

I climbed back into the van and watched as the other men took their seats. Ricardo was the last one in, carrying a giant bottle of Absolut Vodka in one hand and a large bag of miniature Kit Kats in the other. This both impressed and intrigued me.

"Interesting combo," I said. Ricardo smiled, his perfect teeth gently prying open what was the first of many Kit Kats. We had a two-hour drive ahead of us, and from what I'd heard, the last hour was nonstop switchbacks. As we bounced back onto the highway, all I could imagine was chocolate-flavored vomit spraying all over the car. I was grateful for the front seat.

"So," said Ricardo. "You have gone to Portillo before?"

"No. This is my first time."

"One week?" he asked

"Yep. One week."

"And then where? Home? Home is where? United States?" he asked.

"Well . . ." I paused, wondering if I should tell him the whole story. "No, not home. After that I'm heading down south and then into Argentina. Home is Canada."

"Wow! Great! That's a big trip! A few months, yes?" he asked before translating the conversation for the rest of the men in the car.

"Well, actually, it's a bit longer than that. I'm . . . well, let me try to say it in Spanish, and if I make a mistake, maybe you can help."

Ricardo nodded with enthusiasm.

"Yo esquiar todo el mundo."

"You're skiing all of the world?" he asked, confused. "I think you made a mistake."

"Hmmm . . . nope. No mistake," I said. "I'm skiing around the world. Portillo is my first stop. I'm trying to ski four million vertical feet over the next ten months. I haven't learned how to say that part in Spanish yet."

"How much is four million feet?" he asked. I could see him making calculations in his head.

"It's a lot," I responded. "It's like going down Mount Everest from the summit all the way to the sea about a hundred and thirty-five times. It's more than I've ever skied, like in my whole lifetime, and I've been skiing since I was three."

Ricardo shook his head in disbelief, and then proceeded to translate what I'd said to the rest of the group. I'm not sure why, but I was a little nervous about their reaction. Lots of people knew about my trip, but they were mostly friends and family. This was the first time I had told people I'd just met.

Hugo sat up in his seat. His eyes got even bigger. They were so big, I thought they might pop right out of his head.

"Mierda, señora! Estás loco."

Ricardo quickly translated, "He said, 'Shit, lady! You're crazy.'"

"Yeah, thanks," I said with a laugh. "I got that part, and it's not the first time I've heard it."

As I told people about my plans and the monstrous goal I'd created, I noticed a pattern. Almost every single person thought I was crazy, and I'm pretty sure you can guess how my mother responded. As it turns out, if the vast majority of people you know start calling you crazy, at some point, you start to believe them. You start wondering if they're right, you start questioning your ideas and doubting your decisions, and then finally, if you're like most people, you just lock everything away in a closet for thirty-five years.

It would take a long time for me to realize that the you're-crazy response was a cue to move forward, all guns blazing, and to learn that divine interventions and the ideas born of them aren't meant to be understood right away, especially by other people. But back then, if I got a response with even a hint of "You've totally lost your mind" woven within it, it triggered something I'll call a woolly ball of goat shame.

Because Jaggers, even the men, don't give up everything they've worked hard for. It doesn't matter if there's a goal involved, one that provides some kind of answer to "What's next," Jaggers don't blow all their savings on some mystical message they saw on a blue tin sign. Jaggers don't see "mystical messages." They get married. They have kids (that's another goat pun, by the way. I'm sorry, but I couldn't help myself). They work hard and make money. They create a life that's safe and sound.

But here's the thing I came to realize—you only need one other person. One warm-blooded body besides your own who sees soundness in your insanity. One person to give you the permission you're desperate for. And lucky for me, that one other person showed up in the right place, at the right time, like my very own version of Yoda.

. ·•.

IN JANUARY OF 2009 I attended a birthday party for a friend. The celebration was being held at a small Italian restaurant, and while I was drinking wine in a darkly painted, dimly lit hall just outside the washrooms, I bumped into Ran. Ran is a former colleague and friend. He's a massive man who towers over most people, and he's Israeli, which means his accent gives his already deep, booming voice a rather commanding lilt. At first glance he's not someone you want to bump into while drinking wine in a darkly painted, dimly lit hallway, but almost every memory I have of Ran is of him with a slightly mischievous, shit-eating grin on his face. He's a pussycat, a large, intimidating-looking, formidable-sounding pussycat, and I was happy to chat with him between slurps of Chianti.

Ran asked me if I was going to be heading up to Whistler that weekend, and after I told him that yes, of course I was, he did something strange. He took a few small steps toward me. We were already standing fairly close to one another, so his forward march felt a little bit awkward. I had never known Ran to be a close talker. Then he craned his head in ever so slightly and took another shuffle forward. I shimmied a bit to the right.

"I have a friend in town," he whispered. "He's from Israel, and he's up in the mountains."

I paused my sideways shuffle.

"He snowboards," Ran continued, "and it would be great for him to ride with someone who knows the mountains as well as you."

I nodded and took note of Ran's voice. It was clear, serious, and uncharacteristically quiet. The tone implied that he was revealing something important. It was as if he was giving me a set of instructions, a firm directive as opposed to a suggestion or request.

"I don't normally introduce people to him," he said, "but I think you're ready. Here's his number. Make sure you call him."

"What exactly do you mean by 'being ready'?" I asked. And although I wasn't sure why we were being so secretive, I leaned in and whispered the rest. "Ready for what, Ran?"

Ran took a step back and laughed loudly, and with his voice back to its normal volume and cadence, he bellowed, "Wow! Stephanie. Where is your trust?" He smiled his trademark smile and handed me a piece of paper with his friend's phone number written on it. I tucked it into my wallet and promptly forgot all about it.

Two days later, I got a call from Ran.

"Why haven't you called my friend?" he asked.

"Oh, shit!" I said. "Ran, I totally forgot."

"I'm going to tell him you're calling him now," Ran replied.

His tone was clear. This was no time to lollygag.

I called his friend, and we agreed to meet for sushi a few hours later. Just before I hung up the phone, I asked Ran's friend how I would find him. I was hoping for some small descriptor, the color of his shirt or something, so I could pick him out in the crowd. Instead he said, "Just ask for the King of Sushi. They'll know who you're talking about."

The King of Sushi? Who called himself the King of Sushi?

Upon arrival, I did as instructed: I asked for the King of Sushi. I expected a blank stare or maybe an eye roll, but instead, as if I'd just turned from pumpkin to princess before her very eyes, the hostess bowed.

"Yes, of course," she said. "Right this way." She turned around and escorted me to a large booth in the back of the restaurant. And there sat Joseph, on a large tatami throne.

He was wearing jeans, a slightly wrinkled T-shirt, and a zip-up hoodie. His dark, curly hair was both kempt and unkempt, like he'd paid attention to the styling only to become bored partway through. He had smooth skin and deeply set dimples and seemed young, perhaps my age.

I removed the paper from my chopsticks and snapped them open. Joseph asked me how I knew Ran. A curious light bounced through his eyes, and as he spoke, I knew my initial guess of his age was off.

He's older, I thought. Thirty-five, maybe thirty-six.

Joseph did most of the ordering, because apparently that's what you do when you're the King. When the sake arrived, he lifted his glass and motioned for me to do the same. Our small ceramic cups clinked together.

"It's nice to meet you?" I said. It came out a little more like a question than I had intended.

"It's nice to meet you too, I think," he said, laughter coming forth shyly from just behind his dimples.

Food arrived to our table at a steady pace throughout the night, plate after plate of Japanese delicacies. I watched Joseph eat in what I can only describe as pure gluttony. He devoured the food in front of us, not frantically, but in something more like slow-motion hedonism, taking time to savor every piece. His eyes slowly closed as he placed fresh tuna, eel, and small bits of halibut on his tongue, before dousing them with mouthfuls of sake. At one point in the evening, I noticed him humming.

Was he singing the fish a lullaby?

When dinner was finished, we agreed to meet the next morning so I could show him around the mountain.

"I'm the King of Sushi and have fulfilled my royal duties," he said. "Ran told me you were the Snow Princess, so tomorrow you should show me around."

"Sounds like a deal," I said with a chuckle.

The next morning, I watched this piggish zest for life take over once again. As I showed Joseph different runs and secret stashes of snow, he dove right in. It was like watching a child cannonballing into a summer lake. There was a feverish excitement in his every movement. There was nothing moderate or controlled about the way he rode. It was completely unlike how I'd been taught to ski, and I loved it. I'd never met anyone quite like him. I wasn't sure what he was, but one thing was certain—he wasn't a goat.

Watching Joseph play in the mountains taught me more about skiing than anyone or anything else ever had. His form wasn't perfect, so it had nothing to do with his technical execution. In fact, in many ways I would have described him as clumsy and uncoordinated, but somehow he always managed to stay upright. It was the perfect balance of full-blown surrender and physical control. It reminded me of a performance artist I'd once seen, a woman who literally flung her paint-soaked body against a blank canvas in total abandon. As she created this magnificent mess, the audience was transfixed. She didn't care if the paint dripping from her skin landed on the canvas or the drop cloth she'd placed underneath it. She didn't care if little bits of it splattered on the clothes or faces of the people who watched her. If Joseph had been there to see this woman, I'm almost sure he would have clapped and then turned to me with a few droplets of red paint on his face. "*Shibumi!*" he would say. "That was *shibumi!* Bravo!"

As we skied together over the next few weeks, I heard Joseph talk a lot about the concept of *shibumi*. He'd read about it in a book, a philosophical thriller whose main character was obsessed with living a *shibumi* existence. The word itself comes from Japanese slang, and it's typically used to describe the aesthetic quality of something, like a piece of art or pottery. It translates loosely into effortless perfection, complex but organic beauty, or something that is rough but also elegant. After watching Joseph ride, and after hearing him talk about the concept, I couldn't help but think of his movement as a fitting example, something that was beautiful because it combined wild spontaneity with just a dash of control.

.ੰੰ.

ONE WEEKEND, AS JOSEPH and I were riding the chairlift, he turned to me with a serious look on his face. "So many people are slaves," he said. "That should be your main goal, Stephanie, not to be a slave. There's no *shibumi* in slavery."

"Okayyyy," I said.

"When you're a slave, you end up turning into someone other than who you're supposed to turn into."

I nodded, even though I was unsure what he really meant.

It's important to note that when it comes to being enslaved, or what most people would simply call "gainful employment," Joseph has a bit more freedom than most. This is because he's a gazillionaire. It's not something you would realize or even guess when you meet him because it's not something he flaunts. In fact, the only reason I know about his money is because I Googled him. I was curious about how a guy in his thirties, who still carries all of his cash in a Velcro wallet, could afford to live in a hotel for months at a time. So I did a little digging, and as it turns out, Joseph and a few other partners invented some groundbreaking Internet doohickey, and when they sold the company in the late 1990s, bingo!—gazillions.

It's also important to note that Joseph's money is the reason we're still friends.

Regardless of the fact that I am not a formally trained social scientist, I feel confident making the following presupposition: most male-female friendships start off with some inkling of sexual tension, a little question that pops into each person's head about whether or not "something" is happening. This was exactly the case with Joseph. I thought I was picking up on a very slight chemistry between us, something small but interesting. And then I Googled him and immediately placed our chemistry to the side.

I loved spending time with Joseph, and I didn't want him to think I was doing it just because he had money. I wanted him to know, beyond a shadow of a doubt, that I adored him for him, because I did, and still do. I loved listening to him talk about his philosophies on life, what he was reading, and his witty observations about Canada. It was like talking to someone from a totally different planet, someone who was just visiting Earth for a short period of time, whose mind was blown by all the new things they were seeing.

"The newspapers!" he would exclaim. "They have front-page stories about the salmon population. In Israel they write about the human population, about how many people died and who killed who. But here? No! You must write about the salmon."

All I could do was laugh.

"Also," he continued, "I was at the grocery store and I noticed that the vegetables get little showers every fifteen minutes. Only Canadians would be that nice to their vegetables."

From that point on, tension aside, we stuck to skiing, sake, and long conversations about the perils to the salmon population. It was—well, there's just no other term for it—effortless perfection. My weekends were filled with Joseph, snow, sake, and *shibumi*.

During our time together, I started seeing the mountains I had grown up on, the ones I thought I knew inside and out, in a completely different way. As I watched him ride, I felt myself let go. I gave myself permission to become less disciplined, less constrained. I saw lines where I'd never seen them before. In fact, I gave up on the idea that there had to be lines at all, and I began seeing arcs, and curves, and twists, and turns instead. I danced on the snow as if it were a ballroom floor, wide open and polished white, something I could glide across with grace. I started using speed, something I'd always loved, as a form of meditation to ground myself, to shut off the spigot in my brain, the one that had been responsible for spraying doubt and fear all over the place after my blue-tin-sign revelation.

About a month after the Universe prompted me to raise my restraining device, I was having coffee with Joseph. I had told my family and friends about my idea, and every single one of them had labeled me certifiably insane. I was hesitant to hear yet another person tell me I was a lunatic, but I decided to take a chance on Joseph.

"I'm thinking about taking a year off and skiing around the world," I announced.

He didn't even put down his cup.

"Yes," he said matter-of-factly. "Why would you not do that? That sounds like the most obvious way to spend a year. *Shibumi*! Let's celebrate! We'll have a very piggy feast tonight."

It was all I needed. It was formal substantiation, proof that not everyone believed this was crazy, that I was crazy. Did I care if it came from a man I'd just met, or that he lived in a totally different world than I did, financially or otherwise? No. Did it matter that just a few weeks prior I'd watched him sing a song to a little piece of fish? Was that a marker of sanity? No, and no it was not. All that mattered was that I had permission, external validation I could cling to as I moved through sixteen months of preparation, of saving and spending and squatting.

4

BASE CAMP AND THE SMELL OF SULFUR

AFTER A few hours in the van and approximately 247 switchbacks, we arrived in Portillo. We pulled up in front of a hotel that sat at the edge of Laguna del Inca, a small but striking mountain lake. It was hard not to think the whole thing was a painting. Cobalt-blue skies rose up from behind the bright yellow hotel, and a range of black Andean mountain peaks pierced the sky like giant slate daggers. The tallest of the bunch was Acongagua, a mountain that soars to 22,838 feet. She's a venerable giant, the highest peak outside of Asia, and as I stood on the deck of the hotel looking up at her, I exhaled in awe.

I've done it, I said to myself. *I've made it to base camp.*

It took me just over a year to figure out what I thought "skiing around the world" should entail. It meant wrapping my head around something rather large, and the only way I knew how to do that was to organize the shit out of it. Thankfully, organizing the shit out of things is in the top three of my all-time talents (behind sleeping and playing it cool).

The process began with a Google search about round-the-world flights and the baggage fees associated with monstrously large ski bags. From there I tackled the planning and logistics of the trip with enthusiasm and a high degree of anal retentiveness. I spent every spare moment sitting at my kitchen table looking over calendars, budgets, and weight restrictions for the twenty-plus airlines on which I would fly. I pored over the technical specs for avalanche gear, as well as for ski boots, rubber boots, hiking boots, and rolling travel bags in every possible size. It's one thing to travel through Southeast Asia for a year with a backpack and a pair of flip-flops, but it's something different altogether to tackle a year of winter travel involving boots and bulky jackets. One chunky sweater, and your suitcase is already a quarter full; add ski pants and a pair of running shoes, and you're toast.

Questions ran constantly through my head about all the circumstances and issues I might possibly encounter. I did my best to answer them as they arrived, but the unrelenting pace was tough to keep up with. The questions never slowed, not for sixteen months. I even spent an afternoon sitting in a doctor's office getting a just-in-case-you-get-bitten-by-a-strange-Japanese-monkey-while-skiing vaccination. I wasn't planning to have a monkey gnaw on me, but would I have considered myself well organized without an emergency preparedness section? No.

I also spent a massive amount of time planning the mundane. It seemed like a good investment of time to spend an hour in the toothbrush aisle at the drugstore, attempting to determine which brush, bristle count, and firmness would last the longest and weigh the least. Because when the other travelers' brushes wore out and mine didn't, yeah, who would be laughing then? I could imagine the Universe turning to me. "Well planned," it would say. "Well fucking planned."

The other thing I focused on was money. Although it's true that I was born and bred on a certain kind of privilege, it wasn't the kind that included unlimited access to my parents' bank account. In fact, it didn't include any access to my parents' bank account. Getting their help financially, even in the form of a loan, was out of the question. If I was going to do this, I would have to do it on my own. This was totally fine with me. In fact, it was something I took pride in. That said, it didn't come easy. You see, skiing is a bit expensive. Check that: skiing is mind-blowingly expensive; not quite in the sailing regatta or dressage and show-jumping realm, but pricey nonetheless.

In addition to my day job, I took on as many short-term freelance gigs as possible. I know this sounds like the fast track to prostitution, but it wasn't. Well, in a way it was, but that's only because I had so many clients that I lost track of their names, which is something I assume ladies of the night have a similar problem with.

The timing couldn't have been better for my fling with quasi-prostitution. The 2010 Winter Olympics were on their way to Vancouver, and for the year leading up, I scored extra work with two public relations firms who were overloaded with Olympic clientele. I also picked up a contract with an international market research firm, tacked on some freelance blogging, and, when I could, lent a hand, in exchange for cash, at a friend's catering company. During the month of the games themselves, I rented out my apartment and dumped the savings into my bank account. And finally, as if the gods themselves were spurring me on, my bank called and asked if I would like to take advantage of their lower rates and refinance the mortgage. I said yes, and because I took the call as a sign that the Universe's chips were stacked in my favor, I also asked if they would be willing to extend me a line of credit to help pay for a ski trip around the world—although it's important to note that the words "ski trip around the world" remained in my head, and what really came out was "an investment I am looking to make." This was a massive shot in the dark; in 2010, what bank in God's name would give a twenty-eight-year-old a line of credit for an investment for which they had no actual documentation? As it turned out, my bank was apparently in God's name, because their response was, with actual enthusiasm, "Yes, we would be happy to do that for you."

By the time I left in July 2010, I had saved about $30,000, refinanced my apartment, secured a tenant to cover my mortgage, and taken out a line of credit that would cover the rest of the trip and then some. Additionally, the ten months ahead of me were carefully (aka anally) mapped out, including what I had determined to be the most important piece of it all: the goal, the amount I would ski. After factoring in travel, a short break between the southern and northern hemisphere seasons so I could rest my legs, as well as the potential for each season's beginning and end (when the snow begins to fall and when it starts to melt), I figured I would have about thirty-two weeks of skiing. My dad and I regularly skied with an altimeter, a watchlike instrument that measures vertical feet skied. I knew a relatively challenging day for me on the hill was around 25,000 vertical feet. I did some calculations based on skiing that amount five days a week (I was going to treat this like a job) over the course of the trip, and I landed on 4 million vertical feet. It was official—I had the carrot for the end of my stick.

To put this into perspective, this was more than I'd skied in my lifetime to date. It's a number that would take the typical North American skier about twenty-five years to complete. Even if you were a ripper and skied a solid thirty-day season, you'd still be looking at a five- or six-year project. The goal was monstrous. There were two reasons for this.

The first was that monstrous goals were an integral part of my life as a Markhor ram. While the idea of being a lazy ski bum for a year was attractive, I wanted something more. The other reason was that having a goal made the whole thing seem a little less crazy. It gave me a purpose, something to explain the moment I saw the oh-my-God-Steph-has-actually-lost-her-mind look wash over someone's face. As soon as I was able to provide a sound motive, a sturdy goal of some sort, it was like the world could go back to spinning on its regular axis.

Also, people don't like things that are gray. They don't like the murkiness involved with not knowing, even if it has nothing to do with them. People like to pinpoint, peg, and pigeonhole. When someone asks you what you're doing, you can't really say, "Well shit, John, that's a good one. I'm not really sure." We want to put people in a box, and then we want to label that box with a big black marker so we understand where it fits in the world.

I honestly can't think of many people who can pull off the color gray. Jamie Lee Curtis might, and maybe a few of those hipsters doing that lavender shade of gray, but that's it. The rest of us need something more defined, more concrete, like chestnut, or red, or 4 million vertical feet.

With that number, I was able to create a purpose, a reason for pressing pause on my life that made sense to people around me. Once I had the goal, I was just ramming it up, chasing the tick mark for another giant box—nothing out of the norm for a compulsive ribbon collector. People knew where to put me and how to define me—and more important, so did I.

.ˑ.•.

I MADE MY FIRST mountaineering mistake within three hours of arriving at Portillo. The base of the resort sits at 9,449 feet. This elevation would be a big deal for most people, and for a gal coming directly from sea level, it was a very big deal, but in my excitement it hadn't occurred to me to pay heed to the altitude.

When we arrived at Portillo, there was no snow—like actually none. Every lift was closed, but rather than sit and sulk about it, I told myself it was nothing to worry about. It was early in the season, I still had nine months and twenty-nine days of skiing ahead of me, and besides, I saw a sign in the lobby for an all-ages Ping-Pong tournament!

In the first match I was paired with an adorable six-year-old. I fought tooth and nail for every point I got, which was one. He creamed me. Postgame, my ego and I hit the gym for a quick work-out, and then I joined Ricardo and the remnants of his bottle of vodka for a short hike. About an hour later, the altitude struck me. My nose started bleeding at seven o'clock, and by eight I had a throbbing headache.

I spent the next day in bed, and although it wasn't the way I wanted to start my trip, it didn't really matter. The mountain was closed that day, and the one after that. I was disappointed, but I continued to tell myself I had nothing to worry about. I still had nine months and twenty-seven days of skiing ahead of me, and as an added bonus, the mountain closures allowed me to catch my breath, in a very literal sense. They also meant I was able to take in everything else Portillo had to offer, which was a lot. The place was . . . how do I put my finger on it . . . an *exact* combination of *Dirty Dancing* (*en español*) and Club Med (with ski equipment).

Portillo came complete with movie screenings, master's-level hot-tubbing, and nightly tango classes. The only actual difference between it and Club Med/*Dirty Dancing* was that no one called me Baby when I went to the staff quarters. They called me some-thing else, but even with my fluency in pig Latin, it was just out-side my linguistic grasp. Regardless, I dove in and waited for the snow while engaging in regional wine tastings and fiercely competitive round-robin Jenga, pronounced "yeng-ga" in Chile. Other than skiing, there really is nothing like pushing wood in front of a crackling fireplace, glass of Chilean Malbec in hand.

On day four, just enough snow had fallen to open a few of the lifts. I spent the rest of the week scraping down bare slopes, and although I did my best to dodge the wide patches of gravel, they inevitably caught me. I felt like I was skiing over a series of jerky washboards, bits of rock snagging the bases of my skis, grinding my feet to a gravelly halt while my body continued on its way.

During those days I managed to lurch through almost 90,000 feet, something I could have done with relative ease in two or three days at Whistler. I certainly wasn't blown away with the progress, but I wasn't disappointed in it either, especially considering Portillo's main lift system, the glorious, efficient, clearly-made-by-a-set-of-skilled-engineers contraption: the Slingshot.

Portillo had two of these rigs, and as their name suggests, they sling more than they lift. The whole thing is essentially a large pulley system with a giant metal cable that runs from the bottom of the mountain to the top. Unlike most lifts, the cable didn't have chairs or a series of T-bars. Instead, it used two giant metal triangles—one attached close to the top of the pulley, the other near the bottom. Five side-by-very-close-side circular seats/industrial-strength Frisbees dangle downward from the base of each triangle. I assumed that meant five people could be slung in one go, and by golly, I was right.

To load the Slingshot, the seats are placed carefully between the left and right unmentionables of each skier before they are sent flying to the top of the hill. It should be noted that wily South American youth are typically put in charge of operating the contraption, so the pace at which you sling depends highly on whether they find human rag dolls entertaining.

When my turn came, I loaded on, ensuring that both ski tips were facing up the mountain. Although I clearly invaded the personal space of my neighbors in the process, mounting the Frisbee was relatively easy. Staying on it as we were catapulted up the hill was a whole other question. It reminded me of that time I went waterskiing with four other people, getting knocked around as we slammed into various bumps, wakes, and waves, all at different times.

Oh, wait, that never happened. After riding the Slingshot, I know exactly why.

At the top, we were charged with getting off, Portillo style. After being flung uphill, my four new BFFs and I absorbed a few mini slingshots as the system bounced to a rather violent halt. It reminded me of that time I went bungee jumping with four other people—oh, wait, that never happened either, and after riding the Slingshot, I know exactly why.

Figuring out how all five of us were going to dismount while the whole apparatus bobbed up and down was a feat in and of itself. Our ski tips were pointed uphill. Were we to do a 180-degree turn in some glorious, synchronized ski dance? Were we to attempt a simultaneous jump turn, and just cross our fingers that we all made it without any ski- or pole-inflicted injuries? Were we to ski down the hill backward? Yes. Those were the options. That was precisely what we were expected to do.

Although grateful for the opportunity to perfect the multi-person ski ballet routine I'd been working on for years, I was ready to move on by the end the week. My altimeter and I were hoping for a place that had more snow, and lifts that, say, lifted.

On a side note, my recommendation to anyone wanting to ski in Portillo is to put some serious thought into Cirque du Soleil training prior to arrival. Either that, or arrange a handful of table tennis lessons in advance, so your ego isn't destroyed by a six-year-old named Alejandro. I wish you the best of luck.

My next stop was a place called Termas de Chillán, a small ski resort about seven hours south of Santiago. I took a morning shuttle from Portillo to the central bus station, and then I hopped on a series of southbound buses en route to Chillán.

They say traveling is the perfect way to test a relationship, and after a day of travel through central Chile, my luggage and I can both attest to the validity of that statement. We passed, but only because, as a solo traveler, I was inseparable from my bags. To leave my gear in the middle of a South American bus station so I could zip off to the loo was not an option. Doing so would have been the equivalent of saying to the forty-odd people who were standing around, "Please rob me. Please steal everything you see here. No, really, I'd love for you to have it."

To be quite frank, my Dove Beauty Bar complexion and big blue eyes were probably already saying that, so I did my best to communicate otherwise. My giant ski bag looked more like a body bag than anything else, so I used that to my advantage and tried to give off a clear don't-fuck-with-me vibe. I didn't get robbed, so I think it worked.

Navigating through the station with my bag was another story. That part did not work as well. The bag itself was about six feet long, and with all of my ski equipment it weighed close to eighty pounds. It was like dragging a horrendously overweight toddler behind me, one who was refusing to walk on his own.

I also had a cross-body purse, which contained anything I might need to access quickly—my camera, wallet, and passport, a snack, water, and something to read—and on my back was a packed-to-the-brim forty-liter backpack. It contained my computer and all of my ski clothes, including outerwear and underwear. Last, I had a rolling suitcase, home to my toiletries, a small first aid kit, two pairs of shoes, and a handful of winter clothes (as opposed to ski-related apparel). Ask anyone I've ever traveled with, and they'll tell you I'm a packing magician. Seriously. It is one of my greatest strengths—it comes right after sleeping, playing it cool, and organizing the shit out of things. And actually, now that I think about it, maybe it's just one of the ways I organize the shit out of things. I don't overpack, I don't underpack, I perfect-pack. Everything I took with me would be put to good use. My luggage and I were like a family of Irish Catholic potato farmers circa 1935—yes, even little Declan is expected to work. I suppose the only difference is that any decent Irish Catholic family would never have forced its largest members to ride for five hours in a filthy compartment underneath a bus.

As I hauled my bags from bus to bus and through each of the depots, I couldn't help but notice my surroundings. Five months prior to my arrival, the region around Termas de Chillán had been pummeled with an 8.8-magnitude earthquake. Five hundred and twenty-five people lost their lives, and the impact of the catastrophe was still reverberating. Many of the roads in the area looked like open wounds. We drove by huge slabs of scarred and buckled pavement, and deep cracks that led to gaping holes. The damage wasn't fresh, but it was clearly far from healed.

When I got to the actual resort, I found that many of the buildings had been condemned. They were taped up and empty, large pieces of concrete still lying where they'd tumbled. I'd never seen that kind of destruction, a whole chunk of the earth torn open with no one rushing to sew it back up. It wasn't what I was used to. Where was the cleanup crew? Why hadn't everything been put back together, so people could move on with their lives and pretend like nothing had happened? Who was going to come along and sweep things under the rug? I recognized that most of the answers to those questions were socioeconomic, political, or even cultural, but it didn't matter. I looked out the window at the wreckage. Something about the fact that it just sat there, so open and exposed, spoke to me. I'd never seen vulnerability close up like that before.

Nevados de Chillán itself is one of Chile's most active volcanoes, and the region is full of hot springs that bubble away just beneath the crust of the earth. As I skied, I noticed bits of steam rising up from pockets of snow just beyond the area boundary. The smell of sulfur gently curled through the air as I made my way down the rolling hills and the smooth, wide-open slopes. One thing was 100 percent clear: I wasn't in Whistler anymore. I'd made it through base camp and crossed into a whole other world, the surface of which I'd just scraped.

5

THE MEAT SEATS, LENTIL SOUP, AND BOBBY BROWN

I LEFT Chile with just under 150,000 vertical feet, my gear smelling slightly like rotten eggs. I boarded a bus that drove farther south, straight through the heart of Patagonia and on into Argentina. We went up over a mountain pass that had just been covered in snow, heaps and heaps of it. The trees looked like giant white blobs that were sitting on top of thick white whipping-cream clouds. It was a wintry paradise. The young man in the aisle across from me was wide-eyed with wonder, the kind really only seen in kids.

"Nieve. Mucho," I said.

I guess he managed to pick up on the fact that Spanish wasn't my native tongue, because he responded in broken English.

"I'm from Peru," he said. "I never see snow." He held his hand in the air with his pointer finger raised. "First time."

I smiled. "Beautiful," I said. "It's beautiful."

Although it looked like the middle of nowhere, my Peruvian

neighbor got off at the next stop. I liked to imagine him making up for lost time and doing snow angel after snow angel, or maybe running with excitement to the closest pole just so he could stick his tongue on it and see if it really was such a bad idea. I imagined such scenarios with a giant smile on my face until the moment the bus pulled into its final station—a town called San Carlos de Bariloche, and my home for the whole month of August.

I'd heard a lot of amazing things about Bariloche, but not a single person had mentioned that it's basically a real-life Willy Wonka's. There are chocolatiers on every corner. And in the middle of the block. And close to the end, but not quite at the end of the block. It is as if the streets are paved with dulce de leche and ground-up cacao seeds. The smell of fresh cocoa wafts out from the doors of chocolate shops and the bags of Bariloche's sweet-toothed tourists. In any other place in the world, this quantity and quality of chocolate would be the focal point, but in Bariloche, it's hardly a blip on the radar. To understand that is to understand just how much the city has to offer.

Located smack in the middle of a pristine national park, Bariloche is physically stunning. Skiers, trekkers, and mountaineers flock to her like pilgrims, all year round. A looking-glass lake sits at her feet, and like the queen that she is, she wears a crown of Andean mountains atop her head, which then runs west before crumpling to a beautiful close in the south. Combine her natural beauty with her German gingerbread-style architecture, and Bariloche stands out as a better-looking version of Switzerland, which I didn't know was possible. To put this in human terms, it would be like discovering that Gisele Bündchen has a more attractive sister, one who's gone completely undiscovered, and whose skin is made with actual Cadbury Creme Eggs.

A friend of mine visited Bariloche a year prior to my arrival. Why he left is unknown to me, but he did, and when he got home, he convinced me I needed to visit. Based on his rave reviews, not one of which mentioned the fact that the town was essentially made of Mars Bars, I planned a one-month stay. In that time, I lapped Bariloche up like the giant fountain of chocolate fondue that she is.

My landlord met me at the bus station and helped me get settled into a small apartment on the edge of town. He introduced me to the owner of the wine shop located directly below me, showed me what keys were meant to unlock what doors, and taught me how to go about lighting the finicky Argentine stove without burning the whole building down. When he left, I went out onto the small deck and sat there for an hour. It was cold, but I was mesmerized by the view. I could see the whole lake from that deck. The winter sun skipped low across the water, and every shade of blue and orange spilled across this giant liquid canvas. I felt myself fully relax. My shoulders dropped, and out came a huge sigh of air. It made me wonder just how long I had been holding my breath.

The only issue with Bariloche was that I didn't know a soul other than my landlord. This wasn't typically a concern for me, but since I would be in one place for a whole month, I figured it would help to make a few friends. I didn't want loneliness turning into a month-long orgy with a few pounds of red meat, a gallon or two of Malbec, and a ménage à trois of white, milk, and dark chocolate. I could already hear the slurping sounds, see the red juice dribbling from my chin, fingers covered in melted caramel.

Apparently my landlord suspected a similar outcome, and in an effort to save his apartment from impending semisweet doom, he e-mailed me the next day. It was an introduction to another of his tenants, an American guy who was in town for the month, just like me.

"You're both gringos," he wrote, "and you're both here for a month. I thought you should meet."

Apparently that gave us enough in common to warrant hanging out. North American death-by-gluttony avoided.

Pete was a Californian on a self-proclaimed "skibbatical," a month-long sojourn from his job as a manager at REI. We met the next day at Tony's Parrilla, a tightly packed and dimly lit grill on Bariloche's main drag. Pete brought a friend, another Californian he knew from the outdoor industry who was, very coincidentally, in the same area at the same time. Pete's friend's name was Chris, and so began a twisted version of *Three's Company* (like, imagine if the whole show had been written, shot, and edited from Janet and Chrissy's point of view).

As we worked our way through introductions, as well as a massive platter of meat, a few things became clear to me. The first was that Pete and I were Janet and Chrissy. The second was that Pete had been given to me as a gift from the gods. I adored him from the moment we met, partially thanks to his talent for making other people instantly comfortable. He has puppy-dog brown eyes, a fully shaved head, and deep smile lines that curve around each side of his mouth. Everything about him is warm and friendly, but he also has a rough, soulful edge. Something about him told me he could hold his own at Burning Man, possibly trance-dancing while wearing a space suit after dropping a shit-ton of MDMA. Basically, if Carol Brady and Keith Richards made a love child, Pete would be it. I know that's hard to imagine, but so is a woman whose skin is made of Cadbury Creme Eggs—and you managed that, so I'm pretty confident you can make this leap too.

The third thing that became clear was that Chris, on the other hand, had boundaries. Big ones. They started with his beard because, well, everything started with Chris's beard. It was a thing of manly glory. It was so thick and luxurious that it actually looked like a cat had just gone and curled up on the bottom of his face. That said, his boundaries continued well past his facial hair. It was as if he had some invisible but impenetrable wall all around him. I immediately sensed that he was not a hugger. In fact, I thought twice about shaking his hand, or touching him at all. I think I wound up patting him gently on the shoulder or something; whatever it was, it was totally awkward. But what else are you left with when someone has a cat on their face and a giant moat around them, complete with a rusty drawbridge that hadn't been lowered in years? Chris wasn't mean or anything, but he was standoffish and aloof. And for an in-your-face-extrovert like myself, standoffish and aloof is difficult to navigate, which is why I decided to give him some space.

The final point of clarity for me that night was that even with my new friends, the possibility of being victim to my own gluttony was high. We sat at a table beside the meat display, and yes, you read that correctly: The Meat Display. These seats had a premium view of premium cuts, and you could simply point at what you wanted. The three of us ordered about twenty pounds of steak, which came with an additional three pounds of gristle, as well as a few tomatoes. I devoured roughly half and instantly became a regular at Tony's. Every time I went back, I told them I wanted to sit at the table with the meat seats.

Though I've always liked red meat, I'm not typically a carnivorous monster who simply points at the pieces of flesh I'd like cooked for me, only to gobble them down on top of a tomato. But all the skiing was bringing out a voracious appetite in me. I found my rhythm in Bariloche, and I also discovered that to keep it, I had to be fueled with high-quality calories. I can't say for sure, but I'm almost certain the "hunger for life" I demonstrated that night was the reason Pete befriended me.

Pete and I skied together almost every day that month, from the moment the lifts opened until the moment they closed. Most of our days were spent at Cerro Catedral, a large resort located about thirty minutes southwest of Bariloche. Chris only joined us at the resort about once a week. He had a different agenda—one that involved mostly reclusive behavior and solo exploration of the mountains outside Catedral.

It only took a few days for Pete and me to develop a basic routine—which, in an attempt to fully immerse ourselves in the Spanish language, we referred to as our routine-o. I woke up each morning at 7:20, made breakfast, brewed some exceptionally strong coffee, and massaged the little muscles on the bottoms of my feet with a lacrosse ball I'd packed for that very purpose. At 8:00 I would grab my backpack, pop my skis and boots over my shoulder, and walk around the corner to the bus stop. Pete would be waiting there to greet me, with a big smile and a cigarette dangling from the corner of his mouth.

"Morning, *chica*," he would say, and then, motioning toward the cigarette, he'd add, "When in Argentina."

When the bus arrived, we would forcefully stuff ourselves and our gear between the fifty or so Argentines on their way to work and the handful of skiers headed up to the mountain. As the bus bounced along the road, our sole focus was to hold on to our gear and stay upright. No matter how hard we tried, though, the occasional piece would fly through the air as if some sort of ski-based bomb had exploded in our hands. Upon arrival at the resort, we'd disembark from the bus and then elbow our way through the throng of people who were gathered—as opposed to lined up—at the bottom of the ski lifts. In South America, a cluster of people somehow works better than an orderly queue.

I actually got quite good at this, quickly understanding that the key is to avoid eye contact while pretending not to care that your skis were being ruined as you slid them over anything in your way. It's like parking in a really tight spot and not giving two shits about repeatedly sideswiping the cars on either side of you. Unfortunately, right when he needed Keith Richards's DNA to show up, the Carol Brady in Pete would take over. He was too nice. I always got to the front, only to have to wait for Pete as he please'd and thank-you'd his way through the masses.

After all that, we skied. All day. Like maniacs. Until the entire resort was empty. I became conditioned to the feelings, and even more so the sounds, of skiing at Cerro Catedral. The snapping, smacking, and clacking of equipment colliding in the lineups. The whirring of the lifts, and the slight rustle of the wind. The whisper of my skis as they gently slid across the snow at the tops of each run.

I always paused for a little longer than normal when I got off the lifts at Cerro Catedral. It was hard not to. From the top of the resort you can see the entire valley. Sugar-coated mountain peaks sit high above the tree line and then roll into thin folds of forest. Cedar trees, Patagonian cypress, and thick swatches of bamboo are all mixed up together in a sparse and uneven pattern, running from the mountains all the way to the shore of the glass-topped lake. I stopped to look out at that view every day we skied there, and every time I felt grateful.

Once we were ready to go, I slid my hands through the straps of my ski poles, snapped my boot buckles closed, and skated forward. The sound of our first few runs depended on the temperature, which was typically warm in the day, freezing at night. Sometimes I heard a dry squeak or a soft slice as the edges of my skis dug into the surface layer of snow, but more often than not I heard a shearing of metal on hard-packed snow and ice. Occasionally, when the temperature spiked and then held through the night, the snow would be warm and wet in the morning, making a damp *shush*ing sound as we pushed through it.

Then came the sound of the wind as we picked up speed, and we always picked up speed, because speed is one of the reasons I ski—the adrenaline of it, the wind on my face. On calm days the sound of the wind was smooth, a slight ripple as the air found small pockets of material to pull at. My lift ticket flapped gently at my waist, and my inhale was as deep as my exhale. It was easy and freeing. On colder, windier days, the sound was different. There was a crackling to it; the wind would snap through my first two or three layers, all the way to my skin. It was irritating, like a fan set on cool and aimed directly at the tops of my quads. Pins of wind hit my cheeks as we fled down the mountain.

The sound my own body made zipping down the hill varied as drastically as the sound of the wind. Sometimes I sang, a little alto ringing across empty hills as we danced down groomers, arms wide as if I was embracing the sweet, warm air, Annie Lennox's "Little Bird" playing on my iPod.

"Do you know that you're singing out loud?" Pete asked one day with a chuckle.

It was harder to sing when the skiing required a little more effort. On those runs my breathing became more labored, pulsing in and out as I wove my way through the handful of people who were paused mid-mountain. When I skied like that, my breathing had a steady rhythmic count. I was a yogi on snow.

Other times, when we leaped off small ledges, dodged through thickets of bamboo, or slid into steep little chutes, my breath became hard. On those runs the sound of my heartbeat overtook. It was a heavy drumbeat. I could feel it coming up through my body and into my head—a muffled gallop as I moved powerfully, thighs pulsing, through big snow, thick, chunky, moguled snow, heavy, damp snow, huge white pillows, all moving underneath me like an ocean.

It was rare, but on occasion we got into terrain that was out of my league. I'm a good skier, but I'm not a great one, and that's not modesty—it's the truth. I wasn't that kid who spent weekends in race camps. Unless they need extras for the après-ski portion of the movie, I'm not about to star in the next Warren Miller film. There were times I had to focus, like *really* focus, and in those moments, I heard nothing at all. I must have been holding my breath because I don't remember a single sound, not until I got to the bottom, until the blur of white and blue became clear again and I was loading back onto the lifts.

I would land with a *thud* as the chairlift swung around the corner, my thighs no longer able to move from standing to sitting with any kind of grace. I would slide my poles under my left leg and pop open the buckles on my ski boots, offering a short reprieve to my aching feet and my battered toes, which spent most of the day slammed up against the front of my boots. When they could wiggle once again, I would lean back and take it all in. The aged, secondhand chairlifts sounded like an old blender spinning and groaning as we were carried up to the top once again. People chatted in high-speed Spanish, and I watched other skiers as they moved like ants across different parts of the mountain.

Everything about my time in Bariloche was bliss. I felt as though I was unleashing myself, pouring raw energy all over those mountains. And with Pete by my side, acting as Robin to some sort of badass skiing version of Batman, I felt invincible, like I could charge right into my future, like I was doing the exact things I thought this trip was all about—ramming all over the place, proving I was one of the guys, pissing like a dog on every single hydrant I spotted. I felt as though I had all of Patagonia in a headlock, like I could just knuckle right in and give it a noogie any time I wanted. Joseph was right. This was *shibumi*.

Of course it helped that physically, I was stronger than ever before. Over the span of my life I've been described as an athlete, but never a natural one. Coming into this trip, I knew I would have to prepare myself physically, and I did. In the year before I left, I threw myself into a murderous fitness routine. I worked with a trainer named Alex for many months, and he taught me the difference between split squats, lateral squats, one-legged squats, and Bulgarian squats. I trained, and I trained hard. I lost about five pounds of fat, and packed on fifteen of muscle. To this day, when people talk about dry-land training, I throw up a little in my mouth.

And the training paid off. I felt like I was an actual Pegasus on skis—a stunningly powerful Black Beauty–esque kind of horse mixed with a white-rumped swift, which, by the way, is the fifth fastest bird on the planet (very conveniently, it also has a white rump, so we're alike in more ways than one). I was skiing harder, stronger, and faster than ever before. Combine that with the perfect partner in crime, and for the whole month I felt as though I was living inside the pages of a children's book called *The Pegasus and Pete*.

While Pete and I did our best to disregard anything and everything that had the potential to hold us back from skiing like maniacs, there were some inescapable distractions, ones that forced us to stop about every thirty minutes to take in some prize Cerro Catedral moments. These became an integral part of our everyday routine-o.

First were the heated conflicts, both verbal and physical, with the resort's lift turnstiles. In an effort to reduce lift-ticket scams, some genius in the operations department installed a gate of turnstiles, complete with mechanical ticket scanners, at the front of each lift line. This was all fine and dandy except for the fact that the above-described genius installed the turnstiles in the summer, neglecting to account for any snowfall whatsoever. This meant that in winter the turnstiles were the perfect height for dwarfs, small children, garden gnomes, elves, and, to be honest, most South Americans, but awkwardly low for me and just about knee height for Pete. To make matters worse, they didn't work all that well. To scan your ticket, you had to get into a bending crouch, not unlike a limbo position, and then rub your scent on the machine. If that didn't work, you were forced into a slow dry hump (still in a limbo position) in an effort to get the ticket dangling from your pants-pocket zipper directly underneath the scanner. The image of Pete slow-grinding on those machines could only be described as a 1989 Bobby Brown special.

We also spent a fair bit of time discussing the snow grooming—or lack thereof—at Cerro Catedral. Most resorts invest a fair bit in their snow grooming. Each night, when all the skiers are gone, a handful of burly men (and some women) jump into large machines that look like giant snowplows, only instead of wheels they have mechanical caterpillar legs. The machines are called snowcats, and the burly men (and women) drive them up and down the slopes in a meticulous pattern to groom the snow. While doing so, they usually smoke large amounts of marijuana, because it turns the whole process into one long meditation of snowy perfection. Also, it reduces the terror incurred when driving a 16,000-pound vehicle along the side of a cliff in the middle of a very dark, sometimes foggy night. In any case, at the best resorts the snowcats and their totally baked drivers turn chopped-up slopes into smooth, buttery fields of snow so perfectly groomed that it looks like a giant patch of white corduroy. A job well done is marked by the squeaking sound that the small grooves of snow make as your skis glide across the snow's tightly rippled surface.

Other than the cat itself, there are two things a groomer needs. The first is, quite obviously, a decent pipe or bowl—a potato or an empty beer can will do. The second is a clear definition of the fall line—in short, the route a ball would take if it rolled down the hill from the peak. I can't speak to the first need, but I do know that the cat operators at Cerro Catedral didn't have a clue about fall lines. The grooming went more consistently across the hill than down it, and judging by the final product, it actually looked like they may have gone without the cats at all, opting for quad bikes with pieces of chain-link fence attached to the back.

After a morning of humping turnstiles and discussing the state of the snow, Pete and I would pause for lunch. We discovered a small mid-mountain hut that served the most delicious lentil soup on the planet, and we ate there almost every day. About a week in, Pete turned to me with a sheepish look on his face.

"What?" I asked.

He was blushing a bit as he leaned in toward me. "My pee is starting to smell weird," he said.

"Mine too!" I exclaimed.

He was visibly relieved. "Oh, good," he said. "Well, not good, but you know what I mean. I think it's the lentil soup."

"Oh my god. It's definitely the lentil soup," I said as I pushed another heaping spoonful into my mouth.

The soup was like crack, and even though I've never actually done crack cocaine, I can tell you in all sincerity that a bowl of that soup is as close to a hit as you're ever gonna get from a lunch. I felt like Jennifer Connelly in *Requiem for a Dream*. Pete would give me a look on the chairlift at about 11:37 a.m., and from there we would ski directly to our little hut. Then we'd gobble up the salty goodness and laugh like hyenas about everything Cerro Catedral, including the outfits.

If there's one thing my father taught me about skiing, other than the whole going, turning, and stopping part, it's that you should look the part. Whether you're a park rat, a speedster, a backcountry lightweight (because that's the only kind there is), a big mountain hucker, or a free-heeling telemarker, there's a specific style that you want to have. It's a way of communicating to those around you that you know what you're doing, that you belong.

And just as Aspen has rabbit-fur headbands and Switzerland has the ice ax, Cerro Catedral has giant blue bags. Yes, giant blue trash bags, although they have a slight shimmer to them, so you know they aren't actually trash bags. Some versions cinch a bit at the waist, in what seems like an attempt to show a bit of figure. It's an attempt, mind you, that completely backfires. Every single person dressed in a bag at Cerro Catedral—and there were hundreds— looked like a combination of Barney and the beloved McDonald's character Grimace. The bag adds at least thirty pounds to any ass, twelve or so on the thigh, and about seventeen on the upper back.

I saw one guy with a Cape Cod–style sweater tied around his shoulders, *over* the suit. I thought we'd hit the fashion jackpot until I heard Pete gasp.

"Look," he said, pointing at the ticket booth, with a facial expression that communicated he had just seen an animal on the edge of extinction. And then I saw her. A woman donning a rare magenta-colored bag stood in line at the booth. It was the pinnacle of Cerro Catedral style, and we congratulated ourselves on the new heights reached by our routine-o that day.

At about three in the afternoon, Pete and I would clock out our punch cards. Legs throbbing from a day of hard skiing, and bellies aching from hours of comic relief, we would hop back on the bus and head home. Once there, I began my recovery process, a hot/ cold rejuvenation combination known to most skiers as a hot tub and a beer. My body was holding up well thanks to all of my pre-trip training, and I was actually impressed with the strength and stamina I'd built up. Still, on most days I was bone-tired. My legs were stiff and achy, and all of the little muscles in my calves, shins, and feet would tremble as I pulled them out of my boots. If I was going to continue to work them like this for another nine months, rest and recovery was crucial.

I didn't have a hot tub or a bucket for cold beer, but I did have a shower and a bidet, and in a pinch that'll do. When I got home after skiing, I turned the shower to scalding and filled the bidet with ice and a few bottles of very dark beer. I let the piping hot water release any and all tension in my legs, assisted by the frosty, malted beverage simultaneously sliding down my throat. I would stand there congratulating myself on a good day of skiing, and on my top-notch mental capacity for rigging the bidet into something actually useful.

This was my heaven. For six or seven hours a day I was in nirvana on the mountain, and for a few hours in the evening I was in a Valhalla of recovery. I was calm and relaxed, and at the same time I was brimming with energy. That is, until I fell asleep at nine o'clock sharp every night.

I realized then that my pretrip training with Alex had been more than just physical; in many ways he'd trained me to be resilient, to remain unaffected by whatever came my way. Somehow he knew my journey wasn't going to be just about skiing. He knew I would need the type of stamina required to drag eighty-plus pounds of ski gear through twenty-plus airports without losing my composure. He knew I would need mental fortitude, the kind required when patiently explaining to the driver of the minicab in India that yes, we would be able to fit this six-foot bag in the car. We both knew I had some grit coming into all this, but in our work together the sheer power of my will turned into something much stronger, much tougher, than what I had originally brought to the table.

All of this set me up for a smashing success in South America. But I later wondered if the bullish resolve I'd worked so hard to develop was, in fact, the thing I had been most naive about. Because what happens when we rely too much on our resilience, our ability to bounce right back up off the ground? What happens if that mental stamina stops short, or that stubborn goaty well runs dry? What then? Who will take care of our precious egos then?

If you had asked me these questions at the time, I would have just shrugged. I was like a wide-eyed five-year-old running through the playground with my best friend. My hair would have been tousled and messy, and I would have had a thick streak of chocolate across my face. "I dunno," I would have said, palms facing up to the sky, before tearing down the road so I could play a game of hide-and-go-seek with Pete.

This was a time of blissful ignorance, and to be honest, I felt comfortable and perhaps even energized by that kind of blind innocence. Everything about those days at Cerro Catedral was magic. Naiveté and magic.

6

THE RUSTY DRAWBRIDGE AND THE BIG BANG . . . BUT NOT LIKE THAT. WELL, OKAY, MAYBE A LITTLE LIKE THAT.

ABOUT ONCE a week, Pete and I would see Chris and the facial hair he had begun using as a neck warmer. If the snow conditions at Cathedral were precisely as he liked them, he graced us with his presence. I was happy when that happened, but only because it meant more quality time with Chris's car. Getting a ride to the resort meant I was less likely to die on the bus from ski-pole-inflicted wounds, and for that I was grateful. On top of that, Chris's rusty drawbridge seemed to be slowly lowering (very slowly, like the speed at which glaciers travel—or at the very least the speed they used to travel when they weren't dripping all over the place in what has become a global sweat lodge).

We were on the chairlift one day when Chris reached into his backpack and pulled out a small baggie of cookies, all of which had jelly smiley faces on them. I was confused. Chris didn't seem like the kind of guy who would buy jelly-smiley-face cookies. He offered me one, and then I swear he giggled as he bit into the cookie's raspberry-flavored grin.

A week or so later, my mind was blown when Chris invited Pete and me for dinner. He was renting a small cabin on a private lake, and the whole setup was nestled deep in a national park. It was about twenty minutes west of the city by car. The cabin belonged to a friend of a friend of Chris's, which in and of itself was a shock because it meant Chris had relationships—friendly ones, even. Because the place had a small leak on the second floor, Chris's friend was renting it to him for the absurdly low price of $10 a night, thus allowing him to live in luxury as a complete and utter hermit.

Pete and I accepted the invitation, and after a day of skiing together Chris drove us all out to his place. A narrow dirt road led us through a sparsely forested area before it opened up onto a small beach complete with a glacier-fed lake. The house, a white plaster building with dark timber trim, was part cabin, part hut, and all charm. I felt like I was walking onto the set of *Lord of the Rings*.

The cabin was split into two levels. The washroom and a cozy kitchen and living area were on the bottom floor. A gorgeous clay fireplace was tucked into the corner, casting off a glow that filled the entire room. A tiny spiral staircase led from the living room to the second-floor landing, which was big enough for a few single beds, followed by a simple master bedroom and bathroom. The master had a small balcony that looked out to the lake. The water was crystal clear. You could see from the floor of the lake all the way up to the massive spires of rock dangling in the sky, the ankle-bones of the Andes. There wasn't a single person around for miles, and seeing the place, feeling it, smelling it, and hearing its stillness and silence explained a lot about Chris. Whatever it was, he was clearly there to get away from it all.

Upon arrival, Pete took a walk on the beach, I grabbed a spot right in front of the fireplace, and Chris went to the back of the house to take a quick shower. I was enjoying the solitude, and even managed to slip into a bit of a daydream. But I snapped right out of it the moment Chris walked around the corner wearing nothing but a small towel around his waist and a few lingering drops of water on his torso.

I knew Chris was fit—it was a requirement for any of us, given the type of skiing we were doing—but what I didn't know, at least not until he sauntered into the room wearing a towel that was basically just a glorified loincloth, was that he was super fit, like movie-star fit, like the only words running through my head were *Oh my god, oh my god, oh my god.* If it weren't for the fact that I was actually frozen in surprise and admiration, I would have risen to my feet to applaud him. I would have also given serious kudos to his beard for the bait-and-switch, the literal wool-over-my-eyes move it had been pulling on me for the last few weeks, distracting me from what I now saw as the real cat's meow.

Eventually Pete came in from his walk, Chris put on some clothes, and I scooped my jaw back up from the floor. We cooked up a pizza for dinner, uncorked a bottle of wine, and, after a small discussion, decided it would be best for us to stay the night. Chris wasn't terribly excited about driving us back into town, Pete was enjoying the tranquillity of it all, and I was crossing my fingers that I'd catch Chris dressed in a small strip of terry cloth one or three more times.

We drank a little more wine and shared stories, stories that were bigger and longer than the ones we could tell each other in the ten-minute intervals the chairlift allowed. Chris told us about a recent trip he'd taken, a climbing expedition to Jordan. Halfway through the story he got up and left the room, quickly returning with his computer in hand. He wanted to show us some photos. He talked at length about each picture, and while he was telling us about a night he spent with a Bedouin family in Wadi Rum, I realized that his walls were slowly crumbling. There was still a heavily armed checkpoint and a well-equipped roadblock, but as he spoke, I sensed a few bricks tumbling to the ground.

After dinner we all gathered around the fireplace. Pete lay out on the long sofa, and Chris and I sat together on a small couch against the windows. We launched into another conversation about travel, and while Pete was telling us about the handful of years he lived in Alaska, Chris reached out and grabbed my feet.

"Here, let me give you a massage," he said in a whisper, being careful not to interrupt Pete. "It's the right foot, right?"

He was referring to a few comments I had made earlier in the day, about an ache that had been building in the arch of my right foot.

"A massage will help," he added.

Although I was a bit surprised that he was offering, I accepted with a nod.

The foot rub was glorious. Every single moment of it. Chris's hands were strong but gentle, firm but merciful. I sat there and stared as he worked away on my foot.

Who is this guy? I thought, wiping away the drool that had started leaking from the corner of my mouth.

It was a question that stuck with me all through the night, and into the following day.

Who is this guy?

Chris drove us back into town the next morning, and I took the day off to rest and hit the chocolate shops. Images of Chris wearing nothing but his towel lingered in my head.

Later that afternoon, I took a hot shower. When I walked back into my bedroom and pulled open the chest of drawers, I was struck by something—and this time it was not Chris's lack of undergarments but my own. I had officially gone through every pair of fresh undies I had packed.

Using my foundational garments as a calendar to count the days I'd been in Bariloche thus far, I arrived at the conclusion that I only had a few days left before my month was up. I was due to travel farther south in two or three days' time. I was also hit with the fact that it had been well over two weeks since I had washed my sports bra or ski socks, among other things. I wasn't sure if I should be proud about this, or disgusted, or both. I chose the latter, and I started to pack.

On my last night, Pete and I sat in our beloved meat seats and said our final *adiós*. We hugged a long hug and made promises to reunite when I circled back to North America. I wasn't sure what I would do without him. Pete made me feel braver than I was and a little more badass than I'm naturally inclined to be. He gave me an edge, and I was worried about what would happen if I lost it. But instead of expressing all that, I played it cool and went home to get ready for my flight out the following day. I was on my way to Ushuaia, the southernmost city in the world and my last stop in the South American leg of my tour. Chris was my ride to the airport.

Over the last number of weeks, I had learned that Chris had come to Argentina with a few goals. The first was to see if the nonprofit he ran back in the States could get by without him. The second was to decompress after running said nonprofit for fifteen years. And the third was to do some mountaineering, to tackle a few of Patagonia's well-known peaks. One of the most technically challenging places on earth to ski and climb is a place called Fitz Roy. It's best known as the face of the Patagonia brand, that jagged black mountain emblazoned on shirts, jackets, and hats. It was the only thing left on Chris's checklist. He moved out of his *Lord of the*

Rings shire to travel south, but with a storm system passing right over Fitz Roy, he decided to join me for a few days in Ushuaia.

"I'll wait out the weather down there," he said, "and maybe we can ski a few days together."

"Sounds good," I said, noting his uncharacteristically social behavior.

A few weeks prior I had asked Pete about Chris. "What's his deal?" I'd said. "Why is he such a recluse?" Pete alluded to the fact that Chris had a past, and left it at that.

"What do you mean, 'a past'?" I pried.

"I don't know a huge amount about it, Steph," said Pete. "He gave the keynote at a conference I went to, and it was a big deal. It was a great speech. But it was rough. He hasn't had the easiest life. I think he's probably down here doing a little soul-searching. Just cut him some slack. If he seems quiet, there's probably a reason."

Although it didn't answer every question I had, it gave me some insight into why Chris was the way was he was, and it also made me nervous around him. I wasn't scared; there were zero red flags from a safety perspective, and after years of solo travel I trusted my red flag system. It was just that the amount of alone time we now had planned together—in the car, at the airport, on a plane, and at the next ski resort—seemed daunting for the extrovert in me. I wondered what we would talk about. When someone is quiet, I don't really know how to cut them some slack. I get all sweaty-palmed and anxious, and then I just blabber on incessantly about totally random stuff. Basically, I make things awkward.

The only thing I could do was rely on my strength: playing it cool. So I threw my gear in the back of Chris's car, and as we started down the dusty Argentine highway, I tried to be as chill as possible, keeping my rambling thoughts inside my head and my head only. After a while, though, I just couldn't help myself. I took a deep breath, and started to talk. At first I was a bit apprehensive, but it didn't take long for me to turn into a gushing waterfall of words. And much to my surprise, Chris responded. We talked for the next two hours. We talked about my trip and all the people who had said I was crazy. We talked about relationships and why we weren't in them. We talked about the books we were reading and the ones we had read. We talked about where we had traveled, and he told me about his gnarly knee surgery, and his back surgery, and that time he broke his elbow. We talked and talked and talked.

I felt as though I was shedding layers of myself. There had been some sort of cumulative buildup, like I'd been rolling coats of paint over myself for months without even knowing it, and now they were peeling right off.

All of the months of anxious preparation. All of the travel, hauling my bags through multiple airports and multiple time zones. All the speed of these last two months, and all of those freezing cold days on the hill. They all peeled away and left me open and relaxed.

At some point in the conversation, I stuck my hand out the window and felt a warm breeze. I could feel the thick air as it lingered on my fingers and hand, before it moved up my right arm and came rushing into the car. It was early September, and in that moment, I could actually feel the South American winter starting to slip into spring. It made me want to slow everything down. I had been so fixated on the speed of this trip, the tearing, screaming, and flying down mountains. I wanted to pause, albeit briefly.

I should slow down.

I turned to Chris and asked if he wanted to pull over, maybe go for a walk somewhere. We had a little bit left in the drive, but our flight didn't leave until early the next morning. Our plan had been to find a cheap, and therefore quite putrid, hotel by the airport. It was a stunning day. I was in no rush to get to said putrid hotel.

"I know the perfect place," Chris said calmly.

I wasn't sure how he knew "the perfect place," considering we were in the-middle-of-nowhere Argentina, but I went with it.

"Great," I said with a nod. "Whatever's easy."

About twenty minutes later, Chris pulled off the main road and started down a wide gravel path that ran briefly along the highway before veering left onto what seemed like a private road on the outside edge of a property. I saw a basic wire fence marking what looked like an old farm, and eventually we came upon a small gate. Chris got out of the car and lifted a thin wire loop that had been pulled over a wooden post. It seemed clear that he'd been here before, but it was also possible that he was just a really experienced trespasser. I watched as he swung the gate open. The whole area seemed deserted. Suddenly I felt nervous. I scanned my red flag system, and I picked up on a small flash of panic.

Do I really know this guy? Where are we exactly? Is this a smart idea, veering off the road with a man I barely know just because he said he "knows the perfect place"? What the fuck? What do I do?

Chris got back in the car. "We're almost there," he said, an uncharacteristically wide smile plastered across his face. I thought I was going to be sick.

Oh my god. Can I run? Where should I go? Are my wallet and passport close by?

I sat frozen in my seat but prepared myself to bolt. I watched as the narrow road opened up. Shortly after, Chris parked the car.

"We're here!" he announced.

I got out of the car, my mouth open in awe. A series of perfectly stacked log cabins were scattered to either side of us, the largest of which stood at attention in the middle, half cabin, half castle. Horses were trotting around a large ring to our left, and two giant golden retrievers came bounding in our direction, tongues out, tails wagging. In the distance, a thick, Black Forest kind of forest climbed up the side of a jagged mountain, and yet another gorgeous Argentine lake was floating just beyond the cabins. It looked like a sapphire on the hand of a queen. The smell of pine and a wood-burning fire floated through the air.

"This is Peuma Hue," said Chris, the smile still wide across his face. "It means 'place of dreams' in Mapuche, the indigenous language."

I stood there quietly as my pounding heart moved to a slow and steady rhythm. If this was pressing pause, it would do.

The door to the main lodge opened, and a man and woman walked toward us. When they got closer, the man spread his arms out wide to give Chris a big hug.

"Chris! Wow! It's so nice to see you," he said. "How have you been, my friend?" He spoke English but had a thick Argentine accent. The woman stood just behind him, holding a tiny kitten in her hands.

"I've been great, Fernando. Really good," said Chris. "Is Eve here?" he asked. "I'd like to introduce her to Steph." He turned to me. "Eve's the owner," he explained.

"No," said Fernando, "she's away. But come in, come in. We have new little kittens. Let us pour you some matcha, and then you can meet the kittens."

"Great," Chris said. "We're on our way to the airport for an early flight tomorrow morning, and I thought it would be nice to break up the drive. Is it okay if we take a walk so I can show Steph around?"

"Of course, my friend," said Fernando. "But if your flight leaves tomorrow, where are you staying tonight?"

"Oh, we're just going to grab a hotel by the airport," said Chris.

"No, no," said Fernando firmly. "You will stay here, with us. We insist. We can get a room ready for you, and you will stay here. We're having fresh *trucha* for dinner. They caught it this morning.

Besides," he continued, "the roads are never busy in the morning. It will be easy for you to get to the airport from here."

Chris looked at me for confirmation. At that point, I'd swung pretty sharply away from the idea that he was planning to bludgeon me to death in the forest. I mean, it was still possible, but the golden retrievers at my feet, and the fact that the young woman was now bottle-feeding a kitten, suggested otherwise. Add to that a meal of fresh trout, and I was willing to roll the dice.

I shrugged and nodded.

Chris turned back to Fernando. "Are you sure?" he asked. "We don't want to be an inconvenience."

"It's not an inconvenience," Fernando said, "and I know Eve would want you to stay. Why don't you take a kayak out while we get everything ready for you?"

Fernando ushered us toward a boat shed at the edge of the property, and then went back inside the main lodge to have a room made up.

Chris and I pulled a tandem kayak free as he filled me in on how he'd met and become friends with Eve, the owner of Peuma Hue.

"I heard about this place before I arrived," said Chris. "I can't remember how, maybe when I was doing a little research about the area. Anyway, when I got here, I reached out. I really wanted to meet the person who had created all this. So Eve and I had lunch, and it was like . . . you know when you meet someone and have an instant connection?"

"Mm-hmm," I said, nodding my head.

"We had that," said Chris. "Professionally. We've both put our heart and souls into creating things that are designed to help people heal, where they could connect with nature and transform themselves."

Chris was referring to the nonprofit he ran back in the States. He'd told me a bit about it, but I hadn't understood the scope of his work and his passion until that moment. It suddenly clicked in my brain. *Wait, he's a really good guy. Like really, really good. He's like a mountain-man version of Mother Teresa, for Christ's sake.*

Chris continued talking as we walked the kayak to the edge of the water. I climbed into the front as he held the boat steady. He slipped into the back and pushed us gently off the shore, and we started to paddle. Up close, the lake looked like one giant emerald, platinum sparkles streaming behind our oars on every stroke. When we got to the middle of the lake, Chris dared me to put one of my hands in the icy water. We had a contest to see whose hand could last longer. Chris won, but only because I was laughing so hard I could barely breathe.

We paddled a bit more, stopping when we got to the middle of the lake. It was completely silent. In that moment, I felt both lost and found. I had no clue where I was physically, geographically, but at the same time I knew exactly where I was mentally and emotionally. I was overjoyed, filled to the brim with happiness. This trip so far had been everything I wanted and more. I leaned back, looked up at the bright blue sky, and reached my arms out wide. I wanted to grab hold of the moment. I closed my eyes, and when I did, I felt Chris place his hands over mine. He pulled on them gently, drawing my arms even wider, stretching my chest open to the sky. It felt like I was reaching directly into heaven. I didn't want Chris to let go of my hands.

And then all of a sudden, as we were floating in the middle of the lake with my arms spread wide, I felt a jolt, the unmistakable current of electricity.

Here's the thing about electricity, though—regardless of its strength, it is guaranteed to throw you back. It's an instinctual reaction. The moment we see a flash, the second we feel any charge at all, we can't help but flinch and pull back. We can't help but let go of whatever it is we're holding on to.

The jolt had been an instant. And in that instant my hands were back in my lap, and Chris's were on the oars. He paddled quickly to shore.

When we got back to the main lodge, Fernando gave us the key to our room and told us dinner would be ready in a few hours. We rolled our bags down the hallway and unlocked the door. When it swung open, revealing a luxurious queen-size bed in the middle of the room, I had to laugh. It hadn't occurred to me to provide Fernando with any instructions about our sleeping arrangement, which until now had definitely not included Chris and me sharing a queen-size bed.

"Looks like we're gonna be spooning tonight," I said with a grin.

I know what you're wondering. Why didn't she ask for a different room? Or one with separate beds? Or one of those rolling cots, for crying out loud? I suppose I could have done that, but those options seemed both greedy and needy to me, and I don't like to be either of those things. When someone is already going out of their way to accommodate you, when they offer you a free room at a $400-a-night hotel, including a gourmet meal for two, you don't ask for more. You say, "Yes. Thank you. Thank you very much." Plus, I was feeling too relaxed to be assertive, not to mention the fact that being assertive is totally un-Canadian. Sorry, but it is. Besides, I know myself pretty well when it comes to these things. On the prude-to-tramp continuum I fall squarely in the middle. I wasn't bothered by sharing a bed with Chris; I thought of it as a slumber party with a sexy, sexy man, one I would openly ogle while he was changing, but one I had no interest in touching. Okay, fine, maybe there was a little interest in touching, but not in the romantic way, only in the way you would if someone were to allow you to run your hand along the edge of the Venus de Milo.

Even after the electroshock therapy on the boat, I figured Chris and I were both adult enough to navigate the waters involved in going halfsies on a down quilt, and I was right. Chris nodded in what felt like an honest and mature acknowledgement that we were going to be sharing the bed and nothing else.

After that, the evening took its course, the first of which came in the form of champagne and *aperitivos* with the other guests staying at Peuma Hue. Dinner was served at a private table overlooking the lake, with fresh trout as promised, and dessert was devoured in front of the roaring fireplace with a book in hand. While I wasn't completely roughing it on my trip, I certainly hadn't indulged in this kind of luxury thus far, and so I reveled in the evening. I drank a little more wine than usual and just sat with my thoughts, which, in case you were wondering, were: My life is awesome. My life is so fucking awesome right now.

Around ten o'clock, Chris and I returned to our room, made a few awkward jokes, and then climbed into our respective sides of the bed while ensuring a significant amount of room between us.

"Okay. Night," I said.

"Night. Don't steal all the covers," he said with a snicker.

I was lying on my side, facing away from Chris, trying to keep my body as still as possible. My breath was shallow, and then I felt it again. It was just a slight reverberation, a hint of a current, but it was unmistakable. There was another jolt of electricity between us.

Everything that followed was a sleepy blur, not quite conscious, not quite unconscious. At some point Chris's arm unfolded, crossing the imaginary line that ran down the center of the bed. I felt his hand as it came to rest beside my pillow. Minutes, or maybe hours, later, I rolled onto my other side, the edge of my face just touching his forefinger and thumb. I woke up briefly, feeling his hand as it gently stroked my forehead. Slowly our bodies unfurled, inching rather innocently toward one another. Two little magnets in the night. When we woke up the next morning, his body was cradling mine. He was holding me so tightly that I couldn't tell where I ended and he began.

It reminded me of a plant in the sun. There's no brain guiding it, telling it to turn and lean into the light. It's just what the plant does because that's what it was created to do. The instructions are built into every cell.

"It feels so nice being close to you," he breathed into my neck. Another flash of energy moved between us, and in the surge of electricity his words clung to me, pinned gently to my neck for a moment.

What just happened? I thought to myself as I slipped off to the bathroom to wash my face. Did something happen?

I wasn't sure how to answer these questions, but it felt like Chris had finally taken off his mask. Or who knows, maybe I had peeled it off for him. Regardless, his true face had been revealed, and I was a little bit startled by what I found. Not in the way that the woman in *Phantom of the Opera* is startled when the Phantom takes off his mask, but surprised nonetheless. I thought Chris was aloof and standoffish, and now here he was being warm, and open, and dare I say sensitive. Had I found his vulnerable side now that the drawbridge was down? One thing was certain: I'd been wrong about him.

.˙•.

ON OUR FLIGHT TO Ushuaia, we had a layover in a town called El Calafate. The stop gave us just enough time to rent a car, whip down the highway, and sit for an hour in front of the Perito Moreno Glacier, a must for anyone traveling in the region.

Perito Moreno is one of the few glaciers on the planet that is still growing. It is massive, like you-can't-see-the-beginning-or-the-end massive, or if-hell-froze-over-and-was-beautiful-I-think-this-is-actually-what-it-would-look-like massive. Nothing about the glacier itself looks like ice; it more closely resembles a giant chain-mail wedding train worn centuries ago by some mythic bride. Charcoal-gray streaks spill down the fabric, as if the bride herself had run through fields of ash or sharp black stones. The edges are ragged and frayed, scarred by the work of an untalented tailor. I looked at it and wondered if I had years of sediment stitched into my own frayed fabric; I wondered what, if anything, I had carried through my life thus far.

I also wondered how something could both grow and melt at the same time. My measly little human eyes couldn't see the glacier crawling forward, of course, but I knew it was, and not just because I read a brochure in the gift shop. I knew it because I could hear it. The eerie splitting sound, like a deep whisper in the darkness coming from a source you can't quite grasp, and then the loud cracks, like the ones you hear when you drop ice cubes into a glass of 7-Up, only multiplied by the thousands.

As the afternoon sun bore down, I heard the ice laboring for breath, its chest pushing forward with such force that it eventually exploded, cleaving off the parts of itself it could no longer carry. I heard those pieces pop before crashing into the lake below. But they weren't really pieces; they were much larger than that. They were skyscrapers, painted blue, and they were tumbling into a huge body of water below. They pierced the surface, dove down deep, and then came fighting once again to the top, gasping for air, huge waves of water pushing out in every direction. And the cycle continued. The ice groaned and strained in an attempt to adjust to its new size, and then it split, cracked, and cast whole chunks of itself off in an attempt to make room for the new. Except the new was still buried, hundreds of miles away, in a place you couldn't see.

For now, my job was to stand and stare, wide-eyed and a little wet behind the ears, at the tip of an iceberg. But it wouldn't take long for me to feel as if I were standing right on top of it, for me to see just how much of it sat below the surface of the water, and for it all to come crashing down, section by glaciated section. I thought I knew what this adventure was all about. I thought I was in control. But as it turns out, the journey I was on was much bigger than me and my ability to ram all over the place.

You know that's how it happens, right? We get lured toward starting lines and implicated in adventures by some little hook that snags our egos. But the rest, the real reason behind the journey—well, we have to wait for things to crack and cleave off before that is revealed.

I felt Chris at my side, and I noticed that his hand had slipped into mine. I looked up into his greeny-blue eyes, and in that moment I wanted so badly to know what it felt like to swim inside them. He leaned down to kiss me, and oh, the water was warm.

7

THE END OF THE EARTH

A LOT of people refer to Ushuaia as *el fin del mundo*—the end of the world—but for me it felt like a beginning. Most of this had to do with the fact that, upon arrival, I handed my reeking bag of laundry (otherwise known as a large plastic baggie full of well-worn underwear, rancid socks, and sweat-soaked sports bras) to the hotel concierge, but there were other reasons too. By the time we got there, I had skied well over 500,000 vertical feet, and I felt like there was a good amount of energy left in the tank. The last seven weeks had been the appetizer. Now I was ready for the main course, and I found it each morning in Ushuaia.

As I stood on top of the mountains in Argentina's deep south, I was, quite literally, taking in the world from a completely different perspective. Technically, I was at the bottom of the world, but I felt like I was on top of it, like I was doing the exact thing I'd set out to do in the first place. I was planting my Jaggery flag in the snow and claiming everything around me as mine. It was as if I was screaming at the top of my lungs for everyone around to hear, "This is Jaggerville! It's like Margaritaville but snowier!" I felt like the most powerful version of myself. There was no denying it.

Now, someone could have easily argued that how I looked, what I wore, and the way I smelled told a much different story, but I considered all of that proof of my resolve, part of my complete and utter badassery. I was proud of my wet long johns and blackened toenails. The fact that I had holes poking through all of my polyesters, and that I'd taken to wearing a pair of green gumboots on every single non-ski occasion, filled me with satisfaction. Each day I crammed my feet into rigid ski boots, ate waffles made in the back of a grungy van, and drank from dusty beer bottles served as evidence that I was one of the guys. I was pleased with my rapid-growth quads, no matter how pale they were. And I liked that my ski pants, after being ridden hard and put away wet every day, looked as though they'd spent a night or two in a Bogota prison. *Yes*, they screamed, *isn't she gritty?* I was a woman who carried a large knife, some duct tape, and a shovel in her backpack, and I loved it. All of these things, pants included, felt like a badge of honor, and it was one I wore with a highfalutin kind of pride.

If anything was falling away, if any part of me was tumbling to the ground, I felt it was an improvement, something sure to make me better, faster, and tougher. All those people who made cliché comments about Michelangelo were right. The David had always been there; all that needed to happen was a chipping away of the parts that weren't really David. The end result would be a stunning symbol representing strength, courage, and a whole bunch of manly magnificence. Yes, please. I'll take that.

I also felt I was impressing the pants off my dad, which was something I considered an integral part of my act as a Markhor. Ask any impersonator, and she'll tell you that winning approval from the person you're pretending to be is key. It means you've made it. It means the imitation is good enough to fool pretty much anyone. Ultimately, if the House of Chanel gives a bag a thumbs-up, the bag is real.

How did I know I was impressing the pants off my dad? Because skiing was, and still is, a direct route to his heart. My knowledge of this started with a pair of faded blue mittens, hand-me-downs that had made their way from my sister and through both of my brothers to me. They were badly beaten by the time I got them— partially due to the storms they had weathered, but also because of the eight or so years of frozen snot layered on the inside edge of each thumb. Their elastic cuffs were stretched out like an old sock, and they had lost almost all of their puffiness. Visually, they were horrid little things, but it didn't matter—I thought everything about those soggy old mittens was wonderful. I wanted them badly because I knew wearing them meant I was old enough, big enough, and, in my mind, good enough to ski with my dad. Looking back, I suppose they could be considered my very first ribbon.

I still remember the day my mom pulled those gloves onto my hands and pushed my ski boots down into the bindings of my brother's old—and my new—Rossignol skis. There were small roosters painted onto the tips of those skis, and I recall looking down at them nervously before searching for my dad, who was waiting for me lower down on the hill. Skiing with him was, and still is, a very important milestone in the life of a young Jagger.

I saw him through my goggles. He was just a few hundred feet away, his arms outstretched, ready to catch me as I slowly plowed toward him. And there it was. That smile. He was delighted with me, and I knew it.

"Hands on your knees," he said, pride and a little bit of nervousness in his voice. "Hands on your knees, Steph."

I moved down the hill in a jerky stop-and-start motion, arms hovering out in front of me, little mitten-covered hands dangling from the ends of them. I must have looked like a skiing zombie, but it didn't matter, I felt like I was flying.

Eventually, my dad had me ski right beside him. He used his poles to make a little bar for me to hang on to, one he held out at his side. I clung to those poles and we soared down the mountain together, wind on our cheeks, my tiny fists white-knuckling underneath those mucus-covered mittens, holding on tight to both the poles and the moment. If you had pulled down the itchy neck warmer that covered the lower half of my little face, you would have seen that I was smiling from ear to ear. It's the same grin that spreads across my face when I go skiing today. A soul skier was born the day I got those mittens, and from that day on, I knew what it looked and felt like to have my father's approval.

That's what made all of this so perfect. I was skiing around the world, wearing an altimeter on my wrist that my father had given me as a gift before the trip, a gift I interpreted as a sign of both pride and permission. I felt like I was two steps from the top of Everest, two steps from being told I was an authentic Chanel bag. I was doing what I had set out to do, achieving everything I wanted to achieve. I was so close to being what I wanted to be, what I thought I should be. I was holding Jaggerdom in the palms of my hands.

The other reason for feeling like I was the cat's pajamas was Chris. Our glacial kiss at Perito Moreno had turned into kisses (plural), and a whole lot more. For five days straight we explored Ushuaia's main resort, Cerro Castor. We skied well out of bounds, dropped chutes, and dodged around bits of Patagonian rock. We walked across cornices so big it felt like we were on the moon. Massive slabs of ice curled like waves over giant fields of snow. We explored hidden terrain, places where there wasn't a single ski track in sight. We hiked in and skied out, linking figure-eight turns in the deep Argentine powder.

And although the exploring we did at night was of a different kind, it matched and mirrored the physical efforts we made in the daylight. Hearts pounded, thighs quivered, both of us gasping for air.

"Isn't it amazing what two athletic people can do," Chris said one night as he tossed me from the bed and pinned me to the wall in one fell swoop.

If I could have responded, I would have. I think it would have added to the heat of an already hot moment if I'd been able to say something really sexy like, "Stop talking. [*Gasp.*] Keep fucking." Oh, who's kidding who. That's exactly what I said.

.: .

THE WEATHER MOVES QUICKLY in the mountains. As soon as the storm had rolled in, it rolled on. Not because we wanted it to end, but because Chris had Fitz Roy to bag, and I had a flight to New Zealand to catch.

We hugged a long hug and parted ways in the hotel lobby.

"Give me a shout when you circle back to North America," Chris said as he gathered his bags.

"For sure," I replied. "Sometime in March."

Twenty minutes later I gathered my own bags, one of them full of astonishingly fresh laundry. And with that I was ready to leave South America behind for my trip down under. Nothing was going to hold me back from my goal. Blue ribbons were far more important than boys.

PART TWO

MIDDLE EARTH

They cling avidly to what they are—what they were. And then at last the worn-out personality, which should have been molted like the annual plumage of a bird, so adheres that they cannot shake it off, even when it has become for them an exasperation.

—**HEINRICH ZIMMER,** *THE KING AND THE CORPSE*

8

WIND ON THE NIPPLE

A FEW months before I left on my trip, I was driving across Vancouver's Burrard Street Bridge with a friend. The morning light bounced off the water below us, and as we drove, it looked as though a stone was skipping, tiny glimmers of light hopping over the surface of the water. It was spring, and the air was crisp.

"I'm really looking forward to New Zealand," I said as I looked out over English Bay. "I think she'll look just like this. Like Vancouver, like BC. New Zealand is the place I'm most excited about."

Regardless of the fact that I had never been to New Zealand, I had a clear picture of what my experience there was going to be. Physically, I thought the country was going to be immediately recognizable, a spitting-image relative of British Columbia who maybe went a little wild with some 1980s eye shadow. And, as a bonus, we shared a mother tongue, which meant no more pig Latin. New Zealand was going to be similar looking and sounding, and thus familiar feeling.

For months I held firm to my expectations and assumptions, and by the time I arrived, I had convinced myself that traveling through New Zealand was going to be both comfortable and easy. Just knowing I could ask for the washroom without people looking at me strangely gave me great satisfaction. I hated looking lost and confused, and in New Zealand there was no way I could look lost and confused. I could read the maps, I could speak the language, and I loved sauvignon blanc. What could go wrong? This gorgeous little country was going to be my vacation, a six-week reprieve in ten months of travel.

What is the difference between vacationing and traveling, you might ask? Allow me to explain. For me, traveling has always been about going to a foreign place and taking care of yourself while you're there, amid all of the foreignness. It's fun, but it's not as relaxing as going on vacation because you have to do things like use hand gestures to communicate, eat food you're not sure is food, and, in many cases, relive moments of panic from your eighth-grade math class as you attempt complicated currency conversions in your head. Also, you're probably going to get scolded and shamed in some way, via looks of disbelief and/or hand gestures that communicate something along the lines of *You, my friend, are a bumbling idiot and shouldn't be allowed to wander freely in the world.*

In my mind, going on vacation is the opposite. Other than timing your transition from 30 SPF sunscreen to 15, and even down to 8 if you're a real gambler, there's very little panic involved in vacationing. For the most part, you get to speak your own language, eat food you know is food, and use US dollars or even small plastic beads to pay for things. How fun! Being on vacation allows us to engage in lots of mind-numbing things, which is of huge benefit, whereas traveling will include more mind-blowing things—also of benefit, but a very different one. Typically we *go* traveling, whereas on vacation we're more likely to simply exist, like say on a lounge chair, with a drink that has an itty-bitty umbrella in it.

Now, don't get me wrong, I love traveling. I wouldn't have signed myself up for ten months of it if it didn't make me a little weak in the knees. But my mother tongue and I were looking forward to a small vacation.

As it turns out, I was right about New Zealand's looks—her beauty is obvious. I was hit with it before the plane even touched the ground. As we soared over the top of her on my flight into Christchurch, I saw lakes and rivers braided together below us. The water was so bright it looked like a fluorescent turquoise streamer, bending in the wind behind an excited child. I watched the sky in awe as clouds and a whole series of colors moved in and out of view. It was as if someone was shuffling a colorful deck of cards in the sky: some were pale blue, others a deep Prussian color, here a bruised navy, there a dark eggplant. The horizon itself was blood orange, like ripe tangerines sitting on the edge of the earth, just waiting to be grabbed and turned into juice. What I saw from the little window of my plane was more dramatic than I had even imagined. My welcome to the country was big and bold, as if ruby-red peacocks had been let loose to dance all over the place, streaking everything in sight with their color.

And that was just a taste, a small sample of New Zealand's beauty. She is supernaturally natural, a trippy kind of beautiful. She is British Columbia on acid. I'm hesitant to say this because all of Canada will be passive-aggressively mad at me for life, but I can't lie—New Zealand makes BC look like a part-time model in a vacuum cleaner ad. I'm sorry, eh, but it's true. In the six weeks I spent there, I never saw anything ugly. Not a single thing.

When I arrived in the country, I had a smidgen over 700,000

vertical feet under my belt. At a minimum, I was hoping to double that number during my six-week vacation, a piece of Kiwi cake assuming faster lifts and calmer springtime weather.

From Christchurch I boarded a puddle jumper on its way to Queenstown, a small city tucked into the tail end of the Southern Alps. Almost as soon as the propellers began to turn, I heard a few people from the back of the plane begin to sing. Within seconds every single person on board, including the air stewardesses and pilots, had joined in for an exuberant rendition of John Denver's "Leaving on a Jet Plane." I smiled to myself. New Zealand was going to be fantastic.

About thirty minutes later, I was singing a bit of a different tune. Ever since the final verse, the plane had been bouncing through heavy turbulence. At one point, I glanced out the window and was immediately sorry I did. What I saw made me wonder if I had been cast in Helen Hunt's role for a remake of that storm-chaser movie. The guy next to me must have noticed the fear washing across my face, because he turned to me and said, "Just a bit of weather. Tasman's angry, is all."

He was referring to the Tasman Sea, which, I learned, was a body of water forever in the midst of her terrible twos. This was something she demonstrated by launching into a full-blown fit upon my arrival. The fit included howling winds and sheets of rain. And just in case you're wondering, yes, even while dressed as a screaming toddler, New Zealand was beautiful.

As a skier, I came into this trip highly aware of one thing: weather was the single biggest variable outside my control. More than anything else, warmth, cold, wind, rain, sleet, snow—and lack thereof—were the largest threat to my plans. I had been totally okay with this, but that was only because I hadn't yet met New Zealand weather.

My initial reaction to the storm, once the place had safely

landed, was one of joy. The Tasman's temper tantrum looked like an extension of winter, and more snow meant more skiing. Combine that with the fact that I could ask for a glass of water without having to break out my Spanish dictionary, and I resumed my belief that I was in heaven.

I grabbed a cab outside the airport, gave the driver the address of my hostel, and loaded my ski bag into the back of the car. As I slid into the front seat, the driver turned to face me.

"It's a hundrid kay'eem on the nipple," he said.

The rain was beating down loudly on top of the car.

"Excuse me?" I asked.

"A hundred kay'eem on the nip," he shouted.

"I'm sorry, I don't—"

He cut me off. "The wind. You won't be skiing for at least a day or two," he said as he gestured back in the direction of my ski bag.

I was staying at a small youth hostel on the edge of town, and as soon as I pulled my soggy bags through the door, I asked the girl behind the desk if she had a mountain report.

"Yis," she said with an obvious Kiwi accent.

She handed me a sheet of paper. My cabdriver had been right. All four of the local mountains were closed until further notice.

No biggie, I thought. This would give me a few days to get over the jet lag.

I took a nap, went for a run in the sleet, which was not unlike allowing an angry camel to spit directly in my eyes, and got a bikini wax. The joy of walking into a salon and saying, "Bikini wax, please," as opposed to communicating by pointing to my crotch and mimicking a ripping motion, was second to none. The vacation was going well, but it didn't take long for me to get a little antsy, you know, with all that wind on the nipple.

I came to understand, rather quickly, that in order to ski, or do anything outdoors in this tiny country, one had to develop a to-the-minute understanding of the weather. It was not unlike trying to predict the disposition of a teenager. One had to be aware of the infinite possibility of conditions at all times. This included the weather conditions, road conditions, and driving conditions, the rain, snow, and sleet conditions, and the blustery, gale-force wind conditions. This list was conditional, of course, and based almost entirely on whether you had access to snow chains, four-wheel drive, a car, a boat, Gore-Tex underwear, windshield wipers that worked, and a weather forecast every three minutes.

After two or three days, the storm finally moved along and the skies cleared. I decided to ski at a place called Coronet Peak. A fair bit of snow had fallen in the storm, and I was excited for my first taste of Kiwi powder. After doing some research during the oodles of free time I'd had over the last few days, I learned that the best fall line skiing on the mountain was in the back bowls. I wanted to ski a few runs in the fresh snow before spending the rest of the day catching up on vertical, so I took the main lift to the very top of the resort and went directly to the entrance of one of the bowls. When I got there, a small line of skiers had formed, all men, and all eager to score a line or two in the same area.

The line started to move as soon as ski patrol opened the entrance, but it didn't take long before people were jumping out of it, darting around either side of one another in an effort to be the first to the top. They clamored and pushed, and I could have sworn I heard squealing. It was as if they were a parcel of hungry hogs, nosing their way to a spot at the trough. Although I didn't typically take part in this kind of jostling, I was used to it. On a powder day, a little brouhaha jockeying takes place at every resort. But what happened next was brand-new for me.

One of the men behind me started really hustling up the hill. I wondered how many Red Bulls he'd chugged, and if he'd ever seen snow before. He was manic. He came up quickly beside me, but instead of whizzing right by, he slowed just a bit. He gave me a quick up and down, and then said, "Move on over, little lady. This one's for the big boys."

I felt wave of heat rise up from the pit of my stomach, all the way through my chest and neck, until it flashed across my cheeks.

Did he just call me a little lady?

I paused for a moment and watched him scramble up the rest of the hill. The ram in me had been triggered—I could feel those massive Markhor horns spiral right out of my head.

I am NOT a little fucking lady!

I was instantly enraged. Taking my cue from New Zealand, I erupted like a Kiwi volcano, spitting all over the place as if to say, "Oh, yeah? Are you sure you wanna know who the big boy is?"

This guy didn't know who I was. He didn't know about my giant set of balls, and he didn't know I was on a mission to prove I was one of the guys—but he was about to find out. As soon as that chauvinistic little prick passed by, I became set on one thing and one thing only: I would be throwing my cojones directly in his face.

I marched up the hill, my eyes glued to the back of his jacket. When we got to the top, I watched him as he pushed his boots down into his skis. He was panicking a bit, and in the rush of it all he hadn't taken the time to clear the snow from the bottom of his left boot. As a result, the heel of his boot kept popping up from the binding he was trying so hard to force it into.

I walked over beside him and placed my skis directly next to his. I tapped the snow off my boots and pushed them into my skis. Then I turned to him and smiled.

"Go ahead," I said, motioning down the hill with my arm. "Gentlemen first."

He grumbled something under his breath, shoved his boot into his ski, and started down the hill. I watched from above as he took a few turns, and although he was decent, I could tell he didn't have a lot of experience skiing in powder. I took off down the hill and skied up on his right-hand side. And then, when I was *just* ahead of him, I took a hard left turn, and cut him right off. From there, I screamed down the hill. I took wide arcs through the snow, making sure I marked up as much of the run as possible. It was the equivalent of a dog pissing on everything, not just on every bush, or on the corner of each block, but in a constant stream, everywhere.

When I got to the bottom, I was a bit surprised. I thought I'd feel good. I thought I'd feel victorious. I'd just sucker punched the bully! I thought all the kids would gather around, hoist me on their shoulders, and call me their hero. At a minimum, I thought I would be pleased with myself. But I wasn't. Instead, I felt like shit. I skied on my own for the rest of the day, my tail tucked ever so slightly between my legs.

It hit me as I was driving back to the hostel. What I'd done, that whole peacock display, that puffy-chested spectacle of ostentation I'd put on, it didn't make me better than him. In fact, it made me exactly like him. Only a total chauvinist would think someone had to man up to prove themselves. Only someone who was really scared, or someone who didn't feel good enough, or seen, or special in the world, would throw a set of balls around like that, pretending they were a ram.

And then it hit me harder. I recognized that voice. I knew that phrase. For years, for decades, for almost my entire life, I was the one who'd been screaming. I was the one who had yelled, "Move on over, little lady." From the moment I discovered that my head was too big for that red pillbox hat, I'd told myself to move over. I'd shoved my femininity to the side and decided that life was for the big boys and that I was going to be one of them. How could I be mad at someone else for saying the same thing I said to myself daily?

This entire trip was about confirming that I was one of the guys, and the first chance I'd gotten to really man up, I had. But it felt awful. It didn't feel like a big blue ribbon. It felt small and petty. This was unfamiliar territory for me. Up until this point, manning up had always felt good. The excitement in my grand-father's voice when he found out I made the rugby team in high school, and the joy I felt because of it. The rush of adrenaline that coursed through my body when I beat my dad down the ski hill for the first time. The in-your-face pride I felt when I went tequila shot for tequila shot with my brother's best friends, and they nick-named me Frank the Tank (although it's a bit of a foggy memory, I remember beaming in delight).

But this time, there was no feeling of reward. I rubbed my fore-head. What now? I wondered. What do I do now?

And that's how I arrived again at the starting line, back at the very same question that had prompted this grand adventure.

What's next, little lady?

Experience told me to grab a broom and start sweeping, so that's what I did. I swept these questions right under the proverbial rug. I didn't know how to look insight in the eye. That seemed like an awfully uncomfortable thing to do. The only discomfort I was comfortable with was the pushing kind, the speed-and-endurance kind, not the slowing-down-and-getting-patient kind, not the looking-things-in-the-eye kind. And this questioning seemed like an annoying distraction. So I swatted it away like a bug and stuck with what I knew, what I was good at. With my sights still firmly focused on my goal, I kept moving.

9

LEVI MCCONAUGHEY, TWO KINDS OF TOUGH, AND A WI-FI CONNECTION

WHEN I got back to the hostel, I collapsed onto the couch. I hadn't really used the communal area of the hostel because I wasn't a leggy blonde from Germany just shy of her nineteenth birthday, or a twenty-two-year-old from Ireland whose goal was to drink two dozen Jägerbombs before attempting to sleep with said leggy blonde. But it was four in the afternoon, nap time for the young-sters, and the entire communal area was guaranteed to be empty. I sat there for a while, staring at the dingy carpet and the beanbag chairs scattered about the room. I felt like I was in a giant sandbox that was filled to the brim with tiny little bits of my confusion. For the first time in my life, manning up had felt awful, and I wasn't sure where that left me. I let out a sigh, closed my eyes, and leaned my head back on the top of the couch.

A voice cut through the silence. "How was the skiing?" it said.

I opened my eyes and looked up. Standing right in front of me was the tallest, darkest, most delicious-looking person I had ever seen. He was a cool glass of chocolate milk, probably from Bariloche. He had a big smile on his face, and he was eating a banana.

I couldn't speak. Not a word. All I could do was stare.

His skin was beautiful, and he had perfect teeth, perfect curly hair, and perfect salted-caramel eyes. He was gorgeous. He was a brown-skinned Matthew McConaughey.

"I'm Paulo," he said.

He was Paulo.

"I've seen you around," he continued. "You went for a run the other day in that storm."

"Mm-hmm," I nodded, before finally finding enough composure to put a sentence together. "Where are you . . . where are you from?"

"Brazil," he said.

Of course he's from Brazil. He was a Brazilian Matthew McConaughey. He was Matthew McConaughey and Camila Alves's young son Levi, grown up, standing in front of me in all his manly splendor.

He smiled and laughed a little, before taking another bite of his banana. "Want some?" he asked. "I have lots."

I shook my head, but internally my entire body was nodding yes. And not about the banana.

"You should come out with us tonight," he said. "There's a group of us heading to the bar around the corner."

I had already looked at the weather report for the next day— high winds and sleet on the nipple. I knew I wouldn't be skiing.

Why not? I thought. What the hell.

Later that night a gaggle of blondes, a few drunken Irishmen, McConaughey Jr., and I hit the town in style. I wore my rubber boots because they were all I had, and then I got really fancy with an extra layer of Chapstick.

In my mind, my main job that night would be to stare at really good-looking people who were all five to ten years my junior. I would act as wingwoman, helping Paulo score with one of the little Gigi Hadids walking around like giraffes in miniskirts—and that's exactly what I did. I sat on a stool, ordered a vodka soda, and immediately began pointing out beautiful women.

"There, Paulo," I said. "Her. She's gorgeous."

He laughed. "No. Not her."

"Well, that's just not possible. Look at her," I said. "Even *I'm* interested in her! Okay, not your type? Fine. What about her?" I pointed out a feisty-looking brunette, and then a tall Jennifer Lawrence look-alike, and then a stunning girl with short blond hair. This went on for hours, me pointing, him laughing.

A while into this game, as I was pointing out yet another young girl, Paulo grabbed my hand. He gently placed it in my lap, looked me dead in the eye, and very slowly, he placed his hands on either side of my stool. And then he leaned in toward me.

"What if it's you I'm interested in?" he asked.

I almost gagged on my straw.

"Believe me, Paulo—" I laughed. "It's not me. Look at these girls. They're young, and they're gorgeous, and that's what they came here to do . . . *you're* what they came here to do."

His hands stayed firmly on either side of the stool. His toffee-colored eyes held my gaze. There was a long pause.

"What if it's you?" he asked again calmly.

All I could do was stare back.

He took my drink out of my hand, placed it on the bar, and lifted me off the stool. Literally, he lifted me. I felt his right arm slip around my waist, and then he pulled me in toward him. Not once during this Harlequinesque sequence of events did his eyes move from mine.

"I've seen you each day at the hostel," he said as he placed me gently on the ground. "I don't want any of these girls. I want you."

And then he kissed me. At first it was an awkward kind of kiss, because my eyes were stuck wide open in disbelief. This was such a shocking turn of events that I wanted to make sure I actually saw it happening. But when he kept kissing me, when I realized this wasn't going to end, I closed my eyes and collapsed a bit in the knees. He tasted exactly like his eyes looked. Sweet, salty, warm. We left the bar immediately.

I've never felt as though I could use the word *titillating* in a serious way, but it's really the only word that comes to mind when trying to describe that night and the rest of my time with Paulo. I never envisioned being with a man that good-looking (or charming, or thrilling, or lovely in every way), and it's not because I think I'm some beast of a woman with zero game. I know I have a certain appeal, but I also know I'm not a German supermodel. I know what league I'm in, and I know it's well below Paulo's. We're an unlikely pairing, so unlikely that if someone showed photos of us to a focus group and asked about the likelihood of a match, I'm almost certain the respondents would just lean back in their chairs and say, "How about you start with a serious question?" Or, if the respondents were women, they would just sit there with Paulo's photo, only to be escorted out of the room three or four hours later, tears streaming down their cheeks. "Leave the photo, ma'am," someone would say from an intercom in the other room, "leave it right on the table."

To make matters worse, or better (I couldn't tell at that point), Paulo's last name was Romancini. I mean seriously? Romancini? I could not. I laughed when he told me, and this wasn't my regular laugh—this was a full-blown Julia Roberts guffaw, because that's what happens when you literally can't even.

I spent the next few days with Paulo, and everything about it was perfect. I rented a small apartment in Wanaka, a lakeside town about an hour northeast of Queenstown, and I invited him to join me. When the weather was good, we hit the mountain together—and for a Brazilian on a snowboard, I was impressed. When the weather was bad, which it often was, we had sex like two little rabbits, and yet again he left me impressed.

My time with Paulo was pure uninhibited joy, dancing around the apartment and laughing all day and all night. He would strut around in the nude while I lay on the bed, clapping like a small child.

"Again," I would say. "Do it again."

It was glorious. He was glorious. He was the perfect distraction from the questions rumbling around in my head, the ones about what came next and whether or not I was a little lady. Also, considering the lifts were closed on most days, he distracted me from going certifiably insane while waiting for the ski resorts to open.

On our last morning together, I watched Paulo get dressed. He pulled a T-shirt over his head, his curly hair popping through the top, and then he turned to me and said, "You're going to be in Indonesia in a few weeks, right?"

I nodded. He was referring to the short break I had planned between the ski seasons in the Southern and Northern Hemispheres.

"I'm going to be in Thailand at the same time. We should meet in Bali."

I nodded again.

There was no reason not to, no reason at all.

.˙●

A FEW DAYS AFTER Paulo left, I got my first e-mail from Chris. And the next day I got another. And then another. At first, the e-mails were quick notes, just catching up on his time in Fitz Roy, along with a little flirtation. But it didn't take long for our notes to become longer, and a little more, how do I say this, adult in nature. I'm not gonna lie, things were really on fire for me in the titillation department.

I would wake up each morning wondering what salacious tidbits I'd get to read that day, and what I would write in response. I got a pang of excitement each time I pressed send, and even though the content was edging on explicit, something about it felt very innocent. It wasn't as if Chris and I could make good on anything we were writing, so in my mind, it was harmless, adult-only fun, as well as a continued distraction from the tediously repetitive show put on by the New Zealand weather channel.

I was twelve days into my six-week stint in New Zealand, and the resorts had been open for four of them. FOUR. Typically, I would have packed up my things and explored the other bounties New Zealand had to offer, but because of the weather's predictable unpredictability I never knew when the mountains would open. It would have been devastating to be trotting through Middle Earth while staring out at spectacular waterfalls and stunning fjords, only to discover I'd missed the one day Treble Cone had opened.

My time with Paulo had kept me busy, and the cheeky romance that was unfolding with Chris gave me something to look forward to each day, but mentally, I knew little bits of my stitching were coming loose. I felt a low-level frustration settling in. The weather and the skiing (or the lack thereof) were wearing on me, but who was I to complain? I was living the dream, and I was there of my own volition. No one was forcing any of this on me. I didn't have the right to call any of it difficult.

So I stuck to my regular pattern. Any concern that popped up got swept right under the rug. And once the floors were swept, I polished them clean with lemon-scented rationalizations.

I'd done hard traveling before. I'd done a tribal bush clinic with my head split wide open, and border scuffles in West Africa, the ones with guns and rapid-fire foreign languages. I'd once had a man spit directly in my face. That was tough. *That* was ribbon collecting. Ten soggy days in New Zealand, entertainment courtesy of Levi McConaughey, and a series of lusty e-mails? Not tough. Sweep. Polish. Sweep. Polish.

I quickly learned, however, that the world has two kinds of tough. The instantaneous, immediately recognizable, holy-shit-this-is-not-a-good-situation kind, and the kind that slowly but surely wears you down to nothing. New Zealand was the latter. It was not unlike the long, drawn-out emotional erosion caused by the musical ExerSaucer things parents buy for their babies. "Isn't that cute?" cry the teary-eyed parents when they see their kid bounce around and smack the button that plays "Mary Had a Little Lamb." But watch out. A week later, on the fifty-seventh round of that song, that same parent is going to contemplate stabbing themselves in the eye with a fork, but only after they send hate mail to the saucer manufacturer. A perfectly reasonable person, reduced to tears by a six-month-old in a plastic jumpy chair. That was me in New Zealand.

But I did my best to pretend I was totally, blissfully happy (which is what I assume most new parents are doing), in a fake-it-till-you-make-it/anything-to-occupy-my-mind kind of way. I wrote postcards to my granny, I drank copious amounts of coffee, and when it wasn't pissing down rain, I went for long walks. I bought a new pair of skis, read the entire Stieg Larsson trilogy, and penned an open letter to the Tasman wind turbine, politely requesting that it compose itself. I did a ludicrous number of pushups (aka sixteen from my knees—my upper-body strength has never been that good), and I researched the difference between a kiwi, a kiwi, and a Kiwi, discovering that they are, in order, a fruit, a strange-looking and kind of hairy flightless bird, and a New Zealand national, named after the bird. I even tried my best to crack the code of reasoning behind the fashion trend that, regardless of the storms, was sweeping New Zealand's South Island (it was called short shorts, and it was for men, not women).

I drank stupid amounts of beer, and I stood stark naked in front of a mirror because I'd developed a mild obsession with the growth of my thighs. They were fascinating to me. If they'd had hair, I could have sworn I was staring at my brother in the mirror, minus the package part, of course. I discovered a J. J. Cale CD in the rental car and began daily jam sessions to "Cajun Moon" and "High on Cocaine," and I thought for hours about why the plumbers of New Zealand, regardless of progress modeled by other first-world nations, were still using two faucets in their sinks, one for hot and one for cold, versus one faucet with both hot and cold water. I mean seriously, who wants to choose between scalding themselves and simply wetting—but not hygienically cleaning—their hands with cold water? It was a total mystery to me.

I practiced the samba while wearing wool socks, high-waisted long johns, and a sports bra, and when I got tired, I conducted serious research into the name of the musical instrument commonly played in the background of samba music, the one that sounds like a monkey screeching and is used generously throughout both Austin Powers movies. It's called a *cuíca*, by the way. I'm not sure how it's pronounced, but I went with "coo-cha" for fun and then tried to imitate the sound of it with my own vocal cords. I don't recommend that, by the way; I'm pretty sure it could do some serious damage. Finally, not unlike our parent from the ExerSaucer example, I contemplated stabbing myself in the eye with a fork.

It was obvious to me that my mental composure was crumbling, but I forced myself not to look at it. I really am a pro with a pair of blinders. I kept my gaze set on the forecast and my fingers crossed that one day soon, the weather would cooperate.

And it did. One morning, about a week after Paulo had left, I woke up to a little stream of sun peeking out from behind the curtain. I jumped out of bed, pulled the mountain reports up on my computer, and bingo! One of the four local resorts was open. I ate a quick breakfast, threw my gear in the back of the car, and drove to the resort.

When I arrived at the access road (a harrowing gravel path that winds up the side of a mountain in a series of steep, narrow switchbacks), I saw a large chain slung across it with an all-too-familiar sign dangling from the middle:

MOUNTAIN IS: CLOSED

I discovered why after chatting with a few people who happened to be milling about. Rumor was, management had been forced to close the resort for multiple days, not because of weather, but because of . . . wait for it . . . poo. Actual excrement. Apparently, whoever's job it had been to monitor the volume of defecation accumulated in the resort's septic tanks had done (I'm sorry, but I can't help myself here) a totally shit job. It didn't seem possible to underestimate the size of the actual tanks, so the error must have occurred when estimating the cumulative bowel movements the staff and customers were capable of crapping in a single season. According to the story making the rounds, this supposed miscalculation put the septic system so close to its limit that the only option left was to close the resort for a few days while a team of people drove truckloads of shit off the mountain.

Taking this all as a sign from the gods, I left Queenstown later that afternoon.

I loaded up J. J. Cale's choice musical compilation, threw eighty-plus pounds of gear in the back of my rental car, and hit the road in an adventure I called The Great Kiwi Road Trip of 2010: Single-Lane Highways and 10,000 Flocks of Sheep.

.ˑ●.

AS IT TURNS OUT, this was the wrong name for my road trip. What I should have called it was The Great Kiwi Time Warp: Flat Tires and a Possibly Feral Dog. Lesson learned, but if I ever have kids, I'm definitely going to wait to meet them before I go and give them a name.

There had been a few signs pointing to New Zealand's ability to warp time during my first few weeks in the country, the most obvious of which was the men and their short shorts. But the modern amenities in Queenstown had been enough to disguise what was really happening in the South Island. I'd been hornswoggled, but it wasn't long after I hit the road that I discovered the truth: New Zealand was stuck rather firmly somewhere between 1978 and 1983.

It started with a speck of a resort called Ohau—pronounced "Oh-how," as in oh-how-the-times-have-changed—which was located about two and a half hours northeast of Queenstown. It came complete with a midsize lodge and a small ski field, and it was the perfect example of what I'll call The 1979 Kiwi Special.

The lodge itself was a quintessential 1970s ski lodge, and even though I'd never actually been to such a place, I recognized it the moment I walked in the door. It was essentially a version of temporary heaven. If you were asked to stay for the night, you would say, "Ab-so-freaking-lutely," just for the novelty of it all, but if your presence was required for longer than twenty-four hours, you would say, "Kill me now. With that deer antler."

As my chosen murder weapon implies, there was a fair bit of taxidermy mounted on the walls. Bad taxidermy. The eyes inserted into each of the heads of deer and a variety of other animals were so obviously not the original eyes, and the creepiest part about it was that those eyes seemed to stare at you regardless of where you were in the room. They were like taxidermy Mona Lisas.

The place was a relic, a well-cared-for museum of wood-paneled walls and heavy yam-colored drapes. The carpeting was a green, blue, and burnt-orange tartan, the perfect decor if you're looking to disguise throw-up. There was a jagged-looking fireplace in the corner, a beat-up piano, a spongy pool table, and a bar that smelled of stale beer and mulled wine. I took a seat on a teal sofa, a piece that was part of the 1983 refurbishment, and actually wondered if I had entered a time machine without knowing it. At first I was excited: who doesn't want to tour the original set of *Cheers*? "Get a load of this place!" you'd say to the guy next to you. And then, five minutes later, after slurping back a Rob Roy and popping a maraschino cherry in your mouth, one that had been preserving for thirty-four years in a sticky bottle behind the bar, you would add, "Well, that was a trip. Shall we move on?"

The deterioration, although entertaining, was depressing, but it was made up for in its entirety by the views just outside the front door. Inside, Ohau is laughably kitschy. Outside, it's jaw-dropping.

The lake in front of the lodge is so thoroughly turquoise that it's hard not to think you're in the tropics. Add to the lake a set of rolling hills covered in crisp icing-sugar snow, and you can't help but think you've discovered the Hawaiian Swiss Alps.

The ski area in Ohau is small. It has a snow mat (otherwise known as a tiny moving carpet for beginners), a platter tow, and one chairlift—a slow-moving two-seater with a vertical rise of about 1,000 feet. I rode that chairlift all day long and managed just over 25,000 vertical feet. It was fun, but the views weren't enough to keep me around for another day, and the decor inside the lodge was giving me vertigo.

I left temporary heaven the next day and drove three hours northwest to a town called Methven, a dusty little place at the crossroads of Decent and Doable. I found a cheap hotel that drunken leprechauns had been hired to decorate, and as a bonus it included complimentary breakfast at the dated Bavarian restaurant next door. New Zealand was one of the more expensive countries I visited, and at the time her dollar was strong. I couldn't afford to say no to free breakfast, even if it was weak coffee and bratwursty things.

Mount Hutt, one of New Zealand's largest ski operations, is located about thirty minutes north of Methven. I drove there each morning with my belly full of caffeine and cured meat, and I took full advantage of the mountain. I managed a few days of big skiing, 40,000 and 50,000 vertical per, before some serious weather moved in. The storm was like a dump truck full of cement, just a straight shoot of concrete-esque rain pouring from the sky. With no end in sight, I packed my things up and left the next morning.

About a month or so earlier, I'd been told that no ski trip to New Zealand would be complete without skiing at one, if not all, of "the clubbies." After doing a little research, I discovered that clubbies are privately run patches of rock and snow managed by local ski clubs, as opposed to larger, commercial ski fields. Each clubbie comes with bare-bones staffing (often volunteered), extraordinarily sparse amenities, and very basic lift systems—rope tows or old-fashioned pulley systems. There are about a dozen of these club fields scattered throughout New Zealand's Southern Alps, and although they are private, I was told they were open to anyone who was ready and willing. I later learned that the "ready and willing" part was highly subjective, if not a bald-faced lie.

After leaving Methven, I drove another hour or so north to Arthur's Pass, the heart of New Zealand's club-field culture. I pulled into the gravel lot at a place called Flock Hill, which was really a working farm that doubled as a backpacking hostel in the winter. Like the previous two places I'd stayed, Flock Hill was virtually empty. The only two other people on-site were both staff, though this wasn't just because I arrived in New Zealand at the tail end of the ski season. The city of Christchurch, about a hundred kilometers due west, had been rocked by a 7.1-magnitude earthquake only one month prior. The damage had been intense, and most of the locals were consumed with the cleanup; people weren't taking weekend jaunts to the mountains.

This wasn't the first time I'd found myself staring down at the wreckage of a big quake—the devastation in New Zealand was eerily familiar to what I'd seen in Chile. I'm not a superstitious person, but I couldn't help but think about the old wives' tales I'd heard about bad luck coming in threes. Was this some sign from the Gods that something else was going to split open? Was there going to be another shakedown? I settled into the sheep shearer's quarters/empty bunkhouse for the night, feeling a little haunted by the thought of some other seismic catastrophe waiting for me a little farther down the road.

I woke up the next morning, relieved to discover that nothing further had shifted. After grabbing coffee and breakfast, I decided to ski at a place called Porter Heights. I'd heard it was a solid mix between a club field and a regular ski resort, so it seemed like the best place to start. The mountain was similar to Ohau in size and layout, and I put in a few solid days there before heading to Temple Basin, my first *real* clubbie.

This is where the "ready and willing" part came in. As it turns out, a more helpful phrase would be "superhumanly fit," "with hair on your chest," or "'ready and willing' to hike to one's death." I would have been much more prepared if I'd heard that instead.

I parked my car on the side of the road, put my backpack on, threw my gear over my shoulder, and started up a path that had a sign pointing toward the lodge. It didn't take long to realize that the path wasn't a path, but rather a steep incline covered in heavy, knee-deep snow. The laborious trudge, with all my gear in tow, lasted well over an hour, and when I arrived at the top, I was totally spent. I stumbled into what looked like a toolshed–cum–locker room, collapsed on a wooden bench, and announced between gasps, "I'm Steph. I called in advance. Do you have water?"

A skinny and slightly grungy twenty-year-old responded in full Kiwi-speak. "Sweet as," he said. "Ya made it."

My upper body was still slumped over my knees. "Just barely," I said.

"Water's back there, and the duty board's right next to it. Let me know if ya have any questions."

The duty board was a small whiteboard mounted onto a wall in the kitchen, and lo and behold, there was my name.

Staying at Temple Basin was about ninety Kiwi dollars a night, a price that included your day on the slopes, a sleeping bag and bunk in a cramped room, and three square meals. It was a bargain compared to most places, but it came with a catch—you had to earn your entrance (aka the hike in) and your stay (aka the chore you were assigned to complete while you were there). My name was next to "Evening Dish Duty." The whole setup made me feel like I was in some alpine version of a Boy Scouts weekend, one you could only gain entrance to by scaling the side of a mountain while carrying forty pounds of gear. Good luck, little Billy!

It wasn't until I'd put in a full day at Temple Basin that I began to understand the very fine line between raising restraining devices and being totally fucking crazy. Physically, it was the most grueling skiing I'd ever done, and that was before I'd even hit the slopes. If I was looking for an easy way to collect vertical, New Zealand's club fields were not it. The only reason I stayed the course was because a small amount of vertical was better than no amount of vertical, and I didn't have to worry about being overtaken on the access road by a dump truck full of feces.

After a few nights at Temple Basin, I went back to Flock Hill. It was pissing with rain, and about twenty minutes into the drive I got a flat tire. In some miraculous stroke of luck, two men in short shorts saw me right away and pulled over to help.

"You on yer own?" one of the men asked while he was wrestling with the tire jack. Rain was coursing down from the sky.

"Yeah," I responded.

"Hmph," he replied with a nod.

His reaction suggested he was a little impressed but also curious as to what the hell I was doing alone on the back roads of New Zealand. I'd been getting the sense that Kiwis, at least those from the South Island, weren't used to seeing many solo female travelers. When I checked in to hotels or asked for a table for one at a restaurant I received similar looks. People stared blankly at me as if I were some sort of cute but obviously stray and possibly feral dog. Then again, maybe they were staring because I was starting to look like an obviously stray and possibly feral dog.

It had been just over a week since I left Queenstown, and in that time I had taken on multiple days of solo driving, including river portaging and sheep dodging. I had stayed in five different hotels that were, for the most part, devoid of people, atmosphere, and any basic cheer, and I had spent a significant time within the walls of those hotels as a lone-wolf storm watcher. When the weather wasn't spouting off in every direction, I had managed some time on the slopes, but even then I'd only added about 140,000 feet to my total, and doing so had taken a massive physical toll. Long gone was the idea that New Zealand would be a vacation, and that I would be soaring down her hills with ease, all while bumping into masses of friendly skiers. I was already mentally exhausted after weeks of running laps in my own head, and now I was deteriorating physically as quickly as the hotel rooms around me.

The only thing that saved me was Wi-Fi. Signals and hotspots were few and far between, but when I found them, I used them to talk to Chris. Our spicy little e-mails had quickly become richer, lengthier exchanges, and a few days into my Great Kiwi Road Trip we moved from e-mail to Skype. A few days after that, we settled into an almost nightly routine. God bless Wi-Fi and Skype. And God bless Chris.

Thanks to the magic of the Internet, we were able to tour each other's lives. Chris showed me his apartment, and I got to meet his big black dog, Ramsey. I showed Chris the wood paneling and dated duvet covers of my hotel rooms, and he got to meet a whole variety of stuffed and mounted deer. We talked about ski equipment and mountains, and we discovered little tidbits about each other, the meaningless things that make up a person.

"I love rhubarb pie, but I have a pathological inability to shut cabinets and drawers," Chris told me one night.

"*I* love rhubarb pie!" I said. "And there is almost nothing that bugs me more than when people leave cabinets and drawers open!

"I like to dance," I added. "You should know that. Also, do you know that peonies are my favorite flowers because they look like what a rose would look like if you took the stick out of its ass?"

"I am an amazing dancer, like really, really good," Chris replied, "and I don't know what a peony is. Maybe I should find out."

It wasn't all just pies and peonies, though; we also talked about bigger things. He already knew about my 4-million-foot goal, so I filled him in on why I had set it, on my lifelong search for more, bigger, better, on my endless quest for blue ribbons. And he filled me in on his past, the reasons for all of his walls. As we talked, I discovered a surprising depth to Chris. Tucked right underneath his beard was a huge heart and an unexpected worldliness. He was sensitive, well read, and well traveled. He had taken the time to explore religion and spirituality, as well as himself. I watched a mysterious hermit evolve into a curious and compassionate man. It was a discovery I liked.

When the words ran out, we would just lie there and look at one another on our screens. We sat and stared. Through our e-mails, and our time on Skype, I couldn't help but feel as though something bigger was unfolding, although we remained optimistically noncommittal. I noticed myself missing him. I caught myself looking at my watch to see what time it was in California, wondering if he would be awake, or if he would be home from work, wondering if it was too early or too late to call. I knew I liked him, but I wasn't sure if it was because I *liked* him liked him, or if he was just a welcome diversion, something keeping me from becoming a full-blown feral dog, or, God forbid, a rabid one.

One night, my curiosity bubbled over.

"What do you think is going on here?" I asked.

"Well," he responded, "I'm not sure what this is for you, but for me it's one of three things."

"Uh-huh"—I nodded—"go on."

"It could just be this hot and heavy vacation romance, something to show me the kind of love and passion that's possible for me."

"Okay . . . ," I said, wondering what the other two things were going to be.

"Or it could be the same old pattern of 'I've fallen for you because you're totally unavailable and so it's safe for me' . . . and I really hope it's not that one. Or, who knows, maybe it's the real deal. I have no idea, but I'm open to exploring."

"Good. I don't know either, but I like the idea of exploring," I said. "What time can you talk tomorrow?"

10

A NUTCRACKER, AN ITALIAN WOMAN, AND A GRAVEL PARKING LOT

I WAS almost three months into my trip when I finally managed to scrape myself across the 1-million-foot mark. I was happy to hit the milestone, but I was more than a little apprehensive about celebrating. I was behind my projections by almost a month, and physically, I was exhausted. I hit my bed hard at Flock Hill, but it didn't seem to matter. I woke up the next morning, and I was still bagged. I felt as though every bone in my body was saying "Rest. Rest yer weary 'ead" in some Olde English accent they had picked up overnight.

"No," I replied, rather bluntly. I couldn't afford to fall any further behind than I already was.

I got up, ate breakfast, and drove to a place called Broken River. I'd heard good things about this club, but my fake-it-till-you-make-it optimism was dwindling. The tone I'd taken with my Anglo-Saxon bones was a dead giveaway. I arrived at the parking lot after driving for twenty minutes up an access road that looked more like a hiking trail assembled by the blind. As I unloaded my gear from the back for the car, I spotted what looked like a gondola. A gondola! At a club field! I was immediately overcome with joyful emotion.

But as I got closer, I realized it wasn't exactly a gondola. I wasn't sure what it was. Although it looked big enough for people to ride in, it seemed more like a wobbly grain elevator than something designed for the safety and comfort of humans. No one was manning the area, but luckily someone had been nice enough to leave a note:

PULL BLACK KNOB

I pulled the black knob, and the door to the giant metal bucket swung open. Once inside, I saw another note. It was just as thorough as the first:

PRESS GREEN BUTTON

I pressed the green button. A loud beeping noise began, and I scanned the area for a large truck backing up. Nope. No truck. The beeping stopped and was followed by forty-five seconds of total silence. Assuming the whole contraption was broken, I grabbed the handle on the inside of the door and opened it. At that exact moment, the whole thing lurched into action, and the door slammed shut. I took a seat, grateful that my right hand and matching mitt were still attached to my arm. The container, or box, or whatever you want to call it, moved up a jerky metal track. It felt like the uphill portion of a roller coaster, circa 1922. Once at the top, I stumbled out onto a platform made of what looked like thirty or so pieces of old grating, haphazardly welded together. Thus far, Broken River looked, sounded, and felt like a giant death trap, but onward I marched.

I walked down the platform and eventually came upon a ticket booth. The woman standing inside seemed irritated by my arrival, like I'd interrupted her as she was in the middle of helping . . . zero other people. She sold me a ticket, and in a harsh Italian accent she said, "You have a harness, yes?"

I looked down at myself.

Does it look like I have a harness? If I did, clearly I would have used it to create some sort of jimmy-rigged safety clamp for that fucking thing I just rode up in, but you don't see any carabiners dangling from my crotch, now do you?

This was said in the comfort and safety of my own head, and then I looked up rather sheepishly and said aloud, "No, I'll have to rent that from you?" I was pleased with myself for answering a question and asking one all at the same time (a totally Kiwi thing to do), until I began to wonder what in God's name I would need a harness for.

The lovely Italian woman slid a ticket across the counter and then tossed a harness in my direction, along with a roughly cut piece of cowhide that had been sewn into the shape of an oven mitt. The harness itself looked more like a leather belt and had a piece of hinged metal dangling off the right-hand side. The overly polite and totally helpful woman behind the counter must have noticed that my eyes had grown wide. "You'll need these for the nutcrackers. They'll show you how to use them when you get up there," she said, with absolutely zero hint of condescension.

I wasn't sure what the hell I would need a nutcracker for (Christmas was months away), and I wasn't sure how the equipment she handed me would help me use a nutcracker, but I thought it best not to bother her with these questions, as she was so busy with the zero other customers and all. But as I was backing away from the counter, it hit me.

Up there? Aren't we already "up there"?

Apparently not. I scuttled along the metal grating to the other side of the building, and before me was the stairway to heaven—or hell (at that point I wasn't sure, because a lot of things were opposite in New Zealand, like the side of the road you drive on, and the direction in which the toilets flush, for example). After thirty minutes of trudging in the springtime sun—which felt like using the stair-climber at the gym that's next to a really hot, sunny window, all while wearing ski boots, multiple layers of winter clothing, and a weird leather belt with metal danglers, and carrying forty-odd pounds of gear on my right shoulder—I reached the top. And there she was: The Nutcracker. Or at least something I guessed was a nutcracker.

The area around this strange piece of machinery was deserted, but luckily, it also had a note:

NOT FOR FIRST-TIMERS

Shortly after I arrived, a member of the volunteer ski patrol skied up beside me. He stopped, looked me up and down, and then laughed. Obviously stray, possibly feral.

"It's not really for beginners," he said.

"I'm not really a beginner," I responded. "I can ski."

"Have you ever used a nutcracker before?"

"No."

"Well, then, I'd say that makes you a beginner."

I wanted so desperately to scream, but because I am a polite Canadian, I just nodded. "Will you show me how to use it?" I asked, exasperation thick on my voice.

He sighed, and then, with the kind of pity that any warm-blooded human would offer a stray, he proceeded to show me the ropes—and I mean this in the literal sense of the word.

The nutcracker is a large rope-and-pulley system. It was first used in the 1940s, and the technology hasn't changed since. Not one bit. Since 1940. The rope and series of pulleys are waist-high, and they range in length from 600 meters to just under a mile. They are rugged, and they are unnervingly fast.

To ride a nutcracker, you have to pad your glove with cowhide (hence the oven mitt) so that your regular glove, or hand for that matter, isn't torn to shreds when you move to grab the rope. Yes, you heard that right, when you grab the rope, the one whipping by your side at top speed. Once you've got a grip on the rope, you pray that shoulder dislocations are covered in your travel insurance, and then quickly, like within milliseconds, you use your free hand to whip the metal hinge that's dangling from your harness over the top of the rope before clamping it shut with the hand that has just let go of the rope. After that, you hold on for dear life, white-knuckle it past every pulley in fear that your fingers will be ripped clean off if they get too close, and *hopefully* arrive at the top in a sweaty heap after letting go of everything, including potentially your bowels.

By the end of the day I had managed a success ratio of about 2.7 out of every 12 cracks. In the process, I convinced 100 percent of the local skiers that I had Tourette's. This was likely due to the final show I put on at the end of the day, where I screamed in frustration and gave up. After that, I threw my poles, javelin style, toward the stairway, hoping they would bounce right down it and stab that bitch of an Italian woman directly in the heart. And that, my friends, is how you move from feral to rabid. Apparently, all it takes is a nutcracker.

After roughly composing myself, I collected my javelin equipment and stomped my way down the rest of the staircase, only to discover that the Italian lady had closed shop for the day. A good thing for all parties involved, I thought as I turned to the gondola, pulled the black knob, and . . . nothing. The door didn't swing open. I pulled it again. Nothing.

You've got to be kidding me.

I yanked. Nope. I scurried around on the grating and searched for someone who could help. No one. I pulled on the knob one last time. Nothing.

Strange, I thought to myself. Probably because someone who WASN'T FUCKING LICENSED TO BE OPERATING THE THING WAS FUCKING OPERATING THE THING!

Any composure I had clung to was now gone.

.˙●.

SKI BOOTS ARE UNCOMFORTABLE. Point-blank. Skiing in them is doable, as is standing while donning a pair, but doable is a far cry from comfortable. In short, they're designed for going downhill, not for standing upright, and walking in them is another story altogether. Watch any skier walking around in ski boots, and you'll soon understand that it is quite possibly the trickiest part of the sport. It's typically painful, always awkward, and more than a little dangerous. Rigid plastic mixed with ice and snow is not a combination meant for staying balanced and upright. What it's meant for is slipping all over the place, likely at speed.

Even for the most practiced experts, walking in ski boots while on snow, gravel, or pavement is tricky. Walking in them on ice? Well, if you don't have some other form of support, something to hang on to, like a rope, or the shoulder of that seven-year-old who happens to be standing next to you in the ticket line, you're pretty much fucked. Add a slope of any kind to the mix, and you may as well get right down on your ass and start scooting.

So imagine my dismay when, composure already MIA, I found myself at the top of a bush track (Kiwi-speak for a hiking trail) while wearing a pair of ski boots. Dismay quickly morphed into complete and utter terror when I discovered that the bush track was really more of a steep luge course, with black ice and large bits of gravel poking through here and there. I would have moved directly to my butt if it weren't for the hairpin turns and jagged rocks thrown into the mix. I had to walk. There was no other option. It didn't matter that I was already tired from my morning hike up the never-ending staircase, or from spending the majority of the day having my ass handed to me by something called a nutcracker, and then hiking down the never-ending staircase. Even though it came with the possibility of an early death, I would have much preferred a ride down in the rusty old grain elevator. I was actually looking forward to climbing into that rickety little tinderbox. But no, luck was not my lady that day.

I swung my skis over my right shoulder, and with both poles gripped in my left hand, I reached out over the ice and stabbed at it a few times. My poles bounced right up off the surface. The ice was as hard as granite, and it had a thin coat of water melting on top.

I braced myself and started to walk.

The second my boots hit the ice, my legs began to quiver, and it didn't take long before they were in full tremor. I had been warm to start, but by the five-minute mark I was hot. I could have stopped to take off some layers, but stopping meant prolonging the walk, and I wasn't interested in that. At the ten-minute mark I relented and wedged my downhill boot between a rock and a thick patch of gravel, steadying myself just enough to take off my gloves and hat. Five minutes later I paused again to move my skis from my right shoulder to my left, and then I kept walking.

My heels caught a few times, and I lurched forward, skittering down sections of ice before little bits of gravel snagged the bottoms of my boots, bringing me to a jerky stop. When this happened, I could feel different parts of my body snap to attention, quick, tight little contractions preparing me for possible landing while my free arm swung wildly in an effort to keep me upright.

I took a few deep breaths after each fitful slide in a desperate attempt to stop myself from splitting at the seams and turning into a human version of Mount Vesuvius.

Most hikers will tell you that the downhill is harder than the uphill. The impact on the knees is tremendous, as are the aftershocks sent like hot missiles into the quadriceps muscle. By the time I hit the thirty-minute mark, every downward step felt like a hammer landing on the tops of my knees, followed immediately by the sensation that something was slicing deep into my thighs.

When I finally got to the bottom, it felt like my knees were about to spring loose from my legs. I staggered across the parking lot toward the car, and as I did, the anger that had been boiling up inside me finally burst forth. It felt as though thunder was actually rumbling through my body as I hurled my gear to the ground.

After a few moments of this, my body went limp in defeat. I sank to the ground, tipping forward onto my hands and knees, my head hung low.

I was trembling from head to toe, and I began to cry—a deep, blubbery howl. There I was, on all fours in a parking lot, my tears and snot dripping into dark patches of gravel beneath me. I was exhausted, frustrated, and so fucking mad. For weeks, I'd been working to hold myself together, and that day—from the moment I set foot in that grain elevator to the final descent—broke me. I'd been fighting to convince myself that I had everything under control, to appear stoic and strong, but I just couldn't do it anymore. I hated the lack of progress and being behind on my goal. I hated not knowing how to do something, and I hated having to ask a condescending Italian and a smug Kiwi patroller to show me the ropes.

I was angry because anger is a beautiful mask for denial; anger is easier than looking like a fool. I hated looking like a fool. Perhaps it's because I was the youngest, always the one who didn't know how, always the one playing catch-up, always the one who needed a lesson, or their hand held and their tears wiped. For twenty-nine years I'd been the weakest link, the baby, the one who could never quite keep up, measure up, man up.

Get up, I thought to myself. Get up.

I refused to be the weakest link.

I grabbed the hitch of the car and pulled myself to standing. I leaned my weight against the bumper and took a few shaky breaths. I was already behind on my goal. I didn't have time to splash around in a pool of defeat and self-pity. I pulled off my ski boots and dropped them to the ground.

I'm just tired, I thought.

The road and the rancid hotels had worn me down. This was not a breaking point. This was just the Universe telling me to take a day off, maybe to get a massage. My trainer, Alex, had given me physical strength, but he'd also taught me to be resilient; I had the mental and emotional strength to get through this. Maybe the whole thing was going to be harder than I thought, but I'd be fine after a massage and a hot shower.

And that right there was the number-one sign that my ego had taken over. This may come as a shock, but in those moments when you're on all fours in public, when you're wailing at the world, yeah, there's usually a bigger message being sent than "You need a massage."

Strength isn't necessarily defined as our ability to get up when we're knocked down. Nor is resilience found in our ability to continue getting up—over and over again. That's just sheer willpower; that's called being stubborn as fuck. True resilience is different. True resilience is found in our ability to get up, to create space for a message we may not want to hear, to listen like we've never listened before, and then to act on that message—even if that means changing the way we've been hurtling down our path in life for decades. I didn't know that then, but I do now.

Standing there in the parking lot at Broken River, I could hear the Universe gently knocking, a signal that I should at least crack open the door. But I wasn't having any of it. I had worked my whole life to be strong enough, tough enough to barrel through a man's world at pace. I had no interest in changing any of that.

I looked around at the gear strewn across the lot. I just needed to let off some steam, I told myself. Now it was time to pick everything up and move on.

The Universe is smart, though. I had embarked on this journey because I hadn't been able to resist the call of the mountains and a giant 4-million-foot carrot. And the Universe knew that this big juicy finish line was the perfect bait required to set me up for the real journey, the one I didn't yet understand. The one that was being hinted at, whispered in my ear, while I was on my knees in Arthur's Pass.

If only I'd had it in me to respond with cooperation and grace. Unfortunately, I went with obstinacy instead, a special sauce of fear masked as tenacity. I told myself that this was a purple-ribbon day. Maybe not blue, but at least it was purple, proof of my participation, proof of my active movement toward the goal.

Some tiny part of me knew that this was strike two when it came to looking a tough moment right in the eye. But I refused to see this glimmering insight for what it really was: a call to change. Because I didn't want to renovate myself; I didn't want to bring in the wrecking ball, knock down walls, and expose the core of who I was. I didn't want to rewire the electrical, I didn't want to reroute the heating ducts, and good lord save me now, I didn't want to know if there was a crack in the foundation. It was so much easier to get a new throw cushion or two, maybe put a scented candle in the corner. It was so much easier to get up, collect my gear, and keep driving, pretending this never happened.

Here's the other thing I didn't know then, that I do now: the Universe doesn't care if you're not interested in change. Because as much as we might think we're in charge, we're not. The Universe is the true foreman, in charge of the renovation and the demolition that comes before it. Ignoring it won't help. If you don't open the door at first, it will just keep knocking. Its gentle taps will become louder, and if you don't heed the call, it will bang on the wall, and if you ignore all the banging, it will bring out a crowbar and pry you out, no matter how many hideously tacky throw cushions you've piled around yourself.

We weren't at the crowbar stage yet; we were only at a gentle tapping. So I ignored the noise at the door. I gathered my gear, chucked it in the back of the car, and took my place in the driver's seat. And when I got back to the hotel, later that day, I booked myself a massage.

11

THE TALK

THE MORNING after my massage, I called Chris and filled him in on my less-than-awesome day at Broken River. I blamed most of it on that nasty Italian woman. He seemed a bit distracted, so I asked him what was up.

"Bored of the Italians?" I said.

"No," he replied. "It's just I have something to ask you."

"Oh, okay. Shoot."

"What do you think about me meeting you in Japan?" There was a look of excitement on his face, but his voice was quieter than normal, and I could tell he was a bit nervous.

"Really? Are you sure?" I asked. A wave of apprehension rolled through my body.

"Yeah. I think it would be fun," he said. "Let's look into some dates."

While I was thrilled about the possibility of seeing Chris, I also felt sick to my stomach. If Chris came to Japan it meant our optimistically noncommittal relationship was becoming something else, something a little more committal. Although I had discovered a lot about Chris that I liked, I was a few weeks away from taking a break in Bali—the one that included a booty call with Paulo. The idea of meeting Paulo and then Chris a few weeks later didn't sit well with me. I swallowed hard. Chris and I needed to have "the talk," or at least some version of it.

"Hey, there's something I need you to know," I said.

"Mm-hmm, what's that, sweets?"

Okay, this is over. He just called me sweets, and now I'm going to tell him about this random dude, and then we're gonna be done. Oh god, this is awkward.

I started hesitantly. "You know I'm going to Bali soon, right?"

"Yeah. A few weeks."

I nodded. "Yeah, two or three weeks. Well, um . . . someone is meeting me there."

"Okay," he said, waiting for me to continue.

I began to ramble.

"Yeah . . . it's been planned for a while, and you and I haven't talked about being exclusive or really defined what's going on between us, but now that you're thinking about coming to Japan it's starting to feel a bit . . . well, you know, not right, me meeting someone else. It's just . . . I wasn't expecting this. I wasn't expecting us to happen, or to go to the next level, or whatever, and his ticket is bought, and everything's booked, and I'm not really sure what to do because it would be really nice for you to come to Japan. I want you to come to Japan. But before you book anything . . . you need to know about this."

I wasn't sure what I wanted Chris to say. I was falling for him, and I was pretty certain he was falling for me too. I was excited about the idea of meeting in Japan, but I also knew that the chances of a real-deal, long-term commitment type of romance were slim. Our entire relationship was based on five days in Ushuaia, a handful of e-mails, and three weeks of Skype. And we lived in different countries. And I was traveling for seven or eight more months. Even though our calls had been a bright spot in my time thus far, the common-sense gal inside me knew the odds were stacked right up against us.

My eyes were glued to the computer screen as I watched Chris's reaction. He sat up in his chair, folded his arms across his chest, and in a calm, even tone said, "You're right. We haven't talked about being exclusive, and I don't think it would be fair for me to assume you don't have a past. We both have pasts." He continued, "You don't know about any of my relationships, and I don't know about yours. It's okay, I guess. And if we're meant to be, we're meant to be. Everything will work out how it's supposed to. I think I'd still like to come to Japan . . . if that's what you want."

"It's what I want," I said. "It's totally what I want."

By the end of the call I felt a bit better, but things still weren't sitting quite right. I woke up the next morning and saw an e-mail from Chris. Apparently, things hadn't sat right for him either:

> *Steph—*
>
> *I just woke up and I want to share a few things with you . . .*
>
> *I have this really strong sense of purpose in my life about being FULLY who I am. For a lot of my life I withheld big parts of myself, and I've been working really hard to develop the courage to fully own everything.*
>
> *A big part of all this is how I relate to others—the quality, intimacy, and depth of my relationships, with work, with friends, and ultimately, with a partner. Whenever I think about all of this, I think about you and how much I want to share with you. It would be so great to feel like I had a partner, someone who was supporting me, and who I could support, and we could work together to accomplish some really amazing things. I want that for my future.*

*There is a long road from here to there, but you're the first person
I've met who makes me think I can have that sort of future.*

   *I don't know what's going to happen with us, or if something
like that is possible for us, but wouldn't it be great if it could work
out that way . . .*

   *I think that's why I went to bed pretty bummed last night. I was
thinking about this Bali situation and how it made me feel and
the short answer is it doesn't make me feel so good. I don't know
anything about the nature or context of your relationship with
this person, but the potential of you being physical with someone
else knowing the strength of the feelings I have for you feels really
dishonoring.*

   *I got quite up in my head about it last night and it seems like
there are a couple of options:*

   *1. Either her feelings aren't as strong as mine and because of
that she'd feel OK connecting with someone else (and I don't want
to be in a relationship with someone whose feelings aren't as strong
as mine).*

   OR

   *2. Her feelings are as strong as mine, but she's going to disregard
them because it's a difficult/awkward situation (this one I really
don't like because it means we have a disconnect around integrity
and I won't be in a relationship with someone who doesn't share
that value with me).*

   *I understand it is more complicated than that, but that's how
I'm feeling about it right now. I don't yet know what it means for
me, or for us, or for our future together, but I am committed to
staying open and letting what wants to happen, happen. I hope
you have a really nice day. I can't wait to talk to you soon.*
   —Chris

I closed my computer.

···•·

FOR TWENTY-SEVEN YEARS I'VE been best friends with a girl named Sarah. We met in the third grade. Sarah wound up marrying Bri, a great guy she met in the tenth grade. This means that Bri has had to put up with me for close to twenty years (I know, I'm a total genius at math). It's rare for Bri to involve himself in the conversations Sarah and I have, but after two decades of gossip-osmosis, I can confidently say that he knows me a lot better than most people on the planet. He has overheard a lot, and I also know Sarah must tell him a lot (they're best friends too, after all).

One night a few years back, Sarah and I were in the midst of a Skype debate about a romantic interest of mine at the time, when Bri chimed in from the other side of the room.

"Jags," I heard him say. "Let me cut to the real deal here. I've been listening to you two birds talk on Skype about some dude for hours. He isn't for you, and I'll tell you why—he doesn't challenge you. Can I have sex with my wife now?"

All it took was one sentence, and Bri solved the decade-long mystery of my love life. Apparently, I needed someone who challenged me. I'd been on the lookout ever since, and the moment I read Chris's e-mail, I knew I'd found a worthy candidate.

No man had ever challenged me like that. No man had ever called me on my bullshit while also pointing me toward a path of integrity. I knew exactly what to do.

I immediately typed out an e-mail to Paulo telling him I had met someone and, in a rather unexpected twist, was falling for him. I explained that he was still welcome to join me in Bali if he wanted to, but that we couldn't have sex like rabbits, or like any other animal for that matter.

He e-mailed me back right away. He told me that he was sad but that he wanted the best for me, even if it meant some other guy stole his pale-skinned Canadian. He said he still wanted to come and added that maybe it was for the best, that maybe we were meant to be friends. He promised that we would still have fun and that he would be good, and he signed off by telling me he had to go cry himself to sleep.

I said a little prayer and thanked whoever it was that had blessed Paulo with such a magnificent soul, and then I wrote an e-mail to Chris. I was nervous and excited, little bits of energy moving through my hands as I typed:

> *Hi you . . .*
>
> *I want you to know that I e-mailed Mr. Bali earlier today and explained that I have developed feelings for someone and want to do my best to nurture those feelings and explore where they might lead. I told him that I would love for him to come to Bali as a surfing partner but that we couldn't be physically intimate.*
>
> *I think my feelings are as strong as yours, and I give a way bigger shit about being honest and having integrity than about awkward situations and difficult conversations. I'm not sure where we will land either, but I would rather be in unison as we "take off," and I am going to do my best to make sure that happens.*
>
> *xoxo*
>
> *s*

It was a quick note, but I knew we would connect later that day. I couldn't wait to talk to him about Japan, and about what all of this meant. I skied that day, and when I got home, I went straight to my laptop. My in-box was empty.

Shit. Maybe he didn't check his e-mail before work.

I looked at the time: 4:00 p.m. It was eleven in the morning for Chris. He would be home in five or six hours. I could call him then.

The great thing about Skype is that you can see the person you're talking to. The drawback is that you can see the person you're talking to. When Chris popped onto my screen later that afternoon, I knew something was wrong. He was slouching, his arms pulled in close to his body, and his face was long and stern. All the walls I'd seen tumble down over the past two months had suddenly been rebuilt. He looked closed, as in closed-for-business closed.

"Hey," he said. "I didn't get much sleep."

"Did you get my e-mail?" I asked.

"No. What e-mail?"

Oh hallelujah! Thank the Lord!

"So, I got your e-mail, and I sent you one back." I took a deep breath, and then the words poured out of my mouth in one big rush: "I'm in! I'm totally in. I want you to come to Japan, and I e-mailed the guy I am supposed to meet in Bali and I told him about you and about how he could still come but that we couldn't be together, you know, physically, because I met you and I want to give it a go with you and"—I took another deep breath—"I want to give this a chance, with you, with us."

Very slowly, a smile made its way across Chris's face.

"You are so precious to me," he said.

Chris booked his ticket to Japan that night. We were set to meet in six weeks.

12

TWO FALLS AND A SLIVER OF LIGHT

OVER THE course of the next week, I exploded. Twice. I suppose a more apt description would be that I fell, but the nature of these falls was so dramatic that *exploding* is the only word that really works. Both falls were big enough that I was able to pray a full prayer as my body flew through the air. The prayers went something like this: "Holyfuckholyfuckholyfuck."

So, not a traditional prayer, but a prayer nonetheless.

True to an actual explosion, each fall came with an element of power, as well as surprise. And each seemed to happen in slow motion, with the exception of the final descent toward earth, which happened at a Michael-Schumacher's-Formula-One kind of speed. The fact that I walked away from both incidents with nothing broken is miraculous, and obvious proof that the fastidious nature of my prayers paid off.

The first fall happened at New Zealand's largest ski resort, a place on the North Island called Whakapapa, pronounced "Fack-a-papa," which should have been my first facking clue to steer clear. The second clue should have been my hotel, which could have easily served as the set in a remake of *The Shining*. With the exception of the Danish volcanologist staying in room 316, the place was completely empty. In the hallways I picked up on the smell of mildew, the carpeting felt damp under my feet, and the walls were covered in photos of skiers doing backscratchers and spread eagles, wearing puffy, one-piece ski suits in fluorescent colors. It quickly became clear to me that the North Island of New Zealand was ahead of the South, but only by a decade or so.

The worst part about the Kiwi *Shining* hotel was the common room. It looked like the set of a very (very, very) low-budget porn film, without the cameramen and naked people, of course. I spent the majority of my time on the periphery of that room, waiting out a gale-force weather system, and by the end of day two I would have welcomed a video crew and a gaggle of people with their genitalia exposed—anything for some entertainment other than rain, sleet, and wind.

When the weather finally cleared, I drove straight to the resort. It was located on the north face of New Zealand's largest and most active volcano, also known as Mount Ruapehu. The "most active" description is not messing around. There were evacuation how-tos posted all over the place in the event you found yourself outrunning (or outskiing) boiling hot lava.

The season at Whakapapa typically runs until the end of October. I skied there on October 14, and it was clear from the minute I arrived that the season was a day or two from being finished. The parking lot was virtually empty, and the smell of sunscreen wafted through the air. The whole west side of the resort was closed, and the snow at the top of the mountain had a texture that was very much like a Slurpee or a snow cone. It was a combination of frozen slush and little white corn niblets that you pushed around rather than skied through. Regardless, I had a pretty decent day. I met an entertaining local on one of the rope tows, and after we'd skied a few fresh lines in a big, wide-open bowl, he and his family shared mandarin oranges and a few sips of champagne with me. They had packed a couple small bottles of the cheap stuff in their lunch bag, and I gladly partook.

After lunch, I skied a fast, easy run off the top ridge. My plan was to go back up and do laps on that run for the rest of the day. While I was on my way back to the top, a small patch of clouds rolled in, and the light went flat. Not a huge deal. Everything I was skiing was blue-level terrain, something a relatively talented five-year-old could go down with ease. And I had just skied this run, so I knew what it looked like and felt like. I wasn't going to let a patch of poor visibility hold me back. I started down the run at a medium pace, and about three or four turns in I picked up a tiny bit more speed. On my sixth turn, I exploded.

You know that sensation you get when you're walking down a set of stairs, and you think you've hit the last one only to discover there's one more below it? Your back knee buckles a bit, and your body lurches forward. "Oomph!" you say as you look back at the steps, wondering how that last one snuck up on you.

My fall at Whakapapa was kind of like that, only it happened on skis, in the snow, with limited visibility. The flat light threw off my depth perception, and I completely missed a small ledge below me. It came as an unexpected shove, clear off the balance beam. My arms flailed, circling wildly through the air in an attempt to gain some control. I prepared myself for a rough landing, but because my depth perception was off, I hit the ground sooner than expected. Instead of absorbing the impact, I fell to the ground like a limp noodle. It was not graceful.

I lay there for some time. My jacket and pants were bunched up in various places, and I could feel cold, slushy snow melting against my skin. The snow had gone everywhere: down my pants, up my back, around my neck. It was packed into my goggles, which were sitting askew on my face, covering one eye like I was some sort of pirate preparing for winter. I did a mental scan of my body. There was no major pain, but my right thumb was a bit tender—it must have caught in the strap of my ski pole. I lifted my head and looked around before standing up and shaking the snow out of my clothes and my . . . unmentionables.

I skied very slowly to the bottom of the hill. My head was foggy from the tumble, but one thing was very clear. I was done with New Zealand. More specifically, I was done with skiing in New Zealand. Even though the resorts were still open, I called it—the Southern Hemisphere season was over. I'd have to complete the rest of my vertical in the Northern Hemisphere.

From the moment I first arrived in New Zealand, I'd had a tumultuous relationship with her mountains—day after day of weather delays, truckloads of shit, nutcrackers, and more weather delays. It seemed clear that the mountains of New Zealand weren't all that interested in having me on them. I took my fall in Whaka-papa as their final warning.

As I loaded my skis into the back of my car, I felt a great sense of relief. In the past three months, I'd slept in twenty-five different beds. Most mornings, I woke up to some part of my body crying out in pain. Quite often it was my feet. If they could have run away from me, or if there was some way for them to opt out of the remainder of the trip, I'm sure they would have. My right elbow was aching daily, likely caused by lugging my eighty-pound ski bag from my car to hotel lobbies, from lobbies to hotel rooms, and then the next day all the way back to the car. And I was cold. I was cold all the time, even when the sun came out. I had pushed myself to the point of exhaustion, and now I could rest. I could explore New Zealand without having to think about weather, or vertical, or gear, or what decrepit ski lodge I'd be staying in that night, or what type of Bavarian schnitzel it would serve in the morning for breakfast. Would I have a lot to catch up on once I hit the Northern Hemisphere? Yes. Did I care at that particular moment? No. Not one bit.

I drove away from the volcano feeling as though I had actually outrun it. I even congratulated myself for being so intuitive, as if I had avoided some grand disaster.

Over the last month I had started to feel as though the trip had gotten off track, that it had somehow altered course without my consent, and I badly wanted to be back in the driver's seat. I had two weeks left in New Zealand, and as I drove away from Whaka-papa, an image of horses flashed through my mind. What better way to take back control than to get on top of a horse, to grab the literal reins of something big and powerful? Horseback riding seemed to be the perfect answer to all of my problems, as well as a decent solution for rest and relaxation. If there was anything that would help me rebalance, it was time at a dude ranch—the perfect place for a ram.

The next day, as if the Universe had received my message by overnight FedEx, I saw a sign advertising a blissful-looking ranch a few miles down the road. I gave myself an imaginary pat on the back for nailing it with the whole intuition thing, and I followed the signs down a dirt road before arriving at an idyllic-looking place called the Mountain Valley Adventure Lodge.

Twenty minutes later, I was on top of a filly named Jess, heading out on a guided ride. I felt like I was on the set of *Black Beauty*, albeit a trail-ride version of the film. Jess followed the lead of the horse in front of her, and we plodded along a little trail that rose high into the mountains. We stopped at the top of a bluff to take in the view, and I couldn't help but think I'd been right. It was just me and my horse and some glorious nature. I felt totally in control, like I had my shit completely dialed. This was, of course, exactly when the Universe came crashing into the basement with a crowbar.

A heavy gust of wind came up, and the lead horse, who I'll call Spooky McSpookerson, got startled. Spooks did an about-face, and at an astonishing speed, she tore down the path we'd just marched up. My horse did as she had been trained: she followed. I grabbed hold of her reins and clenched my thighs against her with every bit of muscle I had. Much to my surprise, this worked. We galloped down the hill and arrived at the bottom in one piece. But the Spookinator kept going, and when I saw her take a sharp right turn into what looked like the entrance of Sleepy Hollow, I knew I was in for it.

Again, Jess followed. Unfortunately, my thighs and I did not, and I flew through the air like Rudolph the Red-Nosed Reindeer on Christmas Eve. For a few magical moments I was soaring and then . . .

"Holyfuckholyfuckholyfuck!"

I landed with a massive *thud*.

End scene. And horse movie. And me thinking I was in control, or the wizard of intuition, or that I knew anything about anything.

I lay on the ground a little longer after this fall. My right cheek was resting on the earth, and I watched as the guide ran toward me. I heard her asking me if I was all right, but to be honest, that wasn't the conversation I was interested in having. I was too busy demanding answers from the universe.

WHAT THE FUCK? I screamed in my head.

I had been shaken up and chucked clear off course, figuratively and literally. Twice now I had been tipped over and poured all the way out—three times, if you included Broken River. I wanted to know why.

Is this my very own series of earthquakes?

For the next few days, I watched the skin on my ass turn into a deep hematoma. What was peach became deep rose, and then dark purple, light blue, and yellow, before fading all the way back to a smooth rosy pink. My thinking was almost as circular.

A crowbar had been hurled my way, and I needed it to make sense. I needed to feel in control.

This trip is about skiing 4 million feet, I told myself in earnest.

That was the mission I'd given myself, and that was the mission I'd accepted. It never occurred to me that there could be something more to all this than the finish line, so, blinders firmly in place, that's where I kept my focus.

Sure, I'd been knocked off that path once or twice, but if I wasn't supposed to finish, I would have broken my leg or my arm or something, right?

I looked at all the details, rationalized each and every one of them, and came up with the following answer: this trip was still about skiing 4 million feet—just somewhere other than New Zealand.

Another round of congratulations, please—applause for my ability to interpret messages sent from the Universe with total accuracy. Epiphany received. I changed my flights that night and called my friend Josh, fingers crossed that he and his fiancée would be okay with me visiting them in Auckland a few weeks early.

"Of course," Josh said. "Any time you'd like!"

"Fantastic!" I said with relief. "Oh, and prepare your washing machine. Given what's in my bag at the moment, I feel it should be warned about the physical and emotional task that lies ahead."

A day later Josh picked me and my dirty laundry up in downtown Auckland.

"Stiff!" he exclaimed, using the nickname he'd given me when we met. "How are ya? But wait, before you answer, who's this guy Chris? By the looks of it, he digs ya."

We drove to Josh's house, and waiting for me in the hallway was a midsize box.

"Chris sent this?" I asked, pointing to the box.

"Yeah, and there's another in your room."

"I have a room?"

Josh laughed. "Yeah, mate. It's just over here."

Josh's house was beautiful, and clean, and especially in comparison with the rest of New Zealand, shockingly modern. Additionally, there were people in it, friendly ones, and I could walk around in my bare feet without fear of contracting some hideous fungal disease from a piece of moist carpet. Stepping out of a clean shower and placing my toes onto a plush bathmat was pure rapture. During my two-night stay I took refuge in all of it—the crisp sheets, the freshly washed towels, the buckets of cold white wine. It was heavenly. And then there were those boxes from Chris. I tore into those with just as much gusto.

Each box was packed to the brim. He'd sent a long letter, a pair of his pajama pants, and a brand-new toque (Canadian for beanie), as well as seven or eight of what he said were his favorite books, including *The Alchemist*, *The Magdalen Manuscript*, and *The Dance of the Dissident Daughter* by Sue Monk Kidd.

I wondered about the odds of meeting a man who not only read books about the sacred feminine, but also called them his favorites. Apparently, there was still a lot more to Chris than Skype had revealed.

At the bottom of the second box I found a set of CDs, recorded interviews with the writer and mythologist Joseph Campbell.

"I listened to these a long time ago," Chris wrote at the end of his letter. He went on to tell me how much he loved Joseph Campbell, who used mythology to talk about human transformation and the spiritual journeys we take, and in most cases, find ourselves on.

"Given the journey you're in the midst of," he wrote, "I thought you might find these interesting."

I wasn't entirely sure what Chris meant by that, so I tucked the CDs back in the box and spent the next few days walking around Auckland and letting the salty ocean air lick my wounds. After so much time in the mountains, the dense sea-level air was revitalizing. I felt like a wrinkled old balloon taking a much-needed hit from a tank of helium. I looked back at the last six weeks and reflected on the good and the very bad of New Zealand. When I left South America I felt like my most powerful self, like I was dancing just underneath my highest potential, something I had expected to achieve on this trip. How was it, then, that a mere six weeks later, I felt further from myself than ever before?

Was Chris right? Was I in the midst of something larger?

One by one, all of my assumptions about New Zealand had been shattered. The expectations I'd placed on her shoulders chipped away until, by the end of it all, there was really nothing left. New Zealand was not comfortable, nor was she easy. She was grit, the kind you see when you look any Kiwi in the eye, the kind that tells you they're ready to tackle you at a moment's notice. And that's what she had done. She had tackled me. She had pinned me facedown on the ground at the exact time I thought I needed to keep moving.

She challenged me, and I rose in the same way I always had. I rolled up my sleeves, brought every bit of stubborn ram I had to the table, and fought for as long and as hard as I could, and in the end I quit. It had been an amphitheater-style battle, and New Zealand had won.

When I flew to Bali a few days later, there was nothing I wanted more than to close the door behind me, to leave New Zealand where she belonged, somewhere in 1987 perhaps. I wanted to forget the loss and keep moving, because ultimately that's how I believed I would win the whole thing. New Zealand had knocked me down, but I still had the Northern Hemisphere to make it all up and then some, to come back as the gladiator I knew I was. So I slammed the door shut, right in her face.

Good riddance, New Zealand! I thought as I took my seat on the plane.

But here's the thing: sometimes when you slam something hard enough, it bounces back just a little. I know this because that's what happened to me. Without me knowing it, the door remained open ever so slightly, just a crack, just enough to shed a sliver of light on what was really going on.

13

EYE OF THE TIGER

I COULD have flown to Finland, or some other place like Finland, to start the Northern Hemisphere season early, but way back when I was brewing this whole thing up, I'd had just enough foresight to plan a break between the Southern and Northern Hemispheres. Also, I don't like pickled herring very much. What that left me with was four weeks in the Balinese sunshine and one thing to accomplish—I was to fatten myself like a Christmas ham. Over the last three months I had lost seven or eight pounds. Not a massive deal overall, but if I was supposed to go on to ski three times what I'd logged in the south, I knew I couldn't afford to lose more. So it was with happiness and reckless abandon that I dove into a month-long feast of *nasi goreng* and *gado-gado*, with sides of suckling pig and coconut milk thrown in for good measure.

When I arrived in Bali, I wasn't the picture of summertime glamour. It could be argued that I've never been the picture of summertime glamour, but this was definitely the furthest I'd ever been from it. In the fourteen months leading up to my Indonesian arrival, I'd seen two months of fall, three of spring, a whopping nine of winter, and zero—*zero*—of summer. With the exception of my cheeks and the tip of my nose, every inch of me was alabaster. Factor in the muscle I'd packed on, and I was as close as a human can get to resembling a small, pale pit bull.

My feet looked prehistoric. In total, I had four or five toenails remaining, all of which were clinging to the cuticle in a delicate mélange of yellows and purples and inky blues. The single bathing suit I packed had been thrown into the side pocket of my ski bag, still damp from a dip in an Argentine hot tub. After two months in said pocket, the suit had been reduced to a pile of elasticized mesh and loose strings. It was abundantly clear that summer and I were not prepared for one another.

Upon arrival, I bought a vat of sunscreen and a new bathing suit. I contemplated one of those pedicures where the fish nibble at the dead skin on your feet, but I worried it would result in a full amputation, so I went without. I called Chris to let him know I would be back in touch at the end of the week, and I asked the hotel staff to make sure the room had two full beds. Paulo was set to arrive the next day.

What ensued over the following week was a massive exercise in trust, and a whole lot of heat—but only the kind you measure with a thermometer. Paulo had been right. We made great friends. We spent a week laughing, and dancing, and playing volleyball in the water. We listened to Bossa Nova music, and we toured around the island on a rented scooter. Other than clinging to Paulo's waist as we weaved through traffic, and a little help with sunscreen here and there, it was a hands-off occasion. He was the perfect gentleman, and I was, well, a lady.

As soon as Paulo left, I traveled east, checked into a bungalow in a sleepy beach community, and called Chris over Skype.

"So?" he asked pensively. "How was your week?"

"It was fine. It was really nice."

"Mm-hmm," he said, nodding a bit.

"I want to thank you," I said.

"For what?"

"For trusting me. I know that must have been hard."

"You're welcome," he said with a kind smile. We never spoke about Paulo again.

"When do Alix and Whitney arrive?" he asked. "You must be pumped to see them."

Three days later a van carrying two of my girlfriends pulled into the gravel driveway of my beach bungalow. Thus began an extraordinary tan-off—and talk-off. We paused on occasion, but only to reapply sunscreen, or to gorge ourselves on piles of banana pancakes, ginger tea, and anything we felt would taste good when drowned in peanut sauce (which, as it turned out, was everything). We tanned, we talked, and we ate.

Alix is well known in our circle of friends for the pace at which she speaks and her pitch when she's excited, which is pretty much all the time. People who can't understand and/or contribute to a conversation at Alix's speed? Well, there's not a lot of room in her life for slow talkers. So we talked, and we talked fast. We also used a lot of abbreves, which, in case you were wondering, is an abbreviation for *abbreviation*. This is a tactic employed when Alix feels she has to speak at an even quicker pace than normal, say for example when you're catching up on three months of lost time. Luckily, Whitney and I have had years of experience keeping up, so much so that Alix believed we deserved some kind of acknowledgment in Bali.

"You guys are brill," she said. "Standing ovaysh. Just don't abbreviate *country*. Never do an abbreve for *country*."

"Perf," said Whitney. "Got it, now pass the banans."

My conversations with Alix and Whitney have always been the perfect combination of surface-level gossip, absolute hilarity, and deep, life-altering epiphanies. The latter of which is the only time the conversation shifts in tempo.

"Wait. Stop," someone will say, and then, if we're in the middle of something like pouring a glass of wine, or shoveling another bite of peanut-sauce-drenched food into our mouths, we actually stop.

"Did you just say . . . that the dream I had about those birds . . . represents my relationship with *my mother*? . . . Ohmygodyou'reto-tallyrightthisisthebiggestepiphofmylife."

It's also important to note that both Alix and Whitney have their own figurative trophy shelves of accomplishments. Alix is a lawyer, a ball-busting federal drug prosecutor to be exact, and Whitney has a well-established career in public relations, work-ing for big-deal international clients like Microsoft and Nike. Our conversations are typically smart and insightful, and they are, among a few other things, one of the main reasons I am friends with these women, and why I had invited them to Bali. There is no one on earth I adore talking to more. So imagine my surprise when I found myself wishing Alix would just shut up. And Whit-ney, her too. I wanted them both to stop talking.

Shhhh, I felt like saying loudly, with my finger pressed firmly to my lips. But instead I just lay in the sun and ate, nodding here and there as they prattled on.

Chris and I had spoken regularly on Skype over the last two months, but besides that, most of the conversations I'd had were with inanimate objects, like my ski equipment or my rental car, and the vast majority of those took place inside my head. When it came to human interaction I was a little out of practice, but my struggle to keep up with Alix and Whitney had more to it than that. On one hand, I felt a deep desire to connect with the people

I loved. On the other hand, I was struggling with exactly how to do so.

As I listened to Alix and Whitney talk about their lives back home, which were close-to-perfect replicas of the one I had put on pause while I chased yet another blue ribbon, I couldn't connect. I found myself disinterested. Bored by the promotions and raises. Bored by the marriages and kids. Bored by the life that was waiting for me, the one I was supposed to go back to when this was all over, the one I'd worked so hard to build. And it was then, between the conversation and mouthfuls of chicken satay, that I first began to see things more clearly.

I thought my journey was about skiing, about achieving some pie-in-the-sky goal so I could slip back into my previous life, bolstered up by a massive accomplishment that would help me kick more ass than I'd already been kicking. But when I heard my girlfriends talking about their version of that very life, I had an overwhelming feeling that I had been wrong, that somewhere along the way the plan had officially changed without me knowing it.

I heard the door as it creaked open wider. The light began to pour in, and as it bounced off the water, I was blinded by its brightness. I put my hands up over my eyes.

My surprise quickly turned to confusion. I was unsure if I still wanted what I had wanted all my life—and if I had ever wanted it, exactly. And if not, what did I want instead? I was unable to answer. The light was glaringly bright, stripping me of my ability to see anything. I could feel myself cowering a little, squirming in my own body. I was intimidated by the ambiguity. I'd always known what was supposed to happen next, and this realization that my journey was shifting right under my feet was profoundly unsettling.

When did all of this change? I wondered. I was trying to hold on but I felt everything sliding underneath me.

New Zealand. It changed in fucking New Zealand.

It would take a few moments for my eyes to adjust to the light. Exactly what had changed was still a mystery, but one thing was for sure: something had definitely shifted.

.⦁.

I'VE ALWAYS LOVED TO swim, but I'm not a let's-just-splash-around kind of gal. Unsurprisingly, I need a goal. I like to get out of the water knowing I swam a certain number of laps, or that I made it to a tangible point and back. Yet one day in Bali, I decided to float. I just drifted along, letting the current carry me where it wished. The water slipped around me like silk, moving me steadily from one place to the next, and the sun shone down, casting a layer of sparkly glitter over the Indian Ocean. While I was floating, my thoughts drifted back to New Zealand, and how she became what she was.

At some point way back in time, eons and eons ago, New Zealand was part of a supercontinent, defined in entirety by the land around her, the land she had grown up attached to. One might say it was the only land she ever knew. Eventually, though, she cracked off from the supercontinent; perhaps because she wanted to be seen in a particular way, or maybe she had heard her mother repeatedly ask something like, "Where on earth did you come from?"

In response, New Zealand went out on her own for a swim. A big, crazy, blue-ribbon swim that she thought was going to answer all her questions, and prove all the things she wanted to prove. So there she was, doing her laps, swimming circles around each of the oceans, until one day she found herself drifting at sea, flailing a bit in the water. Who could fault her? She was tired and a little lost, because swimming all those laps was harder than she'd thought, and because the moon, and the tides, and the wild currents had thrown her off course.

Eventually, as New Zealand was flailing about, she was struck with the fact that she couldn't go back, that the supercontinent was different than she'd thought it was, and that cracking off from it in the first place had set something else in motion, something else entirely. And then, because this is a completely logical scientific argument, New Zealand was hit with the thought that maybe her swim wasn't actually about swimming but about growing up, finding her own place in the world, and looking under the water to see all of herself—including the things she pushed down and kept hidden in order to fit snugly into the supercontinent like a beautiful piece of an inherited puzzle.

Let's just say all of that happened eons and eons ago, and somehow, over time, New Zealand found her place, and now there she is, anchored in a deep and beautiful ocean, like a noble queen. A queen who, if she saw other endurance swimmers flailing around in the ocean, drowning in the sea, in water made of ego and naiveté and shiny blue ribbons, would throw a life preserver their way. And if that life preserver didn't work, she would throw something larger, to be sure the swimmers wouldn't drown—like a lifeboat, for example. She would do all of this so the swimmers could understand that no amount of manning up would get them where they were ultimately supposed to go, nor would it make them the people they were destined to become.

I had been wrong about New Zealand, and I had been wrong about the amphitheater-style battle we had fought in. She wasn't trying to pin me to the ground in an effort to stop me. No. She was trying to throw me a life jacket. She was trying to reroute me, to slow me down just enough so she could teach me about what it takes to be a woman who stands alone in the ocean, or in my case the mountains. She was trying to give me a lesson about leaving it all behind, about drifting away from everything you know in order to become who you're supposed to become. She was trying to raise some simple questions.

Is this what you want, forever and always? To define your life by your ability to win ribbons at an egg-and-spoon race? Do you want to be the kind of woman whose only way of relating to the world is to man up? Whose idea of success involves keeping part of your identity hidden? Is that really you?

In that moment, I finally saw New Zealand clearly.

Look down, she whispered.

I stood up in the warm Balinese water and tilted my head downward. Bright light skipped across the water. I squinted, peering out at the world with one eye closed.

Look, she whispered again.

I blinked, and finally my pupils constricted, adjusting to the light. I looked down at the Indian Ocean, and it was as if it had been waiting there calmly all along. I stared down at my reflection and I couldn't deny what I saw. I was a tiger, one with bright blue eyes that stared back at me intently. I was transfixed.

Was that what I looked like? If so, I'd had myself all wrong. All these years I'd been wrong.

.˙●

IN JULY OF 1994 I contracted a severe case of food poisoning. The technical name for what I had is *Campylobacter jejuni*, and just to give you a taste of its intensity, I'll tell you that "massive gastrointestinal hemorrhage" is a term often associated with it. So no, it's not "campy."

My family and I were on vacation when I contracted the bacteria. Apparently I ate something bad or (the more likely reason) drank so much lake water that my intestinal tract resembled that of a rotting bird. Long story short, I had explosive diarrhea for days and was forced to stay indoors for the rest of our trip. My mom bought me rice cakes and purified water.

On the second night of my quarantine I was woken up by a particularly startling round of the midnight shits. I bolted out of bed and ran for the bathroom, hoping I would make it in time. I did, and when the evacuation was over, I dragged my limp body back to my room and collapsed on my bed—which, unfortunately, was when my bowels decided to release themselves again. Hot tears poured down my face as I stripped out of my freshly soiled pants.

The next day, there was blood in my shit.

"Okay," said my mom with a worried look on her face, "let's get you to a doctor."

We went to an emergency clinic and the doctor asked me lots of questions about what I had eaten, how much water I'd been drinking, how old I was, and if this had ever happened before.

"Are you sure it was blood in the stool?" he asked.

I nodded.

He turned toto face my mom. "Are you sure?" he repeated. "We don't see that very often with run-of-the-mill food poisoning. Has she had her period yet? Is there a chance it could have been her period?"

"No," my mother said, disbelief in her voice. "No, that can't be. Not at the same time as food poisoning. And she's too young."

But the answer was yes. I was thirteen, and not too young. And that's how I discovered I was a woman—my femininity forever coupled in my mind with diarrhea so explosive I was sent to the emergency room.

A few months later, I was sitting at the kitchen table with my mom and one of my aunts. Much to my embarrassment, my mom began to tell my period story.

"She was so sick," said my mom. "I just couldn't believe it. She even went in her pants one night, poor thing."

I felt my face go bright red.

"And then we found blood in her stool." she continued. "We took her to the doctor, and I was shocked when he suggested it might be her period. But it was, and she's been like clockwork ever since." My mother looked over at me. "Right?" she asked. "Like clockwork."

I nodded and felt my face go from bright red to purple. I was mortified. I reached for the plate of cookies that was sitting on the table, desperately hoping to avoid eye contact with my aunt.

And then I heard it.

Laughter.

Big laughter. The kind that spews out of your mouth. The kind that tells you someone has been trying hard to hold in but just can't, so out it comes in a wild breathy burst. Unbeknownst to us, my eighteen-year-old brother and one of his friends had been standing at the bottom of the stairs the entire time. The. Entire. Time.

I bolted out of the kitchen to my bedroom and proceeded to cry for hours.

There were many examples in my life of people, times, and places that linked shame with femininity, but this served as the strongest. It was the one I could name with clarity. From that point on, I thought of womanhood as something to be embarrassed by, something to be laughed at and made fun of, something that paired perfectly with . . . shit. It wasn't the only reason I tamped down my femininity; I found many others as I moved through life. In fact, this very trip served as evidence that I'd built a pretty large case against it. So imagine my surprise when I saw a few glimmers of femininity looking back at me in Bali. I'd been wrong all along.

This tiger didn't look like something to be laughed at. What I got a glimpse of was much more impressive than that.

.⁚●.

I LEFT BALI AT the end of November with five pounds of flesh on my hips, and a few extra ounces of wisdom. In the moments of silence I'd carved out here and there from my time with the girls, I started reading the books Chris sent. I was struck by one in particular. More specifically, I was struck by one line from within it.

In *The Dance of the Dissident Daughter*, Sue Monk Kidd writes, "The truth may set you free, but first it will shatter the safe, sweet way you live."

PART THREE

THE LAND OF THE RISING SUN

What he must annihilate is his own cherished character, and there is no self-conquest more arduous for the truly virtuous than this one of recreancy to the higher nature, sacrifice of the ideal, denial of the model role that one has striven always to represent.

—HEINRICH ZIMMER, *THE KING AND THE CORPSE*

14

HOT BATHS, A VOICE, AND A RECURRING DREAM

I GET a little anxious when I'm going through customs checkpoints in foreign countries, but this go-round I was a total wreck. My nerves had nothing to do with the Japanese border guards ahead of me, though—they had everything to do with Chris.

As I shuffled through the stanchions, got a nod and a few stamps on my passport, and made my way toward the Narita International Airport arrivals lounge, questions were spinning through my head.

Will I recognize him? What if I don't recognize him? What if I walk right by him? How tall is he again? I wonder if he'll have a beard or not? Was he clean-shaven in our last Skype call? But what if I don't recognize him?

Airport pickups are important. Throughout my life they had always been reserved for family and close friends, so it felt strange to be meeting Chris at the airport, a man who, in many ways, I didn't even know.

Where is he going to be waiting? How is he going to be standing? What will he be wearing?

These were all questions I could answer fairly accurately when it came to my regular airport people, but for Chris I had no idea. I thought about how I should know what the back of his head looked like, because if I knew that, then I'd be able to pick him out in a crowd. That's when I realized I was in a straight-up panic. What was worse, though, was not knowing what to do when I saw him.

Should I put my bags down? Should I hug him? If I hug him, do I do a full hug, or do I keep hold of my stuff and do a one-armed hug? Holy shit, what if I give a one-armed hug to a man who isn't Chris? Oh my god this is bad, this is so awkward. I should have just told him I would meet him at the hotel.

I was mid-spaz when I spotted him, which turned out to be relatively easy. We were in Japan, after all, and Chris is a six-foot-tall white dude. His gorgeous swimming-pool eyes were peeking out from underneath a well-worn navy blue baseball hat, the logo of his favorite ski resort emblazoned on the front. He was wearing a black softshell jacket, jeans that were a tiny bit short in the leg, and a pair of canvas hiking shoes. He had a five o'clock shadow, and everything about his smile and the look on his face said *Get here. Get into my arms.* I walked toward him, dropped my bags at my feet, and folded myself into the middle of his chest. He wrapped his arms tightly around me.

"Hi, Little Bird," he said, whispering softly into my ear. The nickname was from Bariloche. He called me Bird or Little Bird on account of how often I sang that Annie Lennox song while perched on the seat of a chairlift.

"Hi," I said, my body full of relief.

The rest of our hug happened in slow motion, as did the part where he dragged my luggage through the airport and loaded it onto a shuttle that took us back to the hotel, the one he'd stayed in the night before. The elevator ride was in slow motion, and so was the walk down the hallway to the door of the room. But once the door closed behind us, things sped right up, and we immediately made good on every detail from those naughty little e-mails. Every. Last. One.

After a short nap and a quick little snuggle, we hit the road. We had a handful of days before our flight north to Hokkaido, and our plan was to rent a car and drive to an area northwest of Tokyo known for its hot springs and world-class *onsen*s (aka Japanese hot tubs).

The drive from the car rental agency to the outskirts of Tokyo was a breeze. Things became a bit more complicated when we moved from the outskirts to the inskirts, and once there, I felt like we were being asked to do the quickstep after being exposed to a short video demonstrating the Chicken Dance.

From that day forward, I had an easy reply at the ready when asked how to determine the compatibility of two people: "Give them jet lag and a rental car," I would say, "and then have them navigate over, under, into, and around the streets of Tokyo. Oh, and make sure they have zero understanding of the Japanese language and no basic recognition of a single kanji character."

The highway we were driving on looked like a combination of Southern California concrete engineering and Orbit City from Hanna-Barbera's cult hit *The Jetsons*. It was a road in the clouds, and it gave us a view into the sky-pad homes and offices of the 35 million Japanese Georges and Judys in the area. My awe and wonder ended the moment we were required to exit the skyway and make our first turn.

We relied on three things to get through our compatibility test. The first was Chris's skill as a driver. The second was a map printed from the hotel website. And the third was my ability to interpret the map. The map was a bit crude, and by crude I mean it was drawn by a seven-year-old, or at least it looked like it had been drawn by a seven-year-old. It showed one main road leading out of Tokyo (there are actually about five thousand), six consecutive stoplights, a right turn, followed by a left OR right turn, and finally a "downward slope" (that part was written in English) that came to an end at the edge of a river. There were a few kanji characters sprinkled throughout the map, and a red dot indicating the hotel's location.

This meant that, as chief navigator, I was going to have to match the kanji characters on the map with the ones we were driving by at seventy miles per hour. It was a very stressful matching game, kind of like if you mixed Go Fish with professional-level, high-stakes mah-jongg.

When I saw the first road sign, I laughed. It looked like Medusa. The arrows, which I assume were related to the various exits but could have been related to the way in which cockroaches move, snaked around one another and pointed in every which direction. For a brief moment I thought it might be a modern art installation, but at the last second I saw a matching character and yelled, "Turn! Turn here!"

Chris swerved hard to the right, moving three lanes in one go, and we merged onto another highway in the sky. Dynamic duo, one. Medusa, zero.

We made it into the countryside, and based on various codes I cracked along the way, I knew we were in the vicinity of our hotel, meaning anywhere from 1 to 171 miles away. Our blood sugar was dropping as quickly as the sun, so we decided to pull over and search our luggage for random almonds or stale, half-eaten granola bars, items quite often found in the pockets of skiers. I got out of the car and walked around to the trunk. It was a beautiful evening. The roads were quiet, the moon hung in the sky, and there was a thick forest on either side of us.

"Look," I said to Chris as I pointed down the road. "What's that?"

I had spotted a large sign tucked behind a few trees up ahead. From where I was standing, it looked as though it had some English lettering on it, so I walked closer. The sign was carved and then beautifully painted with the following German words:

JAPANISCHE ROMANTISCHE STRASSE

I'm not fluent in German, but I took a stab in the dark.

"Japanese Romantic Road," I said to Chris, and then I started to laugh. "We're on the road to romance."

I looked closer and saw, praise the Lord, a map. It confirmed we were just around the corner from our hotel, and so it was by German intervention that we found our way, as well as our first pattern as a couple—getting lost and then found, usually by way of a perfectly placed sign.

For the next few days we soaked up as much as the Strasse had to offer, including numerous customs associated with slippers, beds that looked like fluffy tatami nests, interesting varieties of "food," and pavement. I know that last one sounds strange, but let me explain: some sections of the Strasse were cut with thousands of tiny grooves. At first we thought they were oddly placed rumble strips, but as we continued driving, we discovered that a song was being created by the vibration our tires made as they rolled over the grooves. The hills were actually alive with the sound of music.

We also visited some of the nearby villages, including a small town called Kusatsu, known for its hot springs and its rank on Japan's list of (this is not a lie) "100 scenic spots of peculiar smell." The odor that wafted up from the hot springs was so bad, so completely foul and rotten-eggy, that every person sauntering around was forced to mouth-breathe. On a side note, I think every country should have a list of "scenic spots of peculiar smell." It would be a wonder for tourism, not to mention romance—they would be the perfect spots to fall in love, which was exactly what Chris and I were doing. Laughing, mouth-breathing, and falling in love.

At the end of each day, bellies aching, we would go back to our hotel and relax in one of the many *onsens*. The property was majestic. A series of stunning pine lodges had been built into a densely forested hillside. A deep, mossy river bed ran down one side of the grounds, home to the clean, cool water that ran from Japan's mountains all the way to its ocean, quenching the thirst of the northern Pacific's salty mouth. The water pooled and eddied in various spots, lingering a while before spraying up in a fine mist and then moving on. Natural hot springs bubbled up in a handful of places along the riverbank, creating large baths for guests to sink into, to melt away in. It was like lying in a pool of warm liquid gemstones.

Chris and I sat naked in those pools, and we watched as other people moved like whispers through the forest, their wooden slippers sliding quietly over the series of bridges that connected one pool to another. On one of those nights, I told Chris about what happened in New Zealand, the version of the story I had recently discovered, and what I thought about some of the books he'd sent.

"I'm not sure this trip is what I thought it was. It's different somehow," I said. "I don't really know what's going to happen, but I feel like a lot of those books you sent were pretty bang on—they all seemed to be about people going on a journey, only to have a different one revealed to them partway through. I think that's what's happening to me."

Chris nodded. "I thought you'd like those books."

"I loved them," I said, "and when I was reading them, something hit me. Even though this whole thing started as some way to prove myself, as some quest for achievement and the validation

I thought would come with it, I realized that it's about something different altogether."

Chris smiled back at me and waited as I continued in excitement. "So when I was in New Zealand I feel like I kind of caught a glimpse of myself for the first time, like I understood once and for all that I'm not the person I thought I was. And I don't think I want to go back to that life. In fact, I don't think I can."

"Mm-hmm." Chris nodded.

"But here's the thing. I have no idea how to be another version of myself. Who's going to teach me how to do that?"

Chris put his hands on either side of my face and looked me right in the eyes.

"I think you might be onto something, Birdie. And"—he kissed me very gently—"I think I can help. I had to reinvent the person I was. I had to decide who I wanted to be as a man, and then go out and create that. I didn't have anyone teaching me. It was all from those books. Joseph Campbell showed me the kind of man I wanted to be in the world. Sue Monk Kidd taught me how to treat women. We'll do this together. You and me and those books."

I felt a bit off-balance, but I was also relieved. Chris was a hand to hold on to. I knew he had wisdom to share with me. I knew he could help me figure everything out. At the very least, I knew he had the patience required as I worked through it.

I sat back into his arms and watched our breath mix together in the air.

.˙●.

AFTER A FEW DAYS of soaking ourselves silly, Chris and I made our way back to Tokyo. We returned our rental car with glee, boarded a flight to Sapporo, the largest city on the island of Hokkaido, and then hopped on a train to a small ski town in the center of the island. We were hoping for snow, but there was none on the ground, none floating down from the sky, and none in the short-range forecast.

In the end, I think that was a good thing. Add skiing to the amount of sex Chris and I were having, and I would have been too exhausted to move. There would have been no energy left for talking, and based on what others had told me, I understood that communication was fairly important when it came to building a lasting relationship. So that's what we did. We had sex, and we talked, and we dined in restaurants that had tiny conveyor belts, little pieces of sushi carried past our table at medium speed.

"I make a really good frittata," Chris said one night as he grabbed a piece of fish from the belt, "and James Taylor is one of my favorite musicians."

"I don't really cook that much," I confessed, picking up what looked like a seaweed salad. "And I hate to tell you this, but I'm too young to understand the true impact James Taylor had on the music scene."

Chris laughed and then, pointing at a very suspect piece of fish, shook his head. "Don't touch that one," he said. "I don't think either of us should touch that one."

He looked back toward me and was suddenly serious. "I have a lot of fear when it comes to being out of control."

"Me too," I responded. "And I'm starting to feel like I don't know who I am anymore. What should we talk about first?"

We burst into laughter. Our conversation that night was long and deep, measured and marked by the number of times that suspect-looking fish circled the restaurant. We talked about Chris's fear, and then we talked about who I thought I was—and perhaps more important, who I wanted to be. Chris asked a lot of questions, and each one of them stumped me. As a goat, I'd never really gone off script.

"Who are you?" he asked, "and what kind of woman do you want to become?"

No one had ever asked me questions like that. I'd never thought about the who, what, and why questions. There hadn't been room for those, not when I was so busy answering the wheres, whens, and hows with my growing collection of shiny blue ribbons.

I wasn't uncomfortable having the conversation, but I wasn't comfortable either. This was uncharted territory, and however gentle Chris was in guiding me through it, I felt cracked open and vulnerable.

When we got back to the apartment, I told Chris I was going to take a bath. I needed solace and a little silence to think things through.

"Okay, sweets," he said. "I'll be right here."

I ran the water and closed the bathroom door. I slipped out of my clothes and slid deep into the tub.

I sat quietly for a moment and looked down at the water.

What now?

A few seconds later, I heard a voice. *You have to start over*, it said. *You're going to have to start over.*

I'd heard voices in my head before, but they'd all been shit-talkers, anxious little tattletales that never seem pleased with what I was up to.

This voice was different. It was deeper and more relaxed. There was something soothing about it.

You're going to have to start over, it said again.

"Okay," I said hesitantly, half of me wondering if getting into a conversation with an invisible voice meant I was going crazy. "What does that mean, exactly?"

Let it all go. Let everything go and start over.

I waited for more, but apparently that was all it had to say.

I've read many books and seen many movies where the main

character has something horrible happen to them, where they're required to start over, to pick up the scraps of their life and move on in some way. I've met people in real life who have had to do the same, people who have had to gather the unspooled threads of their life, people who have stitched themselves back together after they were broken by some awful illness or an accident or a relationship that took them all the way to hell. The whole process seems excruciating, to glue the broken shards of one's life back together. But when you're lying on the ground amid the broken shards of your life, picking up the pieces seems like the obvious next step. Gluing things back together would be the clear first move. I'm not saying it would be easy. I'm not saying I would wish it on anyone, the grueling work involved in rebuilding, in starting over. But isn't it the most obvious thing to do? Isn't that what it means to survive?

The starting over I was being called to seemed different somehow. Sure, I had lost my footing on this trip; that part was apparent. But I wasn't shattered; my life wasn't visibly broken. Was I supposed to bring in a wrecking ball anyway? Was I supposed to dismantle a life that had always been good to me, as well as the beliefs that came with it? The thought of that terrified me. The thought of having to toss away everything I knew about safety and security and comfort, the thought that I might not have a choice.

This idea of letting things go, of becoming unmoored, was scary. Everyone knows that being in the mountains, the big ones, the uncharted ones, all on your own is an awful idea. It's not safe. You're vulnerable, susceptible, an easy target for avalanches and animals, for windburn and sunburn and frostbite, for starvation. I didn't know how to survive in those conditions. There was a reason I'd stuck to skiing in resorts. Being outside the bounds of my life terrified me. My name isn't Edmund Hillary. I am not

Lewis, nor am I Clark. I wasn't okay with the venturing off into the vast unknown, no plan or goal other than pure exploration. I may be naive, but I am not crazy.

I sat in the bathtub and started to shiver.

It's time to get out.

I removed the plug and watched the water slowly drain. As I did, questions about starting over began popping up. The biggest ones, the hardest ones to look at, were about the people I loved. If I did this, would I have to tell them that I was no longer interested in sharing a script? If I walked away from the beliefs they'd built their lives around, would they know I still loved them? Would they still love me?

I climbed out, wrapped myself in a towel, and rejoined Chris in the other room.

"I just heard a voice," I said. "It told me I had to start over. I have no idea what that really means, but I think it's what I have to do."

"Okay, Bird," he said, totally unfazed about the fact that I'd just told him I'd heard some mystical voice. "Do you want to start over there?" he said with a cheeky grin, gesturing toward the bed.

"Very funny," I said. "But okay, yes, that sounds like a decent idea. Let's start there."

.·●.

SOMETHING ABOUT THE CLARITY of this voice had hit me on an intuitive level. I'd been thrown off course enough times on this trip to finally understand that something needed to change, that this journey didn't really have anything to do with vertical feet. I could either forge ahead on my own, my identity in one hand and a hammer in the other, or let fate take its course, never knowing if one day I would be dragged away kicking and screaming, never knowing when or how hard the hammer might come down. Call me a control freak, but I chose option one. Freedom over fear. I didn't know how, but I was going to face this head-on.

I've always had quite vivid dreams. The kind where I wake up in the morning with a clear memory of all the images, characters, and colors that have been floating around in the night. Near the end of Chris's visit, I had one such dream. It was a crystal-clear movie, played out in color on the screen inside my head.

When I woke up the next morning, I felt Chris pull me into his arms. I turned to face him, but before I could say anything, he was already speaking.

"I had a dream last night," he said.

"Mm-hmm. So did I. What was yours?"

Chris stared up at the ceiling. "I had a dream . . . we were in bed, and . . . and you were pregnant."

I felt a line of goose bumps rise up on my skin, from my ankles all the way up to my arms.

"We were sitting on the edge of something," he continued. "A bed, I think . . . and you were pregnant, and I was really worried and stressed. But you weren't. You were calm . . . you had a big, beautiful belly. You were sitting with me, and you kept telling me everything was going to be all right."

He looked at me. I was completely silent.

"That was too much, wasn't it? Too early?" he asked. "I probably shouldn't be telling you that I'm having dreams of our unborn children, right? Sorry. I didn't mean to freak you out. Too much. Way too much."

"No," I said quietly. "It wasn't too much."

I sat up and looked into his eyes.

"I just had the *exact same* dream."

"What?" Chris asked in disbelief.

"No, seriously," I said. "It was exactly the same. You were sitting on the edge of a bed with your head in your hands. You were rubbing your forehead like you were anxious about something . . . and I was sitting behind you . . . my legs were wrapped round either side of you. I was rubbing your back, and I was really, really pregnant, and I just kept saying, 'Everything's gonna be okay. Everything's gonna be okay.'"

Chris and I stared at each other.

"What the fuck?" I whispered. "What does that mean? Have you ever heard that before . . . two people having the same dream?"

"Nope," said Chris. His eyes were wide, and he started to nod. "You're not kidding, are you?"

"No. That was the dream. I was totally pregnant. I was huge. We were sitting at the end of a bed, and my legs were wrapped around you."

After some time Chris looked at me, and he smiled. "I guess we're really doing this."

"I guess we are," I confirmed, smiling widely in return.

Over the past few months I'd fallen for Chris, and now, after a few days in Japan, I knew I was in love with him. But there was more to it than that. I didn't know there could be more to it than love, but the dream confirmed it. The whole thing felt preordained, as if something far bigger than both of us had pointed down from the cosmos and said, "Them. Put them together. They will teach each other beautiful things." I had a distinct feeling that beyond being the guy I fell in love with, Chris was a guide, an integral piece of the puzzle when it came to me starting over, and that in many ways, I was the same for him. The whole romance, passion, and sex part of it just seemed like icing on the cake, which I ate happily, spoonful by frosty spoonful.

There were still a lot of unknowns about our future, however.

Realistic, tangible, of-this-world questions about what was next for us. I still had six months of traveling ahead of me, and we lived in different countries. I didn't know what starting over looked like for me, never mind what it might look like for us. So there I was, sitting in a pile of unanswerable questions, a large bowl of butter icing plunked down next to me.

15

KILTIE TASSELED LOAFERS

IT WAS the beginning of December, and I hadn't skied in six weeks. My original plan had been to take three weeks off between seasons. I'd adjusted it to five after New Zealand tried to knock some sense into me, and now it was six. Before I knew it, six turned into seven, and seven into eight.

Chris left Japan on the first of the month, and when he did, I traveled a little farther east, to a larger resort town called Niseko. I was excited because Niseko was home to four mountains interconnected by a series of fast-moving lifts. It was the perfect place to play catch-up, plus it had oodles of restaurants where people brought you food, as opposed to you watching it move around a conveyor belt like an unwanted suitcase.

But the unusually warm start to the Japanese winter kept on. I woke up each morning to a fresh dusting of snow, but then the temperature would rise and the rain would take over, washing away whatever hope had begun to gather.

I coped as best I could. I took long walks in the slush. I hit the shops. I picked out small dangly ornaments and hung them from the side of my change purse like little Harajuku graduation caps. I went to lunch with my landlord, Hiro, who I obviously referred to as Hero, and I celebrated the Japanese for a variety of things like carrying rhubarb-flavored yogurt in their grocery stores and having vending machines that served hot coffee, hot soup, and hot underwear.

I also spent a fair bit of time offending the Japanese. No matter how hard I tried, they seemed consistently disappointed, confused, and/or deeply offended by my actions, and perhaps even my presence. For example, I pointed at things. Additionally, I made numerous errors when it came to the code of conduct regarding shoes, socks, slippers, bare feet, bathroom slippers, house slippers, and wooden clog-thong slippers, as well as the modesty towels at local *onsens*. Yes, they are actually called modesty towels, and no, I still don't understand the etiquette involved. You'd have to have modesty for that, I suppose.

There were some wins, though. I was able to watch a lot of Robert Redford movies (the only type Hiro had stocked in the apartment), and I increased my proficiency in the Japanese language. Within a few weeks of rigorous study, I was able to identify the characters for "ATM" and "post office," ATM being the easiest because it was literally the English letters *A*, *T*, and *M*. Oh, and I mastered the use of the Japanese toilet, which comes with a whole assortment of buttons to adjust the heat of the seat, the spray of the bidet, and the volume of the music you use when you're, say, masking disagreeable noises. Last, I skied down a small patch of ice in my driveway just to feel the wind in my hair, after which point I wondered what it would feel like to pull my eyeballs right out of their sockets.

And then it hit me. Did I really want to turn this whole waiting game into a remake of New Zealand? That wouldn't be "start-ing over" so much as "doing the same thing I'd always done, for-ever and ever and always." I could pop in a J. J. Cale CD, pen an open letter to the Japanese snow blower, and go crazy, or I could try something new. I opted for the latter. If I had to wait for the weather, I would wait in a different way. This would be my first step in starting over.

I was halfway through my trip, and one of the biggest lessons thus far was about waiting. Waiting in airports, waiting in bus sta-tions, and waiting in lift lines. Waiting for snow, waiting for more snow, and sometimes, waiting for less of it. Waiting for the wind to die down, and for the temperatures to drop. Waiting for the chairlift to start back up, and for the temperatures to go with it. Waiting for a good Skype connection, and to see if the person next to me on the chairlift was in the mood to talk, or if they spoke some English. The whole thing was a massive exercise in patience.

Interestingly enough the root of the word *patience* is found in Latin, *patientia*, and it means—wait for it—suffering. When I looked back, it occurred to me that many of my beliefs about manning up involved suffering. The more I suffered, the more I deserved love and attention. The bigger the war story I came home with, the more important the trip. The more it hurt, the more I could bear the physical discomfort, the more worthy I was. In so many ways I was choosing to suffer, creating situations in which I could prove my strength. My identity was so intricately linked with the idea of toughing it out that you might have thought the two were married. I was a pro at making things harder than they had to be. Could I let all that go? Could I wait things out with grace?

I gently placed my suffering to the side, along with my incessant drive and my obsession with figuring out where, when, and how. I did it so I could start over, or at least attempt to. I did it so I could pick up new questions like who, what, and why. I'm not sure it was entirely graceful, but my eyeballs managed to stay in their sockets, so I considered it a win.

I spent the next number of days curled up on the couch with my new set of questions. I wrote in my journal. I read more of the books Chris had sent me, and I listened to the words of Joseph Campbell. When I got hungry, I went for bowls of miso soup and steaming hot ramen, and when I got tired, I booked some time with a Japanese healer. I sat naked in *onsen*s, a handful of sweet Japanese teenagers giggling at the vulnerable-looking white lady tucked in the corner of the baths. I had an hour-long session with an intuitive, a gift from Chris. She told me to still myself, and I did. I sat in my apartment for hours, watching second-rate storms roll in and roll on. I sat for as long as the Universe wanted me there. I sat until the next step began to reveal itself.

I'd known from an early age I couldn't be my mother, but it took me twenty-nine years, eleven months, and a few weeks in Japan to realize I couldn't be my father, nor could I be the rammed-up version of him I'd constructed for myself.

When I was growing up, I spent a fair bit of time fumbling around in my parents' closet, digging through tissue paper, trying on hats. Looking back, I see a little girl desperately searching for something that fit. But at the time it was just another world for me to get lost in. I remember my father's shoe rack as a thing of glory. Pair after polished pair of what was essentially the exact same shoe—kiltie tasseled loafers in light brown, dark brown, chestnut, burgundy, and black. There may have been a few monk straps in the bunch, but most were loafers. Each pair had a cedar shoe tree, the quality kind, to preserve each shoe's shape.

About once a month, my father would select a few pairs from the bunch, walk them into the basement, and I would watch as he polished them by hand. He had special brushes and cloths, as well as varnishes that matched the color of each pair. Everything fit perfectly into a small box he kept in the laundry room. I loved the sound of the bristles as they hit the shoe, sweeping back and forth across the leather. Shoes were an important part of my dad's life, and because of that I made them an important part of mine.

I was five years old when my mom took me to the Kerrisdale Bootery to select a pair of shoes for kindergarten. I couldn't have been more excited. As the youngest of four, I was a hand-me-down girl, and selecting my own new pair was a rare occasion. I quickly moved away from the sneaker aisle. I wasn't interested in a pair of Keds, or, God forbid, those flimsy little jelly shoes. No. I wanted something with more substance, something that would look right with a shoe tree inside it.

After carefully inspecting the stock, we bought a pair of black patent-leather Mary Janes. I wore them home from the store. Rare was the day I didn't buckle up those shoes. I wore them to school and for all of my play dates. I went to birthday parties in them (obviously), and I'm pretty sure I wore them while running in my first three-legged race. One of my parents' friends nicknamed me "Party Shoes" because I was wearing them with unabashed delight nearly every time he saw me. Delight because I knew they made me daddy's little girl, not in a princess kind of way, but in an oh-my-God-you're-just-like-your-father kind of way. This was an important difference.

I bought my first apartment as a presale when I was twenty-three years old. A year later, when construction was complete, I moved into my brand-new home. I was brimming with pride, and so was my father. The first thing I did when I got there was organize my shoe rack. I filled it with pair after pair of beautifully polished pumps. Green, purple, brown, chestnut, and red. The list could go on. As I placed each pair, I was careful to leave one spot open. Then I held the last pair of heels in my hands. They were perfect, a kitten heel, in black patent leather. I placed them front and center, a daily reminder of everything I thought I was, everything I'd worked so hard to become.

Walking in my father's footsteps hadn't been a difficult thing for me to do. First of all, I'm a truly gifted copycat. As a person with three older siblings, I was guaranteed to develop talent in the realm of mimicry. I watched, I listened, I learned, and after two decades of using my siblings' lives as artful fodder, slipping into a hand-me-down identity was just as easy as slipping into hand-me-down clothes. The other thing that made this easy was the fact that my father and I are cut from very similar cloth. My becoming him was never a case of burlap attempting to spin itself into silk, but rather cotton trying to become a slightly different version of cotton. Think chino to seersucker, or corduroy to oxford.

It never occurred to me that there was anything wrong with this. Looking back, I think it's because I never had to bend that far to be my father, just a little bit here and a little bit there. Save a few details, the imitation was impeccable.

I had spent my life marching down the path my father had paved, and I'd read from his script with ease. I had an entire way of doing and having that felt pretty good. I knew exactly what came next, and I knew what came after that. It never occurred to me that I should factor in the steps of being or becoming, the awkward and often painful carving others had done, the shaping and whittling one has to do to reveal an identity. Why would I go through all of that when the trail was already cut, when I had the perfect fall line laid out right in front of me?

"Because," said Joseph Campbell on a warm winter night in Japan, "if you can see your path laid out in front of you step by step, you know it's not your path."

If I couldn't be my dad, I had to be me. That seemed pretty simple.

I just need to be myself, I thought.

Easier said than done.

I never doubted my ability to complete this journey. Barring a serious injury, not being able to ski 4 million feet simply hadn't crossed my mind. I knew what my ego was made of; I knew the depths of my willpower. I was bound to do it. But this personal journey was different. The tables had turned. I wasn't sure I could just be me; I wasn't convinced that was a feat I was capable of.

.ꞏ.

I WAS STANDING IN a parking lot behind one of Niseko's largest hotels, because that's where the buses pulled in. I wrapped my scarf around my neck and looked down at my watch: 5:54 p.m.

I rubbed the side of my neck. Navigating through Japanese train stations is a feat in and of itself. Doing it with an incredibly heavy ski bag, a large rolling suitcase, and a midsize backpack had been nothing short of a miracle, a miracle that took a toll on my neck.

Most rural train stations in Japan don't have elevators or escalators. Maze after maze of interconnected staircases move people from one platform to another. It's almost as if Salvador Dali came to Japan and painted each station right before your very eyes. In many ways, they seemed like a beautiful illusion, but for me and my luggage, they seemed like a giant fucking nightmare.

Whenever I needed to change platforms to meet a connecting train, which was every single time, I had two options. The first was to hop off one train with all of my gear, go up a set of stairs, walk across a connecting hallway, glide down another staircase, and meet my next train. The second was to lie down on the tracks with all of my gear.

I chose the first option, but I'm not going to lie, I almost always regretted it halfway through the whole ordeal. Because all of the hopping, walking, and gliding with my gear was a lie. What really had to happen was that I pulled my bags with all my might until they somehow squeezed loose from the train. After that, I lugged them up a long staircase. If I had lots of energy, I did it in one go, but most of the time each bag got its own trip. Sometimes I got help from kindhearted strangers, and by sometimes I mean once. When I got myself and all of my bags to the top of the stairs, I pushed everything down a hallway (because at that point I was too tired to drag, never mind carry), and then, without a concern in the world, I yelled, "Bombs away!" as I shoved my gear down the stairs, to tumble to the platform below. If I was lucky, no one was killed, and my train would be there waiting.

It's important to note that none of this includes the parts where I had to get my gear packed, out of a hotel room, into a car, out of a car, through the train station, and to the ticket window. Nor does it include getting out of the train station, into a van, out of a van, through the hotel lobby, and into my room before collapsing.

Over the course of three weeks of performing this routine, I developed a problem—one that radiated down the right side of my neck, all the way into my fingers, as well as into my right shoulder blade and down the side of my back. Although I was fairly certain the train station/luggage combination was to blame, I couldn't help but notice the timing. The dull ache became a constant, stabbing pain on the exact day my parents arrived in Tokyo. It was as almost if my head had whipped back when I sensed their arrival: *What! Who's here?*

I looked down again. The bus was coming from the Sapporo airport, and it was set to arrive at six o'clock sharp.

It was 5:57 p.m.

I was eager to see my parents, but I was tense and jittery. They were arriving just as I'd come to realize I had been a tiger all along, masquerading in a herd of goats—their herd of goats—my whole life. And though I'd seen my tigery face for the first time, I had yet to hear myself actually roar, and I wasn't sure how I was going to do it with my father standing right at my side. Ever since I was little, it had been his voice I'd listened to—it was a beacon, a guiding light bleating in a steady rhythm about right and wrong, up and down, yes and no. How was I supposed to roar now?

I paced back and forth a bit as the dry snow squeaked under me. I looked down at my dark green boots. The snow had arrived a few days prior, huge feathery flakes tumbling from the sky, never letting up. The entire town looked as though a thick duvet had been thrown over it. All of the streets were solid white, and behind the plumes of snow hung an indigo sky. It was the middle of December, and Grand Hirafu, the largest of the four resorts in the area, finally had enough snow to open. The coverage wasn't complete, but I'd managed three days of skiing, dodging large thickets of bamboo whose tops were still sticking out from the snow.

I looked again at my watch: 6:01 p.m.

I watched the bus pull into the parking lot and come to a stop. The side door opened, and the driver got out, followed by two little people dressed all in black. I hurried over.

"There she is, there she is!" said my mom. She wrapped her arms around me, and even halfway across the world, my mom still smelled like my mom.

They were in Japan for just under two weeks, and despite my nerves it turned out to be heaven on earth. It was so easy to slip back into my place within the supercontinent, nestled between safety and security and everything familiar feeling, sounding, and smelling. In a very foreign place my parents were a safe haven; they were kind and comfortable, and they were, finally, a vacation from all of the traveling. And they could help with my bags!

"I can't believe you've been doing this on your own," said my dad as we traveled together through Hokkaido, then onward to Tokyo and Kyoto.

"I've had some recent help," I said, referring to Chris.

"Yes, we heard you had a visitor," said my mom, her eyebrows raised in amusement and curiosity.

I gave them a few details about Chris, but not a lot. They were goats, after all, and if I was going to bleat, it was best that I do it in a moderate tone. Also, we were busy with the when, where, and how of Japan. We spent our days soaking up every bit of the country. We skied, we drank sake, and we tried a plethora of strange pickled fish. We visited Zen gardens and ancient Buddhist temples. We celebrated Jesus's birthday, and then, over a formal Japanese dinner that we giggled rather inappropriately through, we celebrated mine. We took photos of ourselves wearing slippers and thin cotton *yakatas*, and then we went back to the mountains and skied some more.

This wasn't the first time my parents had met me on the other side of the earth, and I was fairly certain it wouldn't be the last. But compared to all the times before, this felt different. On every other journey they had previously joined me for, we'd gone home together, literally and figuratively. This was the first time they would leave me to carry on without them, to continue my solo travel. And, more important, this was the first time I wouldn't go home at all. I didn't know where I would land at the end of all this, but if I was going to start over, I knew my definition of home had to change, regardless of where I wound up in a geographical sense. But how do you redefine home? I understood how to do it in a practical sense, with cardboard boxes and large moving trucks, but emotionally I was lost. How do you define who you were before and who you are now? How do you go about creating a new definition for safety, security, and comfort? Where does your heart go when home is no longer an option?

I started by looking back, to the past, to all the memories I had of life in the herd, memories I saw reflected with clarity in my parents' shining eyes. The house, and the kids, and the bright orange Sundance trampoline—I felt like everything they'd built was staring right back at me, as if to say, *Look at the life you are leaving. Are you sure it's not what you want? Look at all the guarantees it comes with. The warranties. You're just going to leave those on the table? And look at these amazing, beautiful souls. How could you not want to be them?*

I turned my head forward and looked straight out in front of me, the pain in my neck instantly gone.

It's not that I don't want to be them, it's that I can't.

I would once again have to ski out from between my father's legs. I would have to loosen the grip I had on the poles he'd stuck out at his side. And as I unfurled my hands and began to fly off on my own down the mountain, I looked up and saw a storm moving in, a blizzard raging so hard I couldn't tell up from down. The sky was dark and the wind was howling, snow was coming down at every angle, but I didn't panic. I was calm. I'd spent enough time in the mountains to learn that nothing is guaranteed. Outcomes aren't promised, and you're not going to get assurance of some final result. The only commitment the mountains can make is that if you go to them, they'll tell you who you are. They'll reflect you back like a mirror. I learned this toward the end of my parents' visit.

A few days before they were due to head back home, we skied together at Happo-One, one of the largest resorts in Japan. When we got to the top of the lift, I looked out at the mountains.

At this point, the internal storm was quieting. I may not have found my own groove quite yet, but at least I knew I was standing on my own two feet.

"If I'm not them, who am I?" I whispered. "How do I figure this out?"

The voice came back, as soothing as ever.

Well, my darling, you came here to ski. Why don't you start with that? And be sure to thank your parents. They were the ones who taught you to ski, am I right?

I embraced this advice for the next few days. And when it came time to say good-bye, I hugged my parents, popped my skis up over my shoulder, and went back to the mountains.

16

A GIRL NAMED TREE
AND JAPANESE SNOW

JUST BEFORE my parents arrived in Japan, when I was consumed with things like learning to be still and watching Robert Redford movies, I was introduced to a woman named Tree, short for Theresa. I had taken a break from my movie marathon that day and was sitting at a local coffee shop. I was there for a while, a fact I know because I vibrated my way home, a result of far too much caffeine. Just before I pushed *The Horse Whisperer* in for round two, I decided to check my e-mail. There was one from a friend back home, and one from Veronika, an amazing woman I'd met in Argentina.

She was writing to tell me about a friend of hers who happened to be in Japan. She wasn't sure if we were in the same place but suggested that, if we were, we should meet up to shred.

I e-mailed Veronika back right away and copied the woman she had referred to as Tree. I told them I was in the north, in a small town called Niseko, and that I would be there until just before Christmas.

Within seconds, another new message popped up. It was from Tree. She said she was in Niseko, at a little coffee shop on the main street.

As it turns out, Tree and I had been sitting in the same café all morning. We met at a bar about an hour later, and I immediately understood why Veronika had introduced us—Tree and I were clearly part of the same Gore-Tex community. Sometimes, when it comes to your tribe, you just know them when you see them. I get the same feeling when I'm anywhere in the Pacific Northwest. I see hipsters in plaid shirts and tight black jeans, and they're sipping coffee from some small-batch roaster that's right around the corner from their apartment, and I just want to throw my arms around them and yell, "It's you! Thank God! I'm home!" only that would be the opposite of what a hipster from the Pacific Northwest would do, so I just throw them a respect nod and ask them if they know the Wi-Fi code. But I digress.

Tree shook the rain from her jacket, slid the bright pink beanie off her head, and grabbed the seat next to me. Her long auburn hair was wet at the ends.

"Steph!" she said as she leaned in for a big hug. Tree was a hugger. "This is so rad," she continued. "Two Canadian chicks in Japan!"

"I know. It's crazy. You're from Whistler, right?"

"Yep. I've been there for years, but I'm here now. So, you know V. She's pretty kick-ass. She told me about your trip. Shit, that's rad. Wait . . . what are you drinking? Let me order something."

She turned to the bartender and pointed at my drink and then back at herself, while nodding enthusiastically. It was kind of like watching one of the Muppets order a drink, and I mean that in the best way possible. She was bouncing in her seat, her face completely lit up: forehead lifted, eyes wide, gaping smile spread across her face. Her big chestnut-colored eyes were beaming with (I can't believe I'm about to write this, but there's really no other way to describe it) life force energy. Then she turned back to face me.

"Tell me about your trip," she said. "And then we'll do a prayer for some snow, some big, big Japanese pow. They totally need it, eh?"

When Tree walks into a room, heads turn. She's a lightning rod, a flash of raw, palpable energy. She speaks at volume, with intention and well-placed emphasis on Every. Freaking. Word. Her smile, guaranteed to showcase her full set of teeth, is megawatt. So basically, imagine Cindy Crawford yelling, "Fuck yeah!" with her right hand raised up in a Hawaiian *shaka* gesture, and you have Tree.

Tree's physical presence is no less striking—she's five foot seven inches of lean muscle, an athlete to her core, something that's apparent in her every sinewy movement. She's an electric shock of a tomboy, an I-was-playing-hockey-till-midnight-and-I-know-it's-5:00-a.m.-but-do-you-want-to-skin-up-the-hill-for-fresh-tracks-after-I-finish-my-vinyasa-flow kind of gal. She's the type of woman who could win *Survivor*, *The Amazing Race*, and *American Ninja Warrior* at the same time. And although I've never seen her shoot an animal or hook a fish, there is no doubt in my mind she could. And once that animal is caught, there's no doubt in my mind that Tree could also skin it, bone it, and bake it. In the fire she built with two sticks and a stone.

There are numerous benefits to meeting people like Tree, especially when you're traveling, but the biggest by far is that their sole purpose in life seems to be throwing stoke around like it's pixie dust. They are real-life Tinker Bells. And Tree? Tree was Tinker Bell, Peter Pan, and a Muppet, all wrapped up in one.

"Okay, so seriously, let's talk pow," said Tree. "I came all the way over here for Japanese blower, and there's nothing on the ground.

So what do we do? Pray to the Russians? I heard the best storms come from Russia."

I stared back at Tree and smiled.

"I'll take that as a yes," she said. "Let's pray to the Russians."

Tree wasn't the first person sent my way on this trip, but she was the only one who fit so squarely in my comfort zone. I have a hunch it's because of the conversations I'd been having with the Universe. I was on the mountain, ready to ski, telling the Universe something like, "I heard ya. Bring it. Let's do this shit." Or perhaps more accurately, "I heard ya. I'm gonna make some turns, but I really have no idea how to jump into this bad boy, so you're pretty much going to have to spoon-feed me this one." And because the Universe is smart, it started spoon-feeding me, and it started with familiar foods because it knew that swapping a three-decade-long diet of meat and potatoes for something more foreign, like say bananas, would have resulted in me spitting up all over myself. So the Universe gave me meat and potatoes in the form of Tree, something I would recognize, something I could throw my arms around and yell, "It's you! Thank God! I'm home."

I saw Tree's stoke, her big bravado, and her masculine energy. In response, I swung the door wide open. I invited her in, and we spent the next six weeks together, skiing our meat-and-potato pants right off. And then, somewhere in the midst of it all, she shape-shifted into a banana, a beautiful Chiquita banana.

In spite of her tough exterior, it turns out Tree has a soul that is dripping with vulnerability. I didn't discover this until a few weeks in, and it surprised the hell out of me when I did. In retrospect, I think it might have been the reason she was sent to me. Actually, scratch that: I'm certain it was the reason she was sent to me.

But first, the meat and potatoes.

Tree and I skied together for a few days before my parents arrived, and then, after they left, she came down south and joined me in the Hakuba Valley, otherwise known as the Japanese Alps. Once there, we went apeshit, and by that, I mean we were actually like a pair of wild apes. With snow finally on the ground, we went berserk in a way that only two totally rammed-up Canadian gals could.

We lay on every bearskin rug we could find (one) and made "cougar faces" while doing so. We went for sumo dinners and drank giant glasses of beer. We created alter egos for ourselves, alter egos who hosted a made-up midwest Canadian talk show. I was Mo-mo, and she was Terry-Mickey Stojko, Elvis's cousin (and unless you're Canadian or a die-hard figure skating fan, it's not the Elvis that you're thinking of). We snuck flasks of booze into *onsen*s and relaxed more than you're supposed to relax in an *onsen*. We tag-teamed twenty-something drunk Aussies, but not in the way that you're thinking, unless what you're thinking is that we took turns yelling at them to hush up because it was four in the morning and we had mountains to slay the next day. And then we slayed mountains. All morning and all afternoon, we killed it.

This was not starting over—this was doing the same thing I'd always done.

.˙•.

I GREW UP IN a city famous for its cherry trees, meaning I have a memory bank filled to the brim with images of cotton-candy flowers and miniature pink pom-poms fluttering through the air. I know what cherry blossoms look like in the daytime, and I know what they look like at dusk, casting a rose-colored light on the sidewalks, brushing a delicate blush across the cheeks of Vancouver. I know how their petals float to the ground when a breeze slides by, and I know what it feels like to walk over those petals after they've fallen, pastel confetti that sticks to the soles of your shoes.

I never got to see Japan's cherry trees in blossom, but I didn't have to. When Japanese winter is in full bloom, there are only two differences between the seasons—the color, and the temperature. Turn pale pink into winter white and warm breezes cold, and you have the exact same thing.

The best way to describe the snow in Japan is as an illusion, like something straight out of a David Copperfield act. Thick flakes tumble from the sky, burying roads, sidewalks, and eventually cars, implying a density, as if someone had come along and draped a huge white X-ray vest over whole cities and towns. But the minute you touch that heavy white blanket, it turns to dust, slipping through your fingers like smoke, like tiny little feathers made of silk. What seems solid is actually fluid. In some ways, I imagine it's just like flying a plane through the clouds.

It didn't take long for Tree and me to assemble a small crew of like-minded souls, and together we buried ourselves in the snowy vapor. We flew through the snow. We surfed it. We went over it, under it, right through the middle of it. We let it engulf us, as feathery flakes brushed our cheeks and streamed over our goggles and helmets. Clusters of milky-colored chrysanthemums turned into soot as soon as the tips of our skis came near. Waves of snow silently crashed all around us. We moved from mountain to mountain in the Japanese Alps. We hiked along ridgelines and soared down chutes. We ducked under ropes and pillaged wide-open fields of downy soft powder. We even jumped off chairlifts. How else were we to access that perfect, powdery fall line? Once the snow started, it never let up, and neither did we. We soared through 750,000 vertical feet in five weeks, a number that had taken me twice as long to hit in the Southern Hemisphere.

We skied like shoguns making a comeback, and the ram in me was fully resurrected. In fact, if starting over was a test, some version of Lent, Japan would have been proof of my failure. It would have been me up to my elbows in candy wrappers, sugar-rush eye-balls darting back and forth, looking for the next hit. Sure, I was back on track in regards to vertical feet, but when it came to start-ing over, this wasn't it—and I knew it.

I'd locked eyes with myself for the very first time, but the moment I saw something familiar, I went for it. Were the grooves of the pattern I was in too deep to get out of? I had turned away from my tigery reflection, walked back to the familiar field of grass, and grabbed the wool coat that was waiting for me. In some ways I was relieved—doing what I knew how to do felt good and easy and safe. But in other ways I was exhausted—I was tired of being back in what I felt was the same place. I knew I would make it to the end of the physical goal. I knew I could ski 4 million feet. What I wasn't so sure about was who was going to be standing at the finish line.

17

THE LOWLY WORM GOES SKIING

THE DAY began like most days did in Japan. I woke up to a huge dump of fresh snow, had a small stretch, and ate a not-so-small breakfast. Then I walked down to the basement of the lodge we were staying in, to the room where all of our ski gear was kept. I packed my backpack and watched Tree do the same. We weren't in the habit of watching each other load up our packs before skiing, but today was different. We were heading into the backcountry: Tree, myself, and a snowboarder named Quentin.

Our plan was to take the lifts to the top of the Happo-One resort, and then hike up the eastern ridgeline of the mountain. This would take us well outside the resort area boundary. From there we planned on dropping into a series of wide chutes on the north face of the mountain. There would be no patrol, and likely no other skiers to see us. From a safety perspective this was the equivalent of moving from a kiddie pool manned by thirteen lifeguards to the ocean on a day with huge swell, no lifeguard, no coast guard, and no other swimmers in sight.

We weren't idiots; we were all experienced riders, and we'd done our homework. Although none of us had skied this exact route before, we had pored over maps of the area, and we'd checked into the weather as well as the conditions of the snow. We filled people in on where we were going. We knew an old hiking trail at the bottom of the last chute would serve as our path to the main road, and we had arranged for pickup from that road at two o'clock that afternoon. We had green lights on everything, and then we watched each other pack. We each had shovels and probes, and we were all wearing well-charged beacons in case of an avalanche. There was no reason to expect one, but we were prepared just in case.

It was set to be a glorious day. We walked from the lodge to the base of the mountain, where I grabbed a can of supersweet coffee, served steaming hot from a vending machine outside the ticket office, and then we boarded the lifts. We rode to the tippy-top of the mountain. There wasn't a cloud in the sky. The only thing left between us and 5,000-plus vertical feet of deep, buttery powder was a short hike. Thirty minutes tops, at a nominal grade, a cakewalk given my current level of fitness and firm reentrenchment in ram mentality. I threw my skis over my shoulder and started to walk.

About two minutes into the climb I stood corrected about the cakewalk part—"stood," in a literal sense, as I was no longer moving forward. This wasn't a good sign so early into the hike, but I shrugged it off.

Maybe one can of coffee wasn't enough, I thought before laboring on.

About three or four minutes later, I came to another breathless standstill, which was more like a stand-sway. Luckily, my ego was at the ready with a riveting pep talk, one that was eerily familiar after the parking-lot speech in New Zealand. It got me moving, but I felt shaky and unnerved, unsettled by what was going on physically and more so emotionally. I couldn't afford a repeat of Broken River. I'd come too far.

I stopped yet again shortly thereafter, and as I did, I felt something rise up through my body, a sensation urging me to throw in the towel, something building that said, *This isn't your day. Let them go on without you.* I was tempted to trust this instinct, but I didn't want to appear vulnerable. I didn't want Tree and Quentin to see me as weak or wavering. I was just getting used to seeing myself that way, and I wasn't ready to show any of that to others. No. I wanted to be where I'd always been. I wanted to be in the position I'd fought for all my life, at the head of the pack, at the front of the group.

My ego agreed. So I muffled the voice of intuition, put my head down, and kept moving.

Each step took great effort. I felt like I had weights tied to my ankles.

I shouldn't be this tired, I thought. Why am I this tired?

A strong wind was blowing from the top of the mountain, pushing down on me as I climbed. I stared at the tracks Tree and Quentin had left in the snow and did my best to make sure each foot landed within them. It was the easiest way up the mountain, something I knew from years of following paths that others had laid out before me.

I kept on up the hill, and as I did, I felt my heart rate getting faster and faster, my breath getting shorter and shorter. It wasn't too long before my poles slipped out of my left hand. My arms went slack, my skis tumbled, and my knees hit the snow in a soft *thud*. I placed my hands on the ground in front of me and took a few deep breaths.

There I was again. On all fours. Tears welled up in my eyes.

This is going to be so much harder than I thought.

Replace the snow with gravel, and you might think I was reprising my role as the Sugar Plum Fairy from New Zealand's Nutcracker Ballet. But I wasn't. This time I couldn't ignore the crack. I couldn't plaster over it, or cover it up by booking a massage. And this time I knew it had nothing to do with skiing another 1, 2, or 3 million feet. No. This was about the emotional journey, about starting over, beginning again. I wanted so badly to reverse time, to go back to the very beginning of all this, to see that blue tin sign and scream, "Noooooooo!" in response. I didn't want to start over. I didn't know how to start over. This was bullshit. I didn't ask for any of this. But one thing was clear—the fissure was deep. I was too far in to go back.

Why here, why now? I wondered angrily. My body was shaking in the snow, my fear mixed with icy air.

I'm not sure how long I was crouched there, but it was long enough for Tree to make it to the top, stash her gear in the snow, and circle back down to me. She planted her boots squarely in front of my hands, and I looked up. A broad smile spread across her face, the rosy color of her cheeks matching the bright pink beanie she was wearing.

"Gettin' in some cat-cow, Jagger?" she asked.

I sat back on my knees.

"I'm having a bit of a tough day," I said.

Tree nodded. "We all do. Some tougher than others."

"This is going to be harder than I thought," I repeated, this time out loud.

"Yes, but there's just a little bit left."

She grabbed my skis from the ground, threw them over her shoulder, and turned to face the mountain. Her auburn hair blew like a tawny cape behind her.

"Take your time," she said as she started up the hill with my gear.

Not many people had ever seen me facedown in the dirt; I hadn't allowed it. I didn't put myself in situations if I knew I couldn't get through them, because I was afraid—afraid of people laughing and telling me to get up, sack up, and move on, afraid of being called a girl. Afraid of them pointing out the very thing I'd been trying so hard to hide: that I wasn't "man enough" at all. But Tree didn't do any of that. She didn't call me names, and she didn't make me feel any lesser or laugh at me for needing a hand to hold on to. There was no judgment. In fact, she did the opposite. She gathered my belongings and then she gave me the time and space to gather myself.

For the youngest of four, for a little girl who had spent her entire life running in an effort to catch up with people who were always bigger, stronger, and faster, this was a welcome moment of pause. I was invigorated. *You mean no one's going to yell at me for taking too long? No one's going to say hurry up, catch up, man up? You mean someone will just bear witness, compassionately clear the area of the shit I was carrying, and then leave me to sit with myself for a moment?*

The cracks were already there, but Tree gently pulled them apart even farther. She created some space for me to expand just a bit. And she did it with ease, so that I didn't feel rushed to patch it all up and move on. She gave me just enough time to sit and to think and to feel. And it was in that moment, as I sat in the wide-open doorway, the entrance to myself, that my pain and worry melted slowly into peace. I felt I could look ahead, as all the things I was tied to began to fall away. Tree had cleared the way forward.

I rose to my feet.

I can do this, I thought. I can do this, and I don't have to push so hard.

I walked slowly up the rest of the pitch.

The view at the top was astounding: 360 degrees of jagged, ivory-white mountains set against a bright cobalt sky. The entire range rose into the air like roughly cut gemstones, crushed into one single crown. It was as if Mother Nature herself had sat for a portrait with Cézanne. I looked over to Tree, and she nodded.

Have you ever stood on top of a mountain, on the tippy-top of a craggy peak, looking down at the valley you've just risen up from? Have you ever done it on a day that's so clear and so cold that you can see the air right in front of you, not because of your breath but because the sun is rolling through the air in a wave? In my mind, it's like staring directly into the Universe and your very own heart at the same time.

"Well," Tree said, "the powder is waiting. What goes up must come down."

We huddled together, confirmed our plans, and started to make our way down. We took every precaution. We tested the stability of the snow pack, and in case of a slide we skied down one at a time, leaving two people to dig if they had to. We met at prede-termined crests and ridgelines, and we kept one another in sight whenever possible.

The initial section was a wide, open bowl. Tree was the first to go, and I watched as she swung from side to side like a marble. She stopped on a ridge to the skier's right, and then she waved me in. The snow was thick, like a sugary frosting. There was a thin wind crust on top, but once you punched through, it was smooth. I skied down, and Quentin followed.

Next up was a small chute that bent again to the skier's right. Quentin went first, and although we couldn't see the ridgeline where he would stop and wait, he hollered when he got there safely.

"It's fucking gorgeous," he yelled from around the corner, a slight echo ringing through the mountains. "Go for it!"

Tree dropped in, leaving me as sweep for this section. When

I heard Tree's voice, I followed. It was glorious. It was a Japanese dream come true. It was steep and a few feet deep. There was no wind crust. I felt like I was rising and falling at the same time.

And then, I actually fell. I was four or five turns in, and I just tipped over. It was a really strange fall because normally, falling in something that steep meant going for a ride, a cartwheel-somersault-barrel-roll kind of ride where you end up with snow in every orifice. No one just tips over in terrain that gnarly.

"That was weird," I said as I moved to stand up. Once standing, I leaned onto my left foot to shake off a bit of snow, and when I did, my whole left leg disappeared into the snow. I hadn't noticed, but apparently my left ski had come off in the fall.

Really weird, I thought. I'd increased the DIN settings on my bindings right before we left; the higher the DIN, the less likely your ski is to come off in a fall. That wasn't a big fall. My ski shouldn't have come off.

I pulled my left leg out of the snow, and I scanned the surrounding area for my ski. Nothing. I stomped down on the snow to create a platform firm enough for my left foot and scanned the area again. I looked left, right, uphill, and downhill. Nothing. There was only one other place it could be: in-hill.

Fuck.

I yelled down to Quentin and Tree. They were tucked around the corner, just out of sightline, but I knew they would be able to hear me.

"Just took a little bail," I yelled. "Give me a sec."

I popped out of my right ski, planted it in the snow, and got down on my knees. I slid my arms out of my backpack, placed it next to my ski, and unclipped my shovel. This is one of the reasons you travel with a shovel in the backcountry. I started digging in the small area around me, cursing the fact that I had ever, *ever* laughed at the idea of wearing powder cords, little fluorescent streamers that would have unfurled from my ski. That's what I would be looking for if only I'd tied a few cords to my bindings.

I dug for a few minutes, and then, rather suddenly, I felt a jolt of electricity move through my body. A realization swept over me. I abruptly stopped digging.

You're digging a pit in the center of a slide path. No one is above you. No one has a sightline on you. Forget about the ski.

In avalanche safety terms, this was a very stupid thing to be doing. Being in a dangerous place with no eyes on you is one thing. Being there, and then digging a pit into the snow above you? It was a death wish.

When it came to listening to my intuition, my track record was not very good. But when it came to actual danger, I was all ears. The moment I felt the hairs on the back of my neck rise to attention, I started packing my bag. I threw it over my shoulder, clipped into my right ski, and made my way down the rest of the chute and around the corner, flamingo-style.

"Are you okay?" asked Tree. "What happened ba—"

(This is when she noticed that one part of the picture was not like the other.)

"Where's your fucking ski?" asked Quentin.

"Well, I'm not sure exactly." I pointed up the mountain. "It's buried somewhere up there."

I watched as their mouths went slack in perfectly timed synchronization. While their jaws dangled in the air, I filled them in on the fall, my hide-and-go-seek ski, and the subsequent minutes I spent digging myself into a potential avalanche/sudden death scenario.

"I decided it was better for me to leave it. I didn't like the idea of you having to live out the rest of your lives with the burden of my death on your backs."

"Good call," said Quentin.

I looked over at Tree and then back at Quentin. We chuckled with nervous relief before falling silent. All of us were wondering how I was going to ski down the remaining 2,500 vertical feet of powder on one ski. It was the vertical equivalent of a 225-story building in which you had to take the stairs instead of the elevator, and then had to hop down those stairs on one foot.

"Don't worry," I said, "I'll be like the Lowly Worm on skis."

As I made my way down the slope, I whispered encouraging thoughts to my right leg, which mostly went something like this, "Youarefuckingamazingyouarefuckingamazingyou'resofuckin-gamazing."

At some point, I was struck by Baby Jesus himself, and I realized that even though my left ski was missing, my left boot was not. For the rest of the descent, I swapped my ski from one boot to the other after every four or five turns. By the time we got to the bottom, both of my legs felt as though they had knives sticking out from the middle of them, and I was completely out of breath. I turned to Tree and said, "I have a lot of respect [*gasp*] for the Paralympian skiers [*gasp*] that have one leg. [*Deep breath.*] Also, [*gasp*] I know why their poles [*gasp*] have miniature skis attached at the ends."

Unfortunately, we still had a lengthy ski-out to go, so I took a few moments to catch my breath before continuing. By the time we got to the main road my legs were fried. They were just two quivering logs of jelly engaged in a totally unsexual twerk that included my ass cheeks, hamstrings, thighs, knees, and calves. I leaned heavily on my poles, barely able to stay upright. Our preorganized pickup had long since left (we were a few hours later than originally planned), but in some stroke of luck a lovely Japanese couple pulled around the corner and agreed to give us a lift into town. Thirty minutes later we were back at the lodge, heading to the bar.

I couldn't bear the thought of my single ski being thrown in the trash, so I decided to turn it into something useful. I asked Quentin if he had a screwdriver, some industrial-strength glue, and five sake cups he could part with.

"Sure," he said hesitantly.

"Don't worry," I said, "you'll still be able to use them. I'm gonna make something beautiful."

I spent the next hour at the bar screwing and gluing before unveiling a stunning, state-of-the-art shot-ski. Because what else would you make when you have one ski, Weldbond glue, and five tiny ceramic cups?

For those of you who don't know, a shot-ski is a single ski, binding removed, with shot glasses (or in this case, sake cups) mounted to the top. The ski is designed for people to drink en masse. Five people line up shoulder-to-shoulder, lift the ski to their mouths, and drink shot after synchronized shot in perfect harmony. It's a wondrous sight to behold.

I presented the shot-ski as a gift, and it was met with much excitement. The bartender at the lodge held it above his head as if he'd just won the heavyweight title. Every person in the bar went wild, turning into savage animals before our very eyes. I should point out that most of the people there were nineteen-year-old male Aussies on week-long ski vacations, so they were fairly savage to start with, but that's beside the point.

I sat back and watched the jubilation unfold, but not without first participating heavily. As the Aussies around me proceeded to drown what brain cells they had left, I reflected back on the day. If the mountains could tell me who I was, what were they saying? What did I see, what image was cast back to me, as I looked at the mirror, at the many faces carved into the rock?

I saw roughly cut diamonds, almost there, but not quite polished, the color and clarity just now beginning to shine through.

I saw a woman letting go, walking away from the things she had been carrying, surrendering something that, in many ways, she'd already lost. I saw her taking her time, her sweet, sweet time. Under the crust of it all, I saw a lesson, an understanding that starting over, that being reborn as a whole new person, was going to require a death, a burial deep in the snow. I finally understood that it was going to require letting go.

. ●.

I'VE NEVER BEEN IN an avalanche, but I have taken multiple courses about how to survive them. A fair bit of your ability to make it out alive has to do with the gear you have with you and your knowledge of how to use it. You need shovels and probes and avalanche beacons. Helmets help, as do snow saws, slope meters, and crystal cards. "But get rid of the rest," I recall one instructor saying. "That GoPro strapped to your chest, that'll strangle you. Those pole straps you've got your hands through? When the poles go flying, they'll take your arms with 'em, or they'll impale you. Not great way to go. And," he went on, "you won't hear shit coming if you keep those headphones in. Get rid of all that," he warned. "Bring what you need and dump the rest, 'cause you won't make it out alive with all that shit."

As it turns out, life is the same. It's really fucking tough to make it to the top if you're carrying too much, and sister, you're gonna go down hard if you try to ski with a pack that weighs more than you do. You can't keep all that shit. Those beliefs you created, the ones you tied around your neck in an effort to keep you safe, to help you sleep at night—watch out, because one day, they just might choke you out. Let them go, say good-bye, march on.

And for me, it wasn't without worry. It wasn't without wondering how on earth I'd live without these things. "But how will I know I'm good enough," I asked, "or if I'm deserving of love? How will I know any of this if I throw my measuring sticks away? And how will I motivate myself?" I demanded. "Where will inspiration come from if I cast my fear of failure, and my perfectionism, and dear God, all of my rules, into the wind?" And then finally I wailed one last question, "How will I know who I am without all of those things?"

Oh my darling, a voice replied, *that's the point. How will you know who you are if you don't let everything go?*

The voice was back, unwavering. She took the fears right out of my hands, and threw them one by one into the snow. I liked this woman a lot.

PART FOUR

THE VALLEY OF THE SHADOW OF DEATH

His myth, his wonder tale, is an allegory of the agony of self-completion through the mastery and assimilation of conflicting opposites.

—HEINRICH ZIMMER, *THE KING AND THE CORPSE*

18

CHURCH PEWS

I LEFT the mountains of Japan in late January and traded them in for the European Alps. I was six months into my trip, and I'd skied 1.6 million vertical feet. That meant I had four months, five if I was lucky, to get through another 2.4 million. To say I was concerned about this would be an understatement, but an Irishman had been put in charge of my European welcoming committee, so things were looking up.

There really is no better friend than an Irishman who owns his own pub. Through a fortuitous stroke of luck I happen to have such a friend, and through a four-leaf-clover-pot-of-gold-holy-hell-I-think-I-just-spotted-a-lephrechaun stroke of luck this friend, and his pub, happened to be located in a small town at the base of some teeny-tiny little mountains otherwise known as the Alps.

My flight landed in Geneva, Switzerland, and my friend Bunty was waiting for me at the airport. He promptly whisked me across the border into France, and for the next five days I was treated like a real class lass. He handed me the keys to his apartment and directions to the local ski resort, and made sure a bar stool complete with a fresh pint of Guinness was waiting for me each day at 4:00 p.m. Other than reintroducing the cheeks of my ass to cold toilet seats, my transition from Japan to Europe went smoothly.

I could walk from Bunty's apartment to the base of the Grand Massif ski resort. From a linguistic standpoint, Grand Massif translates into something like "The Really Big Massive," a fitting name considering the resort links five huge mountains in the Haute-Savoie region of France. The terrain goes on for miles and miles—in essence, if you can see it, you can ski it. You actually have to be careful near the end of the day, as it's rather easy to end up in an entirely different village than the one in which you started.

Much to my surprise, the weather was warm. The mountains were showing a lot of skin for February, and what snow coverage they did have was melting rather quickly. I found bare shoulders and exposed necklines around every corner, a sure sign that the snowfall had been far less than normal. Regardless, I managed 109,000 vertical feet in three days of sweaty, jet-lagged skiing. I thanked Bunty for the very good craic and moved on to the next stop.

I can tell you with certainty that I've seen some of the most beautiful things this world has to offer, both in my travels and in a life spent as an inveterate voyeur. I've watched the giant equatorial sun light up the rude and rugged coastline of West Africa. I've seen the way a snake moves when it charms. I was there the day my niece claimed her place in this world; I saw her do it with my own two eyes.

I can scan through a thousand beautiful images, but the collection isn't complete without Chamonix. You can't help but be captivated the minute you see her, the way she sits on her throne, high in the mountains of France. It's her duality that does it. Her beauty is a spellbinding mixture of everything in life that is permanent, and everything that, poof, is gone in a flash. Many people have vanished in Chamonix, swallowed up by her ancient jaws of rock and ice. She is a valley of life cast in a granite shadow of death. She stands surefooted betwixt and between, straddling two worlds with ease. And given the messages of birth and burial that came to me from the mountains in Japan, Chamonix was the perfect teacher.

Chamonix is also sacred, a mountaineer's version of Vatican City. Exchange Bibles, flowing capes, and crosses for Gore-Tex, beacons, and boots. Replace rosaries and zucchettos with ice axes and helmets. Swap out a prayer rope for a heavy-duty harness, and church bells for cable cars dangling in the sky. It's all the same. Chamonix is where you come to learn faith firsthand.

Her official reign as the spiritual center of snow began when she hosted the first ever Winter Olympic Games in 1924, but I have a feeling she claimed the right to call herself The Holy One the moment her jagged edges were thrust into the sky, the moment she was anointed with that coronet of ink-black granite.

Upon arrival, I found a small bar on the edge of town and cozied up in a seat by the window. The temperatures in the area had dropped, and a dusting of snow was floating through the air like smoke. I watched as it swirled on the ground and then rose with the wind, curling around the necks of the people walking by. I sipped my hot chocolate and looked across the valley to the Aiguille du Midi, a peak in the Mont Blanc massif. There are peaks in the range much higher than this, some pushing 14,000 and 15,000 feet, but none are as striking as Midi. At her apex is a tapered granite tower pointing directly at the sky. It looked like a pin held firm, ready to pop a giant blue balloon. When I looked at her, I couldn't help but think she was a needle, commissioned by God to mark the small sliver of space between heaven and earth.

I spent the whole afternoon in that spot, sipping my drink and looking out at the mountains, each of which looked bruised and a little bit battered. The snow that had fallen wasn't quite enough to conceal the thin layers of ice. All the stuff that was living right below the surface was slowly becoming exposed. And I realized I was looking at myself, at the parts of me I'd never had the courage to face. I'd never felt as vulnerable or as stripped down as I did when I arrived in Chamonix. So I did the only thing one does in Chamonix—I finished my hot chocolate, and I took myself to church.

The next morning, the thermostat read −31°C (−23.8°F). It would have been easy for me to stay under the covers in my tiny hotel room, coffee in one hand and a book in the other, but I couldn't because I heard what was becoming a familiar and welcome voice.

Oh darling, she said, *It's time. Go on up to the mountains.*

I threw on a few extra layers and I went, hope in one hand and prayer in the other. The skiing that day was screamingly fast. A week of hot weather (like hot enough to melt most of the snow), followed by cold weather (like cold enough to freeze anything that had melted), makes for, well, giant fucking sheets of ice. The conditions were designed for speed, and so was the temperature. I skied as fast as I could, mostly because I wanted back on the chairlift, which was the only reprieve. Don't get me wrong, the chairlift was cold, but when I skied, the cold was so cold that it hurt. No matter how much effort I put into ensuring that my face was covered, the frozen air shot through my neck warmer and scarf, like a thousand bees stinging my nose, cheeks, and chin. Once on the chairlift, I could recover, sitting like a dog, tightly curled, paws tucked, snout away from the wind. I spent the entire morning racing, just trying to get back to that place.

The other reason for the speed was my grandfather. This may sound strange, as my grandfather died in 1997, but on occasion since then I'd felt his presence, even seen him. As it turns out, this was one such occasion.

It happened on my fourth chairlift up. I turned to my right, and there he was, long legs crossed over one another, a big smile on his face. He motioned for me to move closer to him. "Faster," he said as he wrapped one of his arms around my shoulder, keeping me warm. "A little bit faster."

I did as my grandfather told me. I pointed my skis downhill, and I went. There was no time for turning. I found my grandfather waiting for me on the next lift, and the one after that, and the one after that. Once I realized he would be there for the day, I went even faster, doing everything to get back to him as quickly as possible. I flew. It was as if the cords had been cut. The parachute I'd been dragging was no longer there. At some point I was skiing so fast that I could feel my body pushing against gravity, and by the afternoon I felt like I'd crossed some sort of threshold, like I'd moved through a trembling, bat-out-of-hell kind of speed and arrived at a steady g-force warp speed. In other words, I was Jonathan Livingston Seagull on skis.

And so that's how I spent the rest of the day: half of it tucking down a mountain at breakneck speed, and the other half in the arms of my grandfather. Half of it freezing, the other half thawing.

On one of the final chairlifts, my grandfather pulled me in close. "Isn't it amazing," he whispered, "how fast you can go when you've let go of it all. Like a bird. Like a rocket to the moon."

I started to cry.

"Just you and the mountains and God," he said.

I went back every day for the next five days, and there he was, waiting on the chairlift, my church pews, in his navy blue ski suit. It was bliss. It was freedom. It was a safety I'd never known. For the first time in my life, I felt all of the love and none of the fear. And so I broke myself there. I dropped everything I'd been carrying and watched it tumble down the mountain into the shadows of the valley. I became unrestrained. I became unbound.

The fissure had become a giant crevasse. I was wide open. Day after day, I let the mountains pull me further and further apart. I let them shatter me and all my beliefs into thousands of pieces, knowing that I would eventually get glued back together. Somehow. Someway. I let the mountains tear me down, and after each run I sat down on a seat in the sky with my grandfather. I was tattered and torn, unanchored and unfettered, and I was loved—by my grandfather and by me. And by the end of a week I was bone-tired. Yes, I'd added 150,000 vertical feet to my total, but the energy drain was mostly due to the fact that six days in the mountains with God is exhausting. I've heard people talk about having to make a deal with the devil, but in my experience you've got to do the same with God. The only difference is that one negotiation is about what you're gonna get, and the other is about what you're gonna give.

At the end of my week-long conversation with God I was raw and vulnerable, little pieces of me dangling here and there. The mountains had smashed my identity to smithereens, and all I could see were shards. I was left wondering how on earth I would piece them back together. I had wounds that needed to be healed, but I wasn't sure how.

It was probably best to lie down and take a long nap, to meditate in some way amid the bits of broken glass, to sit in a sauna with slivers of myself, or to eat chicken soup with a side of mashed potatoes in some attempt to find a path forward.

Unfortunately, I didn't do any of those things. Instead I gathered up my dangly bits, and I picked up every splinter lying on the ground. I put them in a suitcase with my bleeding heart, and then we all boarded a plane together, because New York City doesn't wait for anyone.

19

A BIRD IN THE BAG AND A CERTAIN KIND OF UGLY

YOU DO crazy things when you're in love. You do things like fly to New York City even though your identity has just been cut into a thousand pieces and haphazardly thrown into a suitcase. You do things like spend an entire weekend having sex with the man you love even though you're behind on what is arguably the biggest goal of your life. You do these things thinking that all of the love and all of the sex will somehow help with the piecing together, and the gluing, and the goal, and the journey in general. You do them thinking you'll find everything you need to move forward, to move on, to build yourself back up, like all the king's horses and all the king's men maybe, fingers crossed, *could* put Humpty Dumpty back together again.

New York City was the easiest place to "meet in the middle," with me coming from Europe and Chris from the West Coast. My plane slid to an icy halt on the tarmac at the John F. Kennedy

International Airport. It was about eight o'clock on a Thursday evening, and everything in sight was frozen solid. My flight would be one of the only to land that night because all of the snow in the world, including the stuff that was supposed to be blanketing the Alps, was falling directly over Manhattan. And Brooklyn and Queens, but mostly Manhattan.

Everyone around me seemed tired and grumpy, but I was filled with that ooey-gooey-I'm-in-love-and-gonna-be-naked-in-an-hour kind of rapture. I was also precisely eighty pounds lighter than normal. All of my luggage, spare a small overnight bag, was tucked into a storage closet in Chamonix. I basically skipped through the airport like a real live Care Bear, with joy shooting straight out of my tummy. It's no wonder people were staring at me like I was insane: it was one of the worst travel days of the year, and there I was dancing through the halls of JFK, a slightly off-kilter expression on my face, with a goggle tan that made me look as though I'd taken the Kardashian master class on contouring a little too far.

I took a cab into the city, checked into our hotel, and watched snow drift down from the sky while lying in our big cushy bed. The entire city was white, and there were barely any cars on the roads. For a brief moment I wondered if it was possible to rent cross-country skis. I figured I could collect a handful of vertical feet on the hills in Central Park. The thought vanished as I realized Chris would be arriving any minute. I showered, slathered myself in perfumey lotion, assumed the most unassuming, come-hither position possible, and waited. And waited. And waited.

After a long delay, Chris's flight eventually arrived, and he slipped into the room at about four in the morning. Unfortunately, my sexy, come-hither position had turned into more of a fetal position by then. At the same moment I felt Chris climb into bed, I noticed a little drool leaking from the corner of my mouth.

"I'm here now, Bird," I heard him whisper. "Roll over a little."

I wiped my chin, did as told, and fell right back to sleep. We woke up late the next morning, curled together like two little spoons in a drawer.

"We're in New York City," Chris said.

"Yes, we are," I replied. "Let's eat bagels."

"Okay, but first tell me about the rest of Japan. Tell me about Chamonix. I know we've already talked about it, but now that your parents and Tree are gone, I want to hear about it again."

We pulled on our clothes and walked through the snow to a small diner around the corner. We ate bagels, drank coffee, and I recapped everything for Chris—Chamonix, and my grandfather, and all the things I let go of.

"I cried for six days on those chairlifts," I said. "In a good way, I think. Apparently, I had a lot to release."

"Yeah," said Chris. "That's what the mountains are for. You know, I spent all those years skiing in Alta as a young man, healing in the mountains. It was a huge catharsis for me. I was an angry, despondent eighteen-year-old. I raged on that mountain every day, and it absorbed all of my pain. And slowly, I let go and the pain turned into joy."

"So at some point it's gonna turn into joy?" I asked hesitantly.

"Yep. You know, that's one of my favorite Joseph Campbell quotes: 'Find a place inside where there's joy, and the joy will burn out the pain.'"

"I love that," I said. "What a beautiful quote. I think for me this has been about releasing my fear of letting go. When I was skiing, an image kept flashing through my mind. You know how I told you about those navy blue mittens, and my dad teaching me to ski?"

Chris nodded.

"The image of my little hands wrapped around those poles," I continued, "I couldn't get it out of my head. It's almost as if I'd never let go, like I just white-knuckled it through life for decades. But in Japan, and in Chamonix, I finally let it all go. It's like my fear was glue, holding my ego in place, and then boom, the glue dried up and crumbled away, taking everything else down with it."

"So what happens next?" he asked.

"I don't really know," I said. "I started by relaxing my grip a bit. I think I've managed to dismantle some of the old, and bury some stuff that needed to be buried, but now I think I have to revive the rest."

"What do you mean, 'revive the rest'?"

"Well, I think it has to do with my femininity. I was thinking back, and it hit me—when I bought my apartment six or seven years ago, something strange happened. I don't love the idea of talking to you about it, but I'm going to anyways."

Chris reached for my hand. "Okay."

"Around the same time I bought my apartment, I started getting my period for two weeks every month, rather than one. I went to the doctor and we tried a whole bunch of things, but we couldn't figure it out. It was exhausting."

"That sounds awful," said Chris.

"It was. But over the years, I noticed something. Whenever I went on vacation, everything would go back to normal for a month, maybe two. It seemed as though whenever I pressed pause on manning up, or stepped away from being the person who soldiered through life, things changed. It's almost like I was forcing myself into this idea of being the 'man' of the house . . . you know, making money, changing lightbulbs, killing spiders . . . not that women don't do those things, or can't do those things, but you know what I mean, right?"

"I know what you mean."

"Well, whenever I stepped away from all that and put some sort of temporary hold on trying to prove myself, everything went back to normal. Everything was regular again."

"What about now?" Chris asked. "What about this trip?"

"Like clockwork. I've been on schedule since the day the trip began. What do you think that means?" I continued before he could answer, "I think it's a clue. I think this is the missing piece to my whole self. The part of me I've ignored, brushed aside, and generally mistreated my whole life needs to be revived. I've got to resurrect the feminine. I have to find out who I am as a woman," I said, "and, to be honest, I have no idea where to start."

"I have a few ideas," said Chris with a grin.

"You do? What, like some sort of vagina-worshipping?" I joked.

"Yes, exactly like that," he said. "Let's go. I know exactly where to start."

I'm not sure how Chris knew what to do, but he did. We went back to the hotel for our first official vagina-worshipping, and I'm not going to lie, it actually was a vagina-worshipping. Chris rested his head on my right thigh and proceeded to speak directly to my vagina. I found this to be horrendously uncomfortable, watching him stare at my lady parts, and talk to them about how beautiful and important they were, and about how much he loved them, and me. My first reaction was to squirm away, and my second was to grab a pillow and put it over my face, but I knew a pillow wasn't going to cover what I was so desperate to hide.

When it comes to nudity, I've never been shy. Just ask the half dozen or so people who refer to me as Nudey Judy because of my propensity to strip off all my clothes and dive into lakes, oceans, or large fountains in fancyish hotel lobbies. But the experience with Chris was different. I had never let someone see me *that* naked, to examine me in broad daylight, and to love and adore me as a woman. That part I kept hidden, or at least out of the way. Most of the sexual experiences I'd had prior to Chris were a bit bereft when it came to really seeing one another as a man and a woman. Sex had been about conquering something, an orgasmic achievement. I was okay with the physicality, exposure, and effort. But vulnerability and emotion? No thank you. Spiritual connection? N. O. Someone seeing me as a woman after I'd spent close to three decades trying to convince people I was anything but? Get the fuck out. Put a pillow over my face. And close the door behind you.

But Chris was changing all of that. I had my very own vagina whisperer. But here's the thing, you can't have one of those unless you actually let them in to whisper. I had to resist the urge to run and hide. I told my hand to let go of the pillow, and to move it to the side. And then I started to cry. No one had ever told my vagina it was loved. No one had ever told me I was totally loved. Some parts, sure. "You've got beautiful eyes," they'd say, or something more simple, like "Nice ass," for example. But not *every* part. No one had ever looked at every single bit of me and told me I was beautiful, or that I was enough. Including myself. I wasn't even sure it was possible. But there Chris was, staring at my vagina like it was the most majestic thing on the planet. Maybe he was right. Maybe I *was* beautiful. Not just bits and pieces of me, but all of me. The yin *and* the yang. What a miraculous concept.

Three hours later, Chris and I were surrounded by a pile of silk.

"I'd like to get you something nice," Chris said as we stood in the doorway of an elegant-looking lingerie shop. We walked in, and I ran my hand down the side of a cream nightgown. We took our time picking out itty-bitty French-looking things and teeny-tiny Italian-looking things, and Chris sat in the dressing room as I tried them all on.

"What about that one but in black?" he suggested as I spun around in a circle, my body covered in bits of lace.

I wriggled my way into the black version of the same bra and panty set and turned to face Chris.

"What? What's wrong?" I asked. He looked like he'd been hit by a truck.

"Nothing," he said. "We're getting that one. You are so beautiful, Bird. So, so beautiful."

We walked out of the store with a handful of lacy numbers in black and cream and dusty pink and went back to the hotel for another worshipping. Along with some emotionally-present-in-every-way sex, the kind where you lock eyes with each other and see everything and nothing all in one gasp. Afterward, we curled up for a nap before getting ready for dinner. I wore my fancy new underwear, and I blow-dried my hair, something I hadn't done in months. I'd forgotten how soft and silky it could be, and I'd forgotten how soft and silky I could be. I felt like a goddess that night. I felt like a goddess the whole weekend. I guess that's what happens when you have your own personal vagina whisperer.

I loved every second of our three-day jaunt, too much, perhaps. Chris had helped me unlock parts of myself I never knew existed. How was I supposed to continue without him? I wanted to stay in New York, wrapped up in Chris's arms and the high-thread-count sheets, but I knew I couldn't. Something in my gut told me I had to keep going. Even if I wasn't sure I could make it, I knew that walking away from the journey I was on would be the worst thing I could possibly do.

Imagine for a minute some fledgling artist or musician who's been slaving away at their craft, and after months and months of this slaving, imagine them finally receiving some grand inspiration. "Hallelujah! *Hallelujah!*" they'd scream as they ran to their canvas, or their slab of marble, or their borrowed baby grand. And they would start painting, and sculpting, and playing music, and they would start to believe in themselves, and most important they would come to some sort of understanding with God, or their muses, or that beautiful, calm voice in their head about what it's all about. So there they are, as their work is beginning to reveal itself, and oh my god it's more stunning than they ever imagined. Now, at that exact point, imagine them rising from their chair and walking away. Imagine them abandoning every bit of energy that was finally flowing forth.

I couldn't do it. I couldn't walk away now, brush in hand, some incomplete image of myself floating in the air like a ghost. If I walked away, I knew I'd regret it. I also knew it was a surefire way of destroying everything Chris and I were building. Walking away would give me something to hold over his head, a person to blame if my life fell short, if I never wound up completing the painting. I could skip off down the road with him, but chances were high that doing so would turn into ammunition, ammunition I didn't want. "It was you!" I could scream in some fight in the future. "I gave everything up for you!" I'd seen others do this, walk away from themselves in favor of somebody else, only to turn that person into the reason they were ruined. That didn't seem fair. My ability to finish this, to find myself, it was on me and me alone. I refused to let Chris be my out, and for me, that was reason enough to stick to my quest.

Darling, said the calm, soothing voice in my head, *just keep going. He'll be waiting.*

On the morning of my flight, I stood in the hotel room in front of the bed. My new lingerie was laid out on top of the sheets, and I was staring down at it, wondering when I'd get to wear it next. I felt conflicted. Continuing on this journey while also figuring out who I was as a woman felt impossible. I knew I needed to do both, but how was I supposed to rip through 2 million more feet while embracing this new feminine side of myself at the same time?

I folded each bra and placed it beside its matching bottom. I wrapped everything together in a few sheets of tissue paper, and I carefully placed the bundle at the bottom of my bag. It would have to wait, I thought. I'd finish the skiing, and when I was done, I would fish everything out of my bag, because, come on, a warrior and a goddess are two different things. Outside of the Amazon or some myth from ancient India, a warrior and a goddess can't live within the same person, certainly not at the same time. I'll just put down the feminine side for now, and then pick it back up when I'm done. That will work, right?

Johnny Castle had answered that question for me some time ago when he said, "Nobody puts Baby in a corner." A woman set free, a finally rising watch-me-now tiger-woman, doesn't let you play her like that. No. She doesn't get placed carefully at the bottom of a bag. What she does is rise like a phoenix from the ashes. In fact, she doesn't even wait for the ashes. She rises while things are still on fire. She flies above it all and fans the flames with her wings. And you know what, I'm pretty sure she's the one who dropped the fucking match to start with, because she knows that in order to rebuild, to start over in the way I was being called to start over, there's gotta be a resurrection, and resurrections burn.

But none of this was clear to me in that moment. I politely asked the woman in me to sit in the corner and wait until it was her turn. I told her it would be different this time, and not to worry, because I would be back, I promised. In the meantime, if she would just wait a few months, please and thank you very much, that would be grand.

Big mistake. Big, three-alarm-fire kind of mistake.

I pulled one of my reeking sports bras over my head and kissed Chris one last time. Little did I know that an arsonist bird with a huge book of matches was waiting in my bag.

.ʾ๏.

I FLEW DIRECT FROM New York to Paris and then caught a connecting flight to Geneva. From there I took a long train ride through the heart of the Alps before reuniting (somewhat reluctantly) with the luggage I'd left in Chamonix. I repacked a few things, hauled my gear over to a friend's house, and loaded everything into a car bound for Italy. A friend of a friend was driving.

It was a two-hour trip at the most, and I'm pretty sure it was beautiful. I can't be certain, though, because after twenty-four hours of straight travel, followed by three days and three nights of vagina-worshipping, and another twenty-four hours of travel, I wasn't able to see beautiful. I wasn't able to see much of anything. I was bagged.

At this point in my journey I knew jet lag inside and out. I knew exactly what to expect, including how many hours post-travel I would spend feeling like a fetus, a tiny little creature helplessly floating around in some paradoxical underwater world where things are both too loud and too quiet, too bright and too dark, where you're awake and asleep, where you can't sit and you can't stand, and where going for a walk to get some fresh air is totally out of the question.

The moment I arrived in Geneva, the jet lag hit me hard, but by the time I got to Italy, I knew there was something else at play. The woozy baby feeling was there, but I also felt a bit nauseous. I had jet lag and jet flu, either that or Ebola. I could barely get out of the car.

As I looked toward the front entrance of the hotel, I realized I was going to be at the mercy of whoever greeted me. This may have been the exact moment I started to believe in God, because the door to the hotel opened wide, and there, standing before me, was the King of Sushi himself.

"The snow princess is here!" Joseph cried.

I gave him a weak little hug, and we slowly walked into the hotel. Two minutes later, I crumpled to the ground. It happened in the elevator. My bones just fell away from their ligaments and tumbled to the bottom of a pale, clammy-skinned sack of skin. I remember grabbing the railing inside the elevator, and then watching my hand slide down the wall in some feeble attempt to steady myself. After that, I don't remember much of anything.

I slept through the early evening and right on through dinner. I got up in the middle of the night, searching for the bathroom. The walk made me nauseous, and when I got there I threw up in the sink and then again in the toilet. I went back to sleep and didn't wake up until 10:00 a.m., when I heard a gentle knocking on the door. It had been an eighteen-hour slumber.

The door to my room slowly cracked open. I watched as Joseph walked toward me and sat on the edge of the bed.

"For a while I wondered if you were dead," he said. "But then I thought to myself, If that's the case, at least it happened in such a nice hotel room."

I looked around the room, and he was right—it was a nice hotel room. It was so nice that it didn't even look like a hotel room. It looked more like a luxury mountain apartment, like something an absurdly wealthy person would build if they wanted to pay homage to the gods, Mother Nature herself as well as the ones responsible for things like *Côté Sud* and *Architectural Digest*.

The room, as well as the hotel (a place called Principe delle Nevi), belonged to Joseph. A few years back he'd fallen in love with the area, as well as the hotel and its owners. After suggesting a partnership, they moved forward with a large-scale renovation of the property. And they had thought of every detail: from the state-of-the-art stereo systems to the showerheads, from the crown moldings to the carpets, from the gorgeous fleet of Swedish women who ran the front desk to the sweet stuffed-animal dog named Shmolik who helped them.

Joseph noticed me looking around the room.

"I made this for Peter Gabriel," he said. "It's super luxury and I need you to stay in it first and give it good energy so Peter will

come. But I'm not sure you can bless it right now. Are you okay?"
he asked. "Are you alive?"

"Barely," I said. "I'm not sure what happened. Maybe I'm just
tired from all the jet lag?" I sat up in the bed and told him about
Chris and the whirlwind trip to New York.

"Ahhh," he replied. "You went to see a man. You probably had
too much sex. Like an American at one of those all-you-can-eat
buffets. Did you get greedy, my little piggy?"

"Probably." I laughed. "In fact, yes. I was greedy and now I'm
exhausted from all the sex."

"Speaking of buffets, you must be starved."

"Not really," I said, "but I should probably eat something."

I crept out of bed, slipped into a pair of jeans, and followed
Joseph down to the dining room.

We sat there for an hour or two. My appetite wasn't where it
normally was, so I sipped some tea and nibbled on the edge of a
croissant while Joseph and I caught up on all that had happened
in the year or so since we had seen one another. At the end of our
conversation he pointed to the window at the far end of the dining
room.

"The Matterhorn is usually right there," he said, "but the clouds
are making you think it's gone. Isn't it interesting how you can
have two things right in front of you but only see one? They're both
there at the same time, but our little human brains get tricked."

Giant Tetris blocks were tumbling into place before my very
eyes. In three sentences, Joseph managed to do what he always
did. He showed me that something sane, something quite ratio-
nal, is often sitting right underneath the surface of the absurd. Of
course a warrior and a goddess could exist in the same person. Of
course they could both be there at the very same time.

The lightbulbs turned on, but perhaps it was too late, or perhaps I was just too tired. Three hours later I was back in my

room, sound asleep under fine Italian linen. I slept for another fourteen hours, right through the night and into the morning. I felt a little bit better, though I could tell I wasn't fully recovered. The nausea was almost gone, but my skin was sensitive to the touch, and even after all that sleep, I still felt tired. I crawled out of bed and walked to the bathroom so I could brush my teeth. By the time I got to there I was dripping with sweat. I looked in the mirror, and my whole face was damp. Not a lovely, glowing, dewy kind of damp, but more of a splotchy, clammy, feverish kind of damp.

Over the next few days it became clear that I had more than a bad case of jet lag and more than a touch of the flu. I had both of those things, along with a blazing hot fever, a the-bird-in-the-bag-lit-all-the-matches kind of fever.

I thought my skin might burn clean off. My whole body was a wildfire. The matches had been struck, the bird was flapping her wings over the flames, and the entire house was burning down. I got out of bed in the middle of the night. My clothes were all damp, so I peeled them off and took a cold shower. It didn't help. I looked down at the floor, and then I just kind of sank down to meet it. The tiles were cool. So there I was, dripping wet from the shower, still sweating, in a heap on the ground. I reached out for the hair dryer, set it on cool, and then blasted it toward myself. At that moment, wet-haired, naked, and clammy, I caught a glimpse of myself in the mirror. Three or four days ago I'd been a goddess in New York, one who had silky hair and wore lacy things, one who came with their own personal vagina whisperer. And now this. I looked like a pile of shit, like a deflated albino seal with kelp for hair. I looked like a hideous, horrible wreck of a person. And I felt that way too, like I'd been knocked off a pedestal, like a wrinkled old bag, collapsed and shrunken on the ground.

I cried. Hot tears rolled slowly down my face, and I turned away from the mirror.

I e-mailed Chris when I got back to bed and told him my whole self was on fire. I told him it wasn't all Alicia Keys had made it out to be, and that I was bitterly disappointed in her for misleading me. Then I told him that I thought this was the resurrection, the way I was going to find out about who I was as a woman. "It isn't the most graceful of processes," I wrote, "but what could I expect after disowning that aspect of myself for, I dunno, twenty or thirty years."

I sent the e-mail, and I thought about it some more. And then it all hit me. I buckled over and started to cry, and not a soft sniffly cry but a wailing one, like an old-Greek-woman-at-a-funeral cry, a professional-mourner cry. It all made sense.

In New York Chris and I had allowed the woman in me to come walking out. But when you force one aspect of yourself under the rug, or you make it live in the basement for thirty years, it's not going to come out looking pretty. By definition, a resurrection means that you're going to bring something back from the dead. I'd read *Flowers in the Attic*, I'd watched the movie, and even the most gorgeous person in the world would look a little ragged if they'd been surviving on arsenic-soaked cookies in some dank little corner of the house for thirty years. There's a certain ugliness to any revival, and I realized that if I really wanted to bring myself back to life, I would have to stare ugly in the eye.

I walked back to the mirror and looked at myself. I did it again the following day, and I did it again the day after that.

I learned a lot during my time in Italy, while my whole self was burning down. I learned I could be a warrior as well as a goddess—an idea that rocked me to my core. And even more earth-shattering? I learned that our growth doesn't depend on our ability to look at beautiful things. It's the opposite. Our growth depends on how we look at the not-beautiful. Only when I sat with the not-so-pretty, ragged, beat-up, torn-down, left-in-the-cold parts of myself was I able to understand the true nature of beauty, that my whole self was far more stunning than a jacked-up ram, solo globetrotting with his ego in hand.

20

AN AWKWARD DANCE AND A REMAKE OF *SNOW WHITE*

THE SMOKE cleared and the clouds moved on. All that was left was the Matterhorn, standing in her rocky glory, the strong Italian sun at her back. I skied underneath her every day, and I did my best to put the pieces of myself back together. I spent my days trying to combine things like speed and stillness, stamina and surrender, resilience and release. These were all things I'd worked so hard to keep apart, but now it was time to see if they'd mix. I wanted to see if I could hold on and let go at the same time. I practiced it for nine days straight.

It was painful at first, because pain is what you get when you ask two enemies to come together, when you ask foes to be friends. The warrior and the goddess in me banged their fists on the table, and they shouted and yelled.

"You've pitted us against each other," they cried, "and now you want us to hold hands and sing 'Kumbayah'?"

"Yes," I said quietly, "that's exactly what I want."

They did it begrudgingly, with anger etched into the lines of their faces. Over time, though, the pain died down and they moved a little bit closer together. They shuffled around like awkward teenagers, keeping each other at arm's length, sort of twirling, kind of dancing. They clodhopped. They stepped on one another's toes. They cursed at each other under their breath.

"You're taking up too much space," said the goddess.

"I got here first," cried the warrior.

"Well, actually—," the goddess replied, but I cut her off before she went on.

"Just keep moving," I said.

And that's what I did. I kept going.

I skied and skied and skied, mostly on just one run because the best run in Cervinia also happens to be the longest. It starts at the very top of Zermatt, on the Swiss side, and then snakes around the Matterhorn toward the Italian side. From there, it moves into the valley before finally coming to an end in a tiny Italian town called Valtournenche. The run is about fourteen miles from beginning to end, and the vertical drop is close to 8,000 feet. I spent most of my days doing laps on that run, my eyes fixed on the snow in front of me, the warrior and the goddess moving along in some ridiculous-looking heel-toe.

Physically, I was the most exhausted I'd ever been, but on this run, the huge swath of it moves like an ocean underneath you, so you just keep going. It doesn't matter if you're exhausted. You don't need energy in that situation, you just need to believe, with all of your heart, that the entire Universe is conspiring for your success. Once you're pointed down a mountain, gravity takes over. All that's required at that time is trust. Trust, and faith in the fact that you'll keep descending, and that somehow, someway, the Universe is going to keep you balanced on top of it all.

So there I was, trying to ski, trying to make my way through the ashes as both goddess and warrior, reminding myself that nothing about this was mutually exclusive, black or white, him or her. This was about the colors somehow coming together, not unlike the coat of a tiger. I could be both, I could be one, I could be all.

I had designed this trip as the ultimate expression of my power, a massive blue ribbon that would inarguably prove I was strong enough, and man enough, and good enough. I thought I'd had to break myself down and turn myself into something or someone else completely. But that was all wrong. This whole thing was actually a search-and-rescue mission. I'd come to find the woman I'd buried. And she'd been there all along. In that moment, I felt like I was watching two sides of a zipper coming together, every tooth sliding into its perfect place, sealing something closed. I felt whole and warm.

This revelation was followed by the voice. It whispered to me, soft and smooth.

Imagine what's possible now.

.˙●.

IF YOU ASKED ME what country had the highest per capita rate of dazzlingly perfect tourism days, I would say Italy. And then I'd wave my hands around in the air for dramatic emphasis and recount why: Verona. Pasta. Wine. Espresso. Firenze. Tomatoes. Rome. Pasta, pasta, pasta. Shoes. Gelato. Wine. The golden sun as it casts a sugary glow on your shoulders and cheeks. Pizza. Limoncello. The. Amalfi. Fucking. Coast. Pizzapastawine. And *The Alps*. Now imagine a magical combination of those things, plus the smell of George Clooney wafting through the air? Hands down. It's Italy.

I've traveled to Italy four times, and I can recall dozens of dazzlingly perfect days. But none stand out as much as the day I landed the starring role in an Italian reenactment of *Snow White and the Seven Dwarfs.*

The plans had fallen into place over dinner. My fever was gone, I'd skied 230,000 feet over the last nine days, and although the warrior and the goddess weren't quite dancing arm in arm, they were doing something that resembled a semisynchronized version of a grapevine.

Principe delle Nevi is what's known as a half-board hotel, where breakfast and dinner are included in the price. It's important to note that breakfast and dinner in Italy are rather different from breakfast and dinner in North America, especially at hotels. This was no weak coffee, greasy muffin, dried-out sausage link, single-serve box of Frosted Flakes kind of breakfast. No, no. This was different; this was sumptuous. It was fine Italian espresso, freshly squeezed orange juice, perfectly flaky croissants, and scrambled eggs that came with a delicate sprinkling of green chives and a drizzle of truffle oil, among other options. I'm pretty sure I saw two German guests salivating like hounds over a bowl of mascarpone cream and small-batch preserves, made in-house by the pastry chef, Marcella. And I'll just say this about dinner—it was, at a minimum, five courses of the most delicious food I've ever eaten in my life. Even on the days I felt shitty, dinner was an occasion I rose to.

Each night I sat with Joseph and the other owners of the hotel, a lovely Scotsman named James who had lived in the area for over fifty years and his partner, Kristin, a Swedish Michelle Pfeiffer look-alike. On occasion, James's son Max would join us. It was a family dinner, the kind Nigella Lawson would whip up and pair with a fleet of vintage Italian wines.

During one of those dinners, as the delicately nutty flavor of sautéed porcini mushrooms and pecorino cheese hit my tongue and my eyes rolled back in my head in delight, I heard James's voice.

"I'm meeting a group of friends tomorrow for a day of skiing," he said.

"Mm-hmm," I replied.

"You and Joseph should join us."

"Yes. Sure," I said.

He could have asked me if I wanted to be murdered in a back alley, and I'm pretty sure I would have given the same response. The food had actually rendered me slightly incapacitated, and don't tell me you don't know what I mean because we've all seen a three-month-old baby postfeeding.

"Great," said James. "You're in for a treat."

"Sounds good," I said. "Now what is that flav—"

"Wild fennel," said Joseph. "It's wild fennel."

I looked over at him and saw that his eyes were completely closed. It was as if rolling backward hadn't been enough for them and they actually had to excuse themselves from witnessing that much pleasure, like they literally could not.

The next morning I met Joseph, James, and five other men at the bottom of the lifts. All of the men, with the exception of Joseph, had been living in the area for decades, and between them there was about two hundred years of skiing expertise and local area knowledge.

"Ah," said one of the men. "We have guests!" And then, waving his arm in the air in a big circle, he added, "The full tour it is! Prepare yourselves, my friends."

And so commenced the *Snow White* reenactment (though just to clarify, all of the "dwarfs" were actually regular-size men). We loaded onto the chairlifts, and I sat and listened as we were slowly carried to the top. Their voices rang out across the hills as they shouted to one another from chairlift to chairlift, gently goading each other as old friends do. Boisterous laughter bounced through the air. It was a gentlemen's version of "Heigh-Ho."

Once we got to the top, we skied to a small kiosk in the shadow of the Matterhorn.

"Un espresso?" asked James.

"Sì," I said. "Of course."

One of the men handed me a small ceramic cup. I was at 12,000 feet, sipping espresso, and looking directly into the eyes of the Matterhorn, one of the most iconic mountains in the world. The skies were completely clear.

We spent the rest of the morning cruising through the trails. We zipped down buttery smooth groomers, soared over sun-dappled rollers, and darted through sparse forests. The scent of warm pine cones and (I swear to God) George Clooney floated through the air.

At around 1:00 p.m. I followed the group as they made their way down a wide trail to the right-hand side of the slope. I saw James stop in front of a small white chapel. He took off his skis and propped them up against the wall of the church.

"It's time for Fritz and Heidi's," he said.

I took off my skis and followed the men down a narrow foot-path. We walked between a handful of picture-book buildings and some older wooden chalets that I was told "were built around the same time Hiroshima was falling."

At the end of the path I saw a large chalet complete with a series of international flags flapping in the wind and a massive cowbell swinging gently in the air. A large wooden patio had been built off the side of the chalet, and to the left a huge, slate-colored diamond rose dramatically into the sky—a close-up of the Matterhorn. The whole thing screamed Hansel and Gretel, but in an Italian, *Snow White* kind of way.

"Prepare for a feast," said Joseph.

"You've been here before?" I asked.

"Yes. You're going to become a little piggy. Like a big . . . what do you call those big piggies?"

"A hog?" I offered.

"Yes. A hog," said Joseph. "You're going to become a big hog, and I encourage you to take on the role with enthusiasm. Go as wild as you think a hog could go."

These were words I had been waiting to hear all my life.

I looked around and saw four or five large wooden picnic tables, each set for fine dining. I followed the group over to the corner of the patio and took a seat on a bench that was covered in sheepskin. It was a beautiful day in the mountains, the perfect combination of warm sunshine and crisp, candy-apple air.

From there, I released my inner hog, as did everyone else.

We ate, and we drank, and we ate and drank some more. Charcuterie platters overflowing with fresh meats, cheeses, sun-dried tomatoes, and roasted red peppers. White wine, rosé, and then red. Braised lamb shank and cutlets of veal, sides of pasta tossed in olive oil and served simply with cracked pepper and parmesan cheese, fluffy tiramisu with thick cream dripping down the sides, and to finish things off, honeycomb with coffee and cognac.

I watched the men laugh as they passed plates of food around the table. Fritz, of Fritz and Heidi, waltzed around in a pair of beige hide-skin pants and a shirt that looked like it could have only belonged to Heidi's great-grandfather. We were there for two hours. Sun streamed down on our cheeks and noses, and I heard the flags flapping gently in the wind, followed by wineglasses clinking, forks gently scraping at the bottom of dishes, and laughter that came straight from the belly.

After lunch, we continued into Switzerland and down into the village of Zermatt. The warm wind hit my face, and my legs felt slightly rubbery from all the wine. The sun was beginning to dip behind the mountains, the perfect time, someone said, for an afternoon toast. We popped into another restaurant for a final glass of wine, and I watched as the sun moved behind the mountains, a slightly cooler air settling in.

"Will you look at that," said one of the dwarfs as he glanced down at his watch. "It's four o'clock already."

The lifts close at 4:30, so in order to get back to the Italian side of the mountain I knew we had to hustle. I put my glass of wine on the table and reached for my helmet. As I did, I noticed that no one else was moving.

I wasn't sure Europeans, especially those of the male persuasion who have spent the entire day marinating in wine, sun, and ski-induced hedonism, really understood what hustle was. I watched them pour a few more glasses of wine as I stood there, anxious to get going. They were laughing and making jokes about bribing the lifties. "Oh, screw it," one of them jested, "we'll just pop in some choppers."

About an hour later, we arrived at the doors of Air Zermatt. I stood corrected. Popping in a chopper had not been a joke.

I'd never been in a helicopter before, and I was giddy. This one had a glass bottom, so it felt like floating through the sky in a giant crystal ball. We soared over the top of the Matterhorn, and I looked down at the peak and then into the valley. The highs and lows were framed in one view, all of it dancing together in a single gorgeous snapshot.

The helicopters landed at the top of the mountain, and we disembarked like a set of totally obnoxious movie stars—the common folk around us had obviously taken the lifts. For our last run of the day, we skied down into Cervinia, aiming to land at Principe's slopeside patio. About halfway down the run, the group paused at a crest. As we were standing there, James skated right up beside me. "Can I offer you a tip?" he asked kindly. "About your skiing?"

"Sure," I said, curious to hear what he had to say.

"Well, you ski like . . . like a woman. Your hips swing a little when you turn," he said. "Watch Max. See how solid his hips are. They're always facing downhill." He went on, "You're a beautiful skier, but I think you could be a more powerful one if you, pardon the expression, took the woman out of your skiing. You're certainly strong enough to do it."

I started to laugh. The woman who had started this trip would have been enraged at James's comment. I'd come a long way.

"You're right," I said, "I am strong enough, but you know what, I'm okay with skiing like a woman. I am one, after all. I appreciate the tip, though."

James gave me a wink, and we continued down the hill.

PART FIVE

THE TRUE NORTH STRONG AND FREE

To let oneself go, yielding trustingly to the ground law that is the secret sense of one's own weightiness, and which, nevertheless, is singing everywhere...is to solve absolutely everything at a stroke. For this is to fall in with the cast rhythm of the universe and to move with it. This is to follow the blindest, dullest, mutest impulse—sheer gravity—yet thereby to plumb to the center of all things; that point which everything must circulate simply because it holds its peace.

—**HEINRICH ZIMMER,** *THE KING AND THE CORPSE*

21

VENTURING INTO THE SLIPSTREAM

I ARRIVED in Vancouver on February 16. I wasn't supposed to be there. I was supposed to be in Austria skiing at St. Anton, Kitzbühel, and then a handful of other European resorts, but I flew back to Vancouver instead.

As soon as we wrapped *Snow White* and the most spectacular Italian day of all time, I went to my room and checked the weather forecast for the surrounding regions. Giant yellow orbs hung like Christmas ornaments above each day for the next ten days. There was no snow in sight. I typed "Whistler/Blackcomb weather" into the search bar and watched the page as it loaded. I did some quick math. Forty-three inches of snow was expected in the next seven days. I was on a flight at the end of the week.

One of the reasons I love flying is the view, the fact that you can see the world from a totally different angle as you soar through the air. And as my flight approached Vancouver, that's exactly what happened—I saw the city I grew up in from a completely different perspective. I hadn't told anyone except Chris, but I'd already decided to leave Vancouver. In many ways I'd already left, and intuitively, I knew I couldn't go back, not yet anyway. It would be too easy to slip back into my old life and my old patterns, to unzip the zipper that had just been pulled up. If I immersed myself in my past again, I worried it would be too easy to lose sight of my future, something I was just beginning to glimpse.

I used to have a recurring dream when I was little. It wasn't a nightmare exactly—no one was kidnapped or bludgeoned to death—but the dream was terrifying nonetheless. It was set in a long hallway. With the exception of a single stream of light coming from the opposite end, everything was dark. A man would appear at the end of the hallway, and then he would walk slowly toward me. The lighting made it so I could never see his face or the details of what he was wearing, but it seemed as though he wore a long jacket or a cape because I could see material kind of floating behind him in silhouette. I could hear the sound of his shoes on the ground as he slowly moved toward me, *click, click, click* as he came closer and closer. When the man got about three-quarters of the way down the hall, I woke up, without exception. He never got closer. I never saw who he was.

I can't remember how frequently I had this dream, but I know it went on for six or seven years because I can remember the books I was reading during that time. I always read before bed, and the strangest part about the whole dream happened *before* I went to sleep. I would be lying in bed totally immersed in Richard Scarry's *Please and Thank You Book* or, as I got older, something about Kristy Thomas and rest of the gang from *The Baby-Sitters Club*, and then I would start to hallucinate.

It wasn't an I'm-on-an-acid-trip type of hallucination because I was a kid and didn't have access to acid at the time, but it was a hallucination nonetheless. It would all start with the book: the words on the pages would change sizes, moving between really, really big and really, really small, and the pictures would pop forward, as if I was wearing 3-D glasses. When the hallucination hit that stage, it made me feel sick to keep reading, so I would close the book and lie flat on my bed. At this point, the hallucinations would move to my body. I felt as though most of my body was shrinking, but some parts, like my hands and my tongue, were inflating, getting bigger and bigger, and heavier too. So heavy I couldn't talk or lift my arms.

I was never scared of this part. In fact, it felt kind of cool. I told my mom about it once or twice, but she never believed me, and I don't blame her. If I had a little girl and she walked up to me in her nightie and told me that the hot-air balloons in her book were floating off the page, and that sometimes, but not all the time, she was as small as an ant but as heavy as an elephant, I would probably pat her on the head and say, "That's nice, dear." So I kept it to myself, in much the same way I kept my true thoughts about my grandma Vera being half witch to myself.

Whenever I had a non-acid acid trip, I knew the dream came next. I would be a bit scared to go to sleep, but eventually, and mostly because I have world-class talent when it comes to falling asleep, I would drift off, and there I would be, a little ball of fear at one end of a hallway. I'm not sure why, but the dream stopped cold turkey when I was about thirteen years old. I never had hallucinations again, except for that one time I took mushrooms. Okay, fine, those *few* times I took mushrooms.

I'd forgotten all about this dream until one night in Europe. I was lying in bed when the shrinking-growing-I-can't-lift-my-arms feeling washed over my body. And the dream was exactly the same. The empty, unlit hallway, the scary silhouette man walking slowly toward me. Closer. Closer. Closer. He was halfway down the hallway, he hit the three-quarter mark, and then he kept going.

Wait, I'm not waking up. He's coming too close.

He was a few feet away from me, and I saw that the coat or cape was actually a long hooded cloak. I watched as he pulled the hood back and dropped it behind his head. I started to panic. My heart was pounding as he came even closer. He stopped in front of me, and I knew I was about to see his awful, terrible kidnapper face. I scanned upward from his feet, moving my eyes up his legs and torso, up his chest and neck, and finally to his face.

It was Chris. His beautiful swimming-pool eyes looked right at me.

I jolted awake. Had it been him the whole time? All those years, had it been him slowly walking toward me?

The whole thing made me feel as though our story had been written for years, that we were always supposed to find each other and be together. From the moment I was a little girl reading books about the Big Friendly Giant, it had been written in the stars.

I told Chris about my dream the next morning. "I don't know what's going to happen," I said, "but I'm going to come to San Diego. When I'm finished with my trip, I'm going to come to be with you." I was rambling. "If that's okay. Maybe I should ask first. Do you want me to come to San Diego?"

"Of course, Bird. Of course I want you to come."

"Okay, my love, I have a little bit left, but I'll be there soon. P.S. No more dark, scary hallways."

.⁀.

MY FOURTH NIECE WAS born the day after I arrived in Vancouver. I went to the hospital and kissed her round face.

"I love you already," I whispered, before making my way to the mountains.

Later that afternoon, I was in Whistler. If I was lucky, and if the temperatures stayed cool, there would be three months of skiing before the ski season melted away. My plan was to stay in Whistler for a week or so before heading down to the States. In the time I had left, I would have to ski 2 million feet to hit my goal. Even with the catch-up I'd done in Japan and Europe, that seemed highly unlikely. But nothing about my journey had been likely so far, so I kept my sights set on my goal.

My friend Mike picked me up at my parents' house.

"Jagger!" he said. "Welcome home! Did you see the forecast?"

"Mikey, buddy, I flew home for the forecast."

"It's gonna be epic," he said.

As we drove through downtown Vancouver and over the Lions Gate Bridge, we caught up on life.

"I'm in love," I said.

"So am I," he replied.

"Yeah, right."

"No, seriously, I'm totally in love," he said before pausing a moment. "With this new gourmet mu-tard I found."

"Of course," I said, "and you slather it on giant wieners, don't you."

"Mm-hmm." Mike nodded as we both burst into laughter.

In many ways it was so good to be home. Our conversation continued at a decent clip as we drove up Taylor Way and onto the Sea to Sky Highway. We chattered on as we cruised past Horseshoe Bay and drove through Lions Bay, making our way around the next series of bends, until finally we were both struck silent by what lay in front of us.

When it comes to looks, mountains are very much like people. Most, if not all, have a signature look, a clearly recognizable feature, like a glacier, or a rock formation, or a bow-shaped mouth. Chamonix has Aiguille du Midi, Jackson Hole has the Grand Tetons, and Whistler? Whistler has Black Tusk, a giant rock made of petrified lava. Once you're far enough along the Sea to

Sky Highway, you can see it towering up from its home atop the Garibaldi Ranges.

As its name implies, Black Tusk looks like a large black tusk—almost as if a single-tusked woolly mammoth hiked up to the top, tipped over on its back for a rest, and then, by accident, fell asleep for all of eternity. Normally the tusk is solid black, an ebony spire pointing to the sky. During the winter the mouth of the mammoth (so to speak) is covered in snow, but the snow never piles high enough to cover the tusk itself. No matter the winter, there the tusk is, poking through the snow like the tip of a freshly cracked Sharpie, an actual permanent marker.

Except this winter. This winter the tusk was gray, a small gray nubbin that left us speechless.

"I know," Mike said after a few moments, sensing my deep-seated awe. "It's already epic."

I could hardly believe my eyes. The amount of snow that had piled on top of the sleeping mammoth rendered Whistler barely recognizable. As we drove on, I noticed other signs of a massive seasonal snowfall. Huge outcroppings of rock were completely concealed by the snow. Centuries-old glaciers were tucked underneath thick, downy blankets of white. Thickets of forest were buried, and giant cliffs were small rolling hills. Ski tracks ran down steep sections of snow in places I'd never seen skiers venture, places that were normally sheer rock and stone. And I'm not gonna lie, Whistler looked good with 60,000-odd tons of white meat on her bones.

I arrived to a record-level base, and while I was there, eighty-four more inches of snow heaved down from the sky. It was as if Mother Nature had put an icing sugar sieve in the sky and set it on heavy. Whistler was full and lush. She was a Rubens painting brought to life, a woman standing comfortably in all of her milky-colored flesh.

With the help of Mike and a few other friends, I tore through 360,000 vertical feet of that snow before boarding a flight bound for Utah.

My original plan was to ski the Rocky Mountains from New Mexico all the way back up to Canada, hitting dozens of resorts, six states, and two Canadian provinces in between. But I was tired. The thought of a solo drive through the Rockies and a different hotel every night didn't seem like the best idea when it came to my sanity. So I picked three spots, and Salt Lake City was the first.

I caught a direct flight to Salt Lake, and as soon as I got off my plane, I started to run. I ran through the airport and into customs, I paced on the spot until border patrol waved me through, and once I was on other side I started running again. I ran through hallways, down corridors, up staircases, down escalators. I ran all the way to baggage claim, because I knew that's where Chris would be waiting.

Chris spent his late teens and early twenties living, working, and skiing in the mountains of Utah, so it seemed like the perfect place to meet. He could show me his favorite resorts, carry some of my bags, and love the hell out of me for forty-eight hours.

We hadn't seen one another since New York. He hadn't seen the wildfire or the ashes, or the woman who had emerged on the other side of it all. He held me in his arms at the airport.

"I love you, my Bird," he whispered.

He put his arm over my shoulder as we walked to the rental car, and he held my hand as we drove to the mountains.

"I'm so happy to see you," he said.

"I'm happy to see myself too," I replied.

Chris and I drove up the Little Cottonwood Canyon and stayed the night in a lodge right at the base of the Alta Ski Area and its neighboring giant, Snowbird. There are very few places to stay in the area because the whole canyon is one enormous avalanche path. Each lodge is essentially a concrete bunker built right into the hill.

Once there, we discovered that Whistler wasn't the only place having a record season. Apparently La Niña had cajoled the equatorial Pacific into throwing a full-blown winter fit, and together they buried every single mountain range west of the Great Plains. An early-season dusting had turned into a coat, a coat had turned into a layer, a layer into heaps and piles, and then on top of the heaps and piles more came blasting down. Even as spring approached, there were no signs of winter slowing. She was on a serious roll.

On the night we arrived, the mountains were throttled with snow, like actually choked off. Thirty-five inches fell overnight (*Thirty-five inches!* That's almost three foot-long subs!), and when we woke up, we were told that the marshal's office had closed the roads, and the resorts, until further notice. Additionally, as a safety precaution, we were to remain inside until the canyon had been bombed and cleared.

"This is pretty common around here," said Chris. "Even in a regular season."

The lifts opened at about the same time we were dug out of the lodge. Lucky for us, the roads remained closed. What this meant was that we would be sharing Alta and all of her 2,200 acres with the handful of other skiers who had stayed overnight.

"We couldn't have been luckier," said Chris, who was almost salivating at the idea of skiing his favorite mountain with three feet of fresh powder underfoot (or, if you want to get technical, "underwaist").

He turned to me on the first chair up. "Okay, Birdie," he said. "You usually aim for twenty-five thousand, right?"

"Yep," I confirmed. "Twenty-five thousand. I was doing more in Whistler, but in this kind of powder, I think we'll be closer to twenty."

I looked at the terrain underneath the chairlift. Everything in sight looked steep and deep. This wasn't going to be a day of ripping groomers.

"No," said Chris, shaking his head. "You'll see. Twenty is going to be a piece of cake on this mountain. We'll probably get closer to thirty or forty."

"If you say so," I replied with a laugh.

By eleven o'clock Chris was starting to look a little beat. "How much have we done?" he asked. "Seventeen? Eighteen?"

I pulled up my sleeve and looked at the reading on my altimeter. We had been skiing hard all morning, but my legs and I knew we weren't even close to seventeen or eighteen.

"We're just below ten," I said.

"What!" Chris cried. "There's no way!"

I laughed and showed him the watch. "A little harder than you thought, eh?"

"Jesus," he said. "How have you been doing this?"

"It helped that I became a woman in Europe," I said. "I'm basically Pegasus. I've got the body of a horse, the blood of Medusa, and wings. I'm like a feminine bird horse, and you might not know this, but feminine bird horses can do pretty much anything. Also, I've been skiing every day for seven months, so, I don't know, I'd say I'm a little bit fitter than you."

"Right," Chris said with a laugh. "You're fit, and you're a flying Medusa."

At the end of the weekend we drove back down to Salt Lake City. Chris caught a flight back to San Diego, and I checked into the cutest little bed-and-breakfast I had ever seen. I spent the next two weeks indulging in a life of lace doilies, bubble baths, and a bed so big and fluffy I actually had to climb up into it as if I was a princess on top of a pea. Oh, and I skied.

Eight world-class resorts can be found in the mountains around

Salt Lake. Eight places to ski within a thirty- or forty-minute drive of my bubble bath. It was the reason I chose Salt Lake: Lots of options, little travel.

I woke up each morning, ate breakfast (served hot), and called on the resorts as if they were reindeer.

On Brighton, and Alta, and Snowbird, and Vixen;

On the Canyons, Park City, Deer Valley, and Blitzen.

Over the next two weeks I added 540,000 vertical feet to my total. Traction was being made, and I was feeling balanced, both soft and strong, basically the human version of Secret antiperspirant. I left Salt Lake with 2.9 million vertical feet and boarded a quick flight to Jackson, Wyoming.

Not unlike Chamonix, Jackson had been a must from the very beginning. I'd heard about one of its famous watering holes, where you actually saddle up at the bar, like on a horse saddle instead of a bar stool. Add to that a tram that zipped you from the valley floor up into the Grand Tetons in under fifteen minutes, and Jackson was a requirement.

The town itself is a little confusing, mostly because it walks an interesting line between pure redneck and 100 percent hippie. For example, Jackson is the kind of place where you can book yourself a spa appointment for gong therapy (which, in case you didn't know, is a therapeutic session with a wonderful lady named Nancy who uses a combination of crystals, tuning forks, and giant copper gongs to adjust your energetic vibrations), and then afterward you can trot off down the street in total "child of the moon" harmony and grab a seat at a tailgating party for the Hill Climb (which, in case you didn't know, is a local snowmobile showdown where everyone who's anyone knows what chew juice is, and uses an empty bottle of Mountain Dew to spit theirs into).

In any case, the week that followed in Jackson was a total blur. Saddles, cowboy hats, vegan restaurants with seventeen flavors of tempeh, tram rides, art galleries-cum-fur shops where you can trade your lifetime earnings for a watercolor postcard or maybe a single hand-stitched leather glove, and of course, cold, light-as-dust snow. I'm not going to lie, I adored every fucking minute of it; as a Canadian, I love a strange brew.

On the day I'd arrived, the sky had puked snow. I had locals telling me they had never seen the mountain quite this dolled up. There was powder everywhere. I felt like I was that woman in the Philadelphia Cream Cheese commercial, bouncing from one cloud to the next in the magical kingdom of soft, fluffy cheese.

I raced through 350,000 feet in nine days, because Jackson is designed for racking vertical. She's also designed for other things, like hucking cliffs, escaping into the backcountry, and providing inspiration for ski manufacturers around the world, but on this trip, I focused on the vertical.

I never started out with monster days in mind, but in Jackson I just couldn't help it. Easy mornings turned into 40,000- and 50,000-foot days. And other times, when I felt like exerting just an ounce more effort, I came in at 60,000 and above. My record day on the hill was a smidgen under 64,000, and to be honest, I don't remember it being that hard.

Perhaps it seemed easy because the conditions were perfect. Perhaps it was because my aura was vibrationally balanced from the gong therapy. Perhaps it was because I'd eaten close to a dozen bison burgers since arriving. Or perhaps it was because over the last two months, through Japan and all of Europe, I had placed all of my fears on the ground. I'd been carrying around so many ideas about success, and what I thought it meant to be a woman, and I'd finally pried all of that loose from the clutches of my precious little ego, pried it all out like you would a stubborn oyster from its shell, shucking, cracking, and scraping so it could be released and replaced with something true. My energy was now free to flow, unblocked, unfettered, and unrestrained, toward something pure, something open, something real. As I skied, I felt as if there were a current of electricity running through my body, from the core of me down into my legs and feet, boots and skis, and finally down into the snow. I was plugged into myself and the ground at the same time, allowing the skiing to become an effortless flow, a serene and constant slipstream that I could slide into and out of with ease.

22

LOVELY DAY FOR A GUINNESS

SOMEWHERE IN the midst of my North American blur, I was struck by the sound of my own voice. After months of stumbling through Spanish, Portuguese, a mumbling English dialect known as Kiwi, and then French, Swiss French, Italian, Swiss Italian, Swiss Swiss, and Japanese, I was reveling in the fact that I could speak English. So I talked. A lot. It was as if every extroverted bone in my body was making up for lost time.

I dove directly into conversation with people, regardless of whether they seemed interested. I couldn't help myself, I just jabbered away. On chairlifts (which was the best, because it gave me a completely captive audience), in lift lines, at ticket windows, and at the bar, the one with the saddles. I talked and talked and talked. Most of these places only allow for brief conversations, ten to fifteen minutes at the most, but I didn't care, I just engaged in an astonishing number of surface-level conversations.

"So, where you folks from?"

"How long are you here for?"

"Nice day, isn't it?"

"Pretty chilly, eh?"

I was a pro at these kinds of exchanges, and I developed some serious skills at fielding similar questions from other overly chatty, borderline intrusive loners like myself.

On occasion, if asked how long I was in the area or when I was headed back home, I answered by telling people about my trip. I would say something about following winter around the world and trying to ski 4 million feet. If and when that happened, I could almost guarantee a response that sounded something like this:

"You're trying to ski four million feet! That's a lot of feet . . . wait, how many feet is that?"

Although tempted to say, "Four million," I knew they were looking for something more, so I gave them my line about Everest: "It's like skiing down Everest from summit to sea a hundred and thirty-five times. About once a day I ski down Everest, and about once a day I ride a chairlift up the same distance."

"That's gotta be some kind of record," they'd reply.

The first few times, I responded by saying, "I dunno. I've never even thought about it." But eventually my answer evolved. "Yeah," I'd say. "People tell me that all the time, but I've never looked it up."

Until the day I looked it up.

I went back to my hotel after skiing one day and Googled "guinness record vertical feet skied." Within seconds, I discovered that everyone had been right. There was a record. According to the Guinness website, a British guy named Arnie Wilson set a record in 1994 for "Most vertical feet skied in one calendar year." The total number of feet skied was 4,146,890.

Hold the fucking phone.

I read it again. 4,146,890 vertical feet skied.

That's only five or six extra days. If I can make it to four, I can make it to four-point-one or four-point-two.

I did some quick calculations in my head. In the last seven weeks I had skied 1,250,000 feet, putting my current total at 3,250,000. To break the record, I would need 900,000 more in five weeks. To do it, I would need everything in my favor until the very end—the weather, my body, my heart, and my mind.

I didn't think about whether it was a good idea or a bad idea or a totally fucking crazy idea. I didn't have to because something just took over; some strange energy moved right through my arms and down into my hands. Within seconds I was back on the Guinness website. Within minutes I had downloaded an application, filled it out, and sent it in.

Next up was an e-mail to my family and friends, as well as a small group of people who had taken interest in my journey. I declared my intention to break the world record for skiing the most vertical feet in a year and pressed send.

All of this, every second of it, had happened on autopilot. It was as if I didn't have a say in it at all, as if I were simply fulfilling instructions sent from the Universe as opposed to setting and stating the goals myself. Nothing about this felt like the same old Steph charging after another blue ribbon. It felt bigger than that, beyond me in some way.

I went to sleep an hour later, wondering what the hell I'd just done.

I was already tired. Four million was going to be enough of a challenge. What the fuck had I gotten myself into?

I woke up the next morning to a few new e-mails, every single one of which could be summed up using the exact expression I'd used: What the . . . ? It seemed my family and friends were just as shocked as I was about my decision. I scanned through each e-mail, and as I was reading the last one, I saw another pop up in my in-box. The e-mail was from Arnie Wilson. As it turned out, one of the seventeen people on my list knew the record holder and had forwarded him my e-mail.

He told me he was the English gent who had broken the record, and he talked about his admiration for my journey, specifically the fact that I was going it alone. Before signing off, he added a piece of advice about the record—he encouraged me to go for it but also not to care, telling me that just doing it was what counted the most.

I e-mailed him back right away and told him how honored I felt that he had reached out. "As you can imagine, I am in full admiration of *your* trip," I wrote. "Especially as you seemed to have skied *every* day. I'm not sure how that is even physically possible!"

I also took the opportunity to ask him a question. Arnie's record was listed in the male category, but the description of his feat mentioned a partner, a woman named Lucy Dicker. There was no mention of a female record, which made me wonder if Lucy skied every foot of the feat, or if she was there as a companion and cheerleader.

"If I'm unable to break the record you set, I'd like to go after the female title. Do you know how many feet she skied?" I asked before signing off.

I skied all day thinking of this mystery woman named Lucy, and in some strange way, I almost felt as though she were with me, adding a bit of grace to my every turn. When I got back to the hotel that afternoon, another e-mail from Arnie was waiting. He told me that yes, she had in fact skied every foot, and that he wasn't sure why she hadn't been recognized. He also told me that, had Lucy lived, he was sure she would have wished me well.

After reading Arnie's e-mail, I Googled Lucy Dicker. I couldn't help but be curious about her death. I assumed it was recent.

Maybe she'd died of cancer, I thought.

No. It hadn't been cancer. I was shocked at what I read. As it turns out, Lucy died in a ski accident only three months after setting the record with Arnie. I read a few accounts of her death, and as I did, I couldn't help but think that she *had* in fact been with me all day, and perhaps, I thought, since the very beginning. Perhaps she knew I needed a guide, someone who had experience, say, in an intricate tango between the masculine and feminine.

I left Jackson a day or so later. I would have stayed longer, but the resorts there close earlier than most, something having to do with the moose migration. Although this seemed strange to me at first, I quickly understood that it was classic Jackson, a perfect blend of redneck granola. It was as if they were saying, *The animals here, including the moose, create a symbiotic relationship with the earth, and we respect their role so much that we leave their migration routes undisturbed. Also, Jimmy here enjoys hunting, so we close early to give him ample time to shoot and mount a few big ones.*

.⦁.

I MADE A PIT stop on my way up to Canada. This may seem counterintuitive, given the fact that I'd just revealed plans to break a world record, but my body was requesting a break. And over the past eight or nine months, I'd learned a lot about what that meant. I learned when to push through pain, and I learned when to stop and rest. Given the fact that my knees were oh so close to launching a full-scale protest, complete with picket signs, megaphones, and a handful of angry people dressed in fleece clothing, I knew this was a stop-and-rest moment.

I called Chris and asked him (wink, wink, nudge, nudge) if he knew of a good place, somewhere I could go to recuperate for a handful of days. Twenty-four hours later he picked me up from San Diego International Airport.

Chris's arms were spread wide, and he had a huge smile on his face. In his right hand he was holding a leash.

"Who's this?" I asked, knowing perfectly well that the huge black dog next to Chris was his best friend, Ramsey. We'd met on Skype a few times, but never in person.

"This is Ramsey!" said Chris.

I crouched down to give Ramsey a snuggle, and as I did, his tail swiped back and forth through the air.

"Rams . . . this is your new mama," said Chris.

We walked out of the airport, and the smell of sunshine, palm trees, and fresh eucalyptus hit my nose.

"Does it always smell like this?" I asked.

"Like what?"

"Like a tropical vacation."

After being in the mountains for so long, I'd become unaccustomed to anything but the smell of snow, pine trees, and filthy long underwear.

Chris asked me how I wanted to rest, and I told him it involved seafood, sleep, a swim in the ocean, and more seafood. Chris and a few surfing buddies owned an old motorboat together, and shortly after I had arrived and filled my belly with a fish taco or two, we jumped on the boat and drove it out off the coast. We anchored and leaped right into the big, salty Pacific. It was perfect. We spent the rest of the afternoon on the bow of the boat, drifting in and out of small naps, Chris to my right, Ramsey to my left, the sun beating down on my skin.

As waves lapped against the side of the boat, I was hit with a memory from my time in Japan. I was on a bus that was slowly winding its way through the Japanese countryside and up into the mountains. I had the window seat, and a delicate-looking Japanese woman sat to my left. It was a beautiful drive. Layers of damp leaves and heavy snow lay on the ground like a handwoven tapestry, and fog hung thick in the air all around us. A handful of farmhouses freckled the landscape, and each had smoke wafting up from the chimney, a soft gray ribbon curling toward the sky. There must have been, no pun intended, fifty shades of gray in that view. Soft gray, blue gray, damp, dark gunmetal gray. I saw smudged charcoal, and bruised shadows, and thick soot that came down in streaks, running from the rooftops to the roads, from the sides of the farmhouses to the pewter-colored pavement. It was a painting, a haunting image coming to life before my very eyes.

The very tiny Japanese lady next to me missed the whole thing. Just to be clear, this wasn't because my comparatively large Caucasian body was blocking her view. I'm sure it was, but that didn't matter because her eyes were glued to the map that sat open in front of her. She studied that map with great focus, looking up only when the driver announced the names of the places we were rolling into and pulling out of. A name would come flying down the middle of the bus, and she would catch it in midair and then, with her finger, she would trace a line from the place we had just passed to the place where we'd just arrived.

This woman seemed so determined to know exactly where she was on that map. I'm not sure what would have happened if for some reason we wound up a little to the left, or heaven forbid, off the grid. She was composed externally, in seemingly perfect control, but everything about her energy told me she was having kittens. I'm not sure what the Japanese translation is for that, but I can guarantee you that's exactly what she was having.

Eventually I stopped staring at her. This was mostly because I realized that if I was having kittens, I probably wouldn't want a large Caucasian woman staring right at me, but also because there was that magnificent gray painting just outside the window. I turned my head and once again was swallowed up by the gray.

But this woman consumed my thoughts for several days following. Eventually I begged the Universe for an answer.

"Why?" I asked. "Why is she so important?"

And then it hit me. I used to be her. I used to be that woman.

I used to live my entire life like that woman and her map. Every event planned out in advance. Plotted, measured, completely controlled. I knew exactly when and where I was expected to be in life, and when that didn't happen—boom, a giant litter of kittens. I used to be completely consumed with the destination, and totally blind to the journey. And, like most people who use maps to navigate their way through life, I had been relying on others to do all the cartography; mine were inherited maps, passed down from a purebred bloodline of goats.

Maps used to make me giddy with joy. The measuring of progress, the rush of knowing I had moved from A and made it to B. Check! Tick! Done! But now, as I lay on the boat in San Diego, reflecting back on my life, I realized the thrill had always been fleeting. Arriving at B, only to replace your map with the one for C, and then D, and then E—well, that isn't as exciting as staring out into the gray while the Universe paints a picture before your very eyes, one that reveals little by little where you're going next.

I felt the salt water drying on my skin.

"I can do this," I said to Chris.

"Of course you can, Bird," he replied. In his tone, I knew he was referring to the record.

"No, I mean this," I said.

I sat up and looked him in the eye.

"I mean moving here, to San Diego, without a plan, without a map, with no idea of what comes next, or what I'm gonna do, or how I'm gonna feed myself besides living off the leftovers in your cupboards and putting hundreds of dollars' worth of fish tacos on my credit card. I can do this. Without knowing a single thing about how, or what's going to happen in the end, I can do it."

Chris leaned over to kiss me.

"We'll be doing that part together, Birdie," he replied.

.ˑ●.

THREE DAYS LATER I flew from San Diego to Calgary, Alberta. I stayed overnight at my aunt and uncle's house and then got on a bus bound for Golden, British Columbia. Four and a half hours later I was standing at the base of Kicking Horse Mountain Resort.

I had planned a five-night stay in the area, and to be honest, if the town of Golden wasn't such a sleeper, I might have stayed there forever. The resort itself has fifty-eight double black diamonds, eighty-five inbound chutes, two or three massive bowls, and a never-ending supply of really, really steep groomers. Essentially, Kicking Horse is a total fucking stallion. I racked up 200,000 feet over five days, and it was, dare I say, easy.

On my third day there the skies were especially clear, so I stopped for lunch at the top of the mountain. As I ate, I stared at the giants unfolding in front of me. The Purcells, the Selkirks, and of course, the Canadian Rockies. It should be noted that these weren't just peaks but giant mountain ranges, three of them lined up spine by rocky spine, spanning out to the north, south, and west of me.

A singular truth had crystallized for me throughout my journey: I couldn't imagine my life without mountains. They inspired me. They freed me. They taught me more than any person ever could. They showed me that life is a stunning contradiction, a test about how many truths we can hold in the palms of our hands at the very same time.

The mountains spoke to me loud and clear, and at the same time they helped me understand the power of silence, and the sounds that live within it. They released me while teaching me about what it feels like to be grounded, attached, and immovable. They taught me about erosion, about the things that crumble away and dissolve, and they taught me about permanence, the things that stand the test of time. And more than anything else, they taught me that you cannot be one thing without the other. There cannot be strength without weakness, light without shadow, man without woman. You cannot be half of yourself and expect to endure.

I reflected back on a conversation I'd had with a friend a week or so prior. We were catching up on life, and I was filling her in on my journey thus far. I told her about the roller coaster of it, the series of ups and downs and twists and turns that had taken me out of myself and back in. It was a big-picture kind of conversation.

I told her I felt like a new pattern was emerging in my life, one that was less steady, less known, but oddly safe and secure. I told her that I was trying to get comfortable with that, and that I felt the big lesson (she's big on big lessons) was to understand and accept that new and greater highs were going to come with new and greater lows.

"So, that's what I'm grappling with," I said.

"Well, good luck with that, Steph," she replied. "I'm just not sure people are going to get on board if that's the way you're driving, and if they do, I can guarantee you they're gonna jump ship pretty quick. You've got to figure out a way to even the keel, girl."

I cried for a long time after that conversation. I was so hurt by her blunt response. But as I sat on top of Kicking Horse, looking out at the wild ocean of mountains, I realized she was wrong. And perhaps *wrong* isn't the right word. Perhaps what I realized was that her truth just didn't fit inside the palms of my hands.

What I knew, what the mountains had taught me, was that life has peaks and valleys, darkness and light. That life is rough, and life is smooth. And that's where we find ourselves. That's where we can carve something out of nothing. We don't find out who we are in the flat, steady, featureless parts of our lives. We find out who we are when we're pinned between rocks and hard places, when we're set loose on steep slopes—a test to see if, once and for all, we'll break free and ski our own line.

23

A FOURTH WIND, FIRE ANTS, AND HOW TO PUT ONE FOOT IN FRONT OF THE OTHER

I CAN talk for hours on end about the logistics of traveling. Well, actually, I can talk for hours on end about basically anything, but I can give a university-level class on the logistics of traveling, as well as mid-length seminars to taxi drivers from around the world about how to fit a ski bag into a minicab. I can provide intricate details about the color and quality of laminate flooring used in most bus stations, and/or the carpets in most airport waiting lounges. I can give workshops on how to select the right lines at customs, where to keep your wallet and passport, and exactly what you will and will not need in your carry-on. I can speak eloquently and informatively on booking, packing, rolling, lifting, running, darting, preboarding, taxiing (multiple kinds), and waiting things out. I can go on about luggage tags, hydration, emergency exits, domestic, international, and maybe even extraterrestrial travel. But the biggest insight I could ever give anyone about traveling is this: you will be exhausted. And that's exactly what I was after Kicking Horse.

The thought of another bus or plane or hotel room made me feel physically ill. I could not imagine pulling my bags one more horizontal foot. Nor could I face the idea of packing, and unpacking, and packing up again. So I didn't. I went to Whistler instead. I took one last bus and one last plane (and another bus, and another one after that), and I dropped all four of my bags on the floor of my parents' cabin. The giant black ski bag, the rolling suitcase, the largish backpack, and the coral tote.

Never again will I lift those bags, I said to myself.

On a side note, I lifted them the next morning because they were blocking the front door, but besides that, never again.

It was the beginning of April, which meant I had about a month of skiing left before the mountains closed. If I wanted to break the record, I would have to ski just over 700,000 feet in that time. I started right away.

I skied twenty-one of the next twenty-four days and averaged 35,000 feet a day. I woke up, I ate, I went to the lifts. On the chair-ride up I prayed, and what I mean by "prayed" is that I listened to Patty Griffin's "Up to the Mountain" on repeat.

Once I got to the top, I skied. I did laps on the chairs that gave me the best vertical ROI, and I skied them over and over and over for as long as I could bear. My left knee had developed an ache over the course of the trip, a dull but consistent pain that dug its teeth in a little deeper every time I turned. My solution was to stop turning. I pointed my skis downhill and let gravity do the work. I felt the snow under my skis as I sped down each run. It was a vibration. My skis ran over frozen grains of sand, and a gentle humming moved through my feet and up each leg. Hour after hour after hour. The only break came by way of small rollers, mounds of snow from which I could catch a bit of air if I crossed them at speed. I could feel my body take flight for a few seconds, and I could hear my skis as they slapped back down on the snow. I skied ten runs, then twenty. I stopped to drink a giant latte. I skied ten more. I ate a hamburger, sometimes two (this is not a joke). I skied ten more. I came home, I climbed into the shower, and I collapsed in a heap on the ground, warm water pelting my legs until the vibrating sensation went away.

The last month was numbing and in many ways boring. I had become accustomed to new mountains, new terrain, and new challenges, weekly if not daily. To get through the boredom, to move all the way to the other side of it, I made each day a long, drawn-out moving meditation. Essentially, for a brief period, I became a Buddhist monk. As I skied, I imagined I was still. Instead of me moving toward the finish line, I imagined it moving toward me, the final few feet getting closer and closer without me having to move an inch. In some strange way, I think this helped me conserve what energy I had left. All I had to do was be a monk and vibrate my way through a few more weeks.

It also helped that I was on my fourth wind. I'd never experienced a fourth wind before, but apparently that's what happens when your brain stops working. Think of it like you would the stages of hypothermia. Your body, smart little thing that it is, decides you can no longer afford to use the energy you have left on something as silly as brain function, so it shuts down. Because of this, I no longer had the mental capacity to decide what to have for breakfast, or what mountain to ski, or what lift to take. I did the same thing every day, because there's no way in hell I would have been able to figure out anything else. The fact that I was a Buddhist monk helped me maintain a positive outlook on all of this.

I knew I was deep in the throes of the final chapter, and I knew my ability to finish this journey had less to do with being able to soldier on or man up than with letting go and simply being. "It would be a mistake to think that it takes a muscle-bound hero to accomplish this. It does not. It takes a heart that is willing to die and be born and die and be born again and again," wrote Clarissa Pinkola Estés. So that's what I did. I skied away the old, and the weary, and the no longer serving. I skied away the idea that I had to be a ram. I prayed. I meditated. I vibrated. I trusted. I let it all go, cleared it all out, so that eventually the new would have space to come rushing in.

We don't really have rites of passage anymore. I suppose baby showers, graduation parties, and weddings might count, but in their current form so many of those events seem to be centered around buying things and getting drunk, as opposed to some kind of emotional transition or spiritual maturation, which, as far as I know, was the original intention. Gone are the days of walking into a forest for a month of fasting in order to come back as a woman. Gone are the week-long initiations that come complete with spiritual elders and hallucinogenic drugs (although there was that one time my aunt and I got a bit tipsy in Morocco). Gone are the rituals and ceremonies that mark the past and welcome the future.

It's possible we ditched most rites of passage because they included elements of suffering, because of the physical pain involved. Pain and suffering are things we humans tend to avoid, at least in an outright, face-on kind of way. Common sense gives us a pretty obvious answer when asked if we want to spend eight days in the jungle surrounded by an army of poisonous frogs. But if we toss the rites and rituals, what are we left with? A planet full of wandering souls? Fully grown adults who haven't matured a day since their eighteenth birthday? Countries of people with overflowing bank accounts but no knowledge of themselves?

This journey was, in many ways, my very own rite of passage, one about growing up, about knowing and owning every sacred ounce of myself. But I'd had no clue where to start. Heck, at first I didn't even know I needed lessons. No shaman stepped forward to announce I had a deep imbalance. No wise woman threw me in a hut for four days of chanting and goddess worship. So in many ways I created my own rite of passage, without really knowing it. Each day I chucked my body down the mountain like it was some sort of sacrificial lamb on skis. And I was nearing the end. I was almost there. If this was a seven-day ceremony involving my flesh and three colonies of fire ants, I was on day seven. I was hours away from transcendence.

And that's exactly when my sister called.

I answered the phone, and even though I was covered in ants that bite and sting, and my brain had stopped working, and I was a Buddhist who had slipped into a vibrating meditation, we chatted. I didn't really have the capacity to tell her that I was deep in the throes of a dark-night-of-the-soul—aka the final stage of a meta-phorical fire-ant metamorphosis—nor did I tell her that giving up now would likely mean losing the woman I'd fought so hard to find, or that I was basing my survival on blind faith and the law of gravity. So we just stuck to small talk.

But at some point in our conversation she said, "So, how's it going?"

The truth couldn't help but pour out. My voice came forth with some strange depth, like the kind you hear when someone's voice is being disguised.

"I'm tired," I mumbled. I'm pretty sure I sounded like hell.

In the olden days, I'm sure my sister would have been one hut over, chanting prayers to the God of Ants to please have mercy on my soul, but it wasn't the olden days, so she did what any sane person would try to do—she tried to save me.

"Steph," I heard her say as she attempted to rouse me from my trance. "Steph, you don't have to do this. You know that making it this far is fine, right?"

Her words came flying at me like darts. I was instantly enraged, which I'll admit, was rather unmonkish of me.

I was in the room when my sister gave birth to her first daughter. I stood at the end of the bed and watched as she bore down, and I was right there as the two of them, her and a little baby girl named Olivia, worked together. "Keep going," I whispered. "Keep going!" My hands were clenched tight.

My sister gripped the bars on the side of the bed as Livy pushed her way into this world with firm resolve. It was the most beautiful thing I've ever seen, the crown of that child's head claiming space in this world.

When you're birthing something new, "making it this far" isn't fine. You have to go all the way. You have to go, and go, and go, until you turn into something else. You have to go until you turn into a daughter or you become a mother.

I didn't have a right to be mad at my sister. She didn't understand I was birthing something new, and if she had, I'm sure she would have whispered, "Keep going," with her fists clenched tight at her side. But she didn't, and I was angry. Buddhism wasn't working out as well as I thought.

Luckily, I didn't have the energy required to stay mad. I was too busy being reborn. I took a deep breath, and then I said, "It's important that I finish. I can't quite explain why, but it's really important."

.∴•.

ON SATURDAY, APRIL 30, I hit the slopes early. I knew that if I got through enough vertical in the morning, the chances of hitting the 4,000,000 mark in the afternoon were high. I wanted so badly to hit that particular milestone on that particular day. Two of my nieces were up for the weekend, and the idea of crossing that line, with those kids in tow, filled me with pride. I was thrilled about the idea of showing them what a woman could do.

I stopped at the top of what we had planned as the last run of the day. I looked at my altimeter. I was 1,000 feet away from hitting 4,000,000, and I knew there were at least 1,700 more feet on the run below us. I pointed to a bend near the bottom of the slope, and I told my sister, my mom, and my dad to wait for us there. They skied down as I gathered my two nieces beside me. They were five and seven years old.

"Will you help me ski this part?" I asked. "Not too fast, but not too slow."

They nodded, their Dora helmets bobbing up and down in the air. Chloe put her hands on her knees and moved her skis into the shape of a pizza—a clear signal she was ready to go.

We skied down the final run, and as we approached the bend, Livy soared up ahead. I felt Chloe move in close behind me, and I bent down into a deep snowplow tuck. Without looking back, I knew she'd done the same. Two little birds flying in formation. At a speed of about one or two miles per hour, we made our way down the final section of the slope.

And I was proud, more proud of myself than I'd ever been. Hitting the original goal made me think of how far I'd come, of the difference between the physical journey and the emotional one.

We had hot chocolates at the base of the mountain, and then we went back to the cabin. I took a small nap that ended up turning into a fourteen-hour sleep, and when I woke up the next morning, the cars were being packed. It was Sunday, the girls had school the next day, and my dad was planning to head into the office. Life went on, and as it did, I moved closer and closer to Guinness.

The next couple of days went well, as did the one after that. It was May, the temperatures were warm, and it seemed as though spring had finally sprung. Patty Griffin's lyrics could not have been any truer for me than they were on those final days:

> *I went up to the mountain, because you asked me to*
> *Up over the clouds, to where the sky was blue.*

In the end I'm not sure who had called me up to the mountains— my ego, a blue tin sign, the Universe itself? Whatever it was, it whispered to me on those final days when I was exhausted, when I couldn't see the path in front of me. It was a sweet voice, telling me softly that it loved me.

On the fourth day of that week, my 160th day of the trip, I broke the record. And, well, that's it. I broke it, had a coffee, and then I skied a little bit more.

I know what you're thinking. You're wondering when I stopped to celebrate. You're wondering when I had the shindig with all of my friends, and some booze, and an ice-cream cake from Dairy Queen, one that had "Way to Verti-go!" written on the top in red-colored gel frosting. "The fire ants," you're crying, "they're gone! Dear god, woman, throw yourself a party or something!"

But here's the thing. Even though I was the one who'd set the goal (plural, if you include Guinness) and created the finish line, and even though I'd chased after blue ribbons for my whole entire life, I realized at the end of it all that the end isn't all that important. I know we need finish lines, because without them no basement renovation would ever be completed, but this trip had taught me about the importance of something else—starting lines. What if we spent as much time glorifying starting lines as we do finish lines? I wondered. What if we cheered as loudly for people the moment they assumed their position in the starting blocks as we do when they run through the tape at the end of the race? This journey made me realize that it's our ability to get to starting lines that prompts all the doors to swing open, that our courage is not found in the words *I finished* but in the words *I started*. What I had come to realize was that starting lines, the moments we respond to the Universe in a scared little voice, nodding that we're in—those are the moments we should be celebrating.

You know when you eat something delicious, and you put the first few bites in your mouth, and you can barely breathe, it's so good? You know that feeling where your mouth gets all slobbery, and you eat a few more bites, and you moan a little bit, and the whole thing is orgasmic? It's so good that you keep eating. A couple more bites, a few licks of your lips, just a few more pieces, and then, oh my god you can't stop. One more. Maybe two. And you know that you're full but you keep going, and you eat, and you eat, and then, on the last forkful, you turn to whoever is sitting next to you, that wide-eyed person who just witnessed you devour an entire plate of brownies, or whatever it was you were eating, and you say, "Oh my god. I feel sick."

Finish lines are kind of like that.

The first few bites in the beginning, and the momentum that's slowly building, and the idea that something is going to happen or be created, or that you're going to experience something close to heaven on earth—that's divine. That should be celebrated. But the end? The last few bites that make you feel sick, but you force it down anyway? Well, I'm not sure those are the moments we should be glorifying. I'm not sure that's what the pinnacle of humanity is really about. I'd spent my whole life glorifying the ending—heck, I have a box full of ribbons as proof of that. But things had changed. I had changed. And by the end of the trip, as a tiger, as a woman, I wasn't interested in all that. I don't want someone saying a toast in my honor when I'm leaning back on the couch with my jeans unbuttoned, belching up small bits of chocolate, I want them to say it when my toe is on the starting line. I think it takes more courage to offer yourself up to opportunity, and chance, and the whimsy of the Universe than it does to come home with your ego in one hand and willpower in the other.

Plus, this wasn't a finish line for me, not really. This was a brand-new beginning. It's true that some kind of roar had burst forth from my tigery throat, but I'm not sure I would have called it triumphant. I had a lot more to learn about life as a jungle cat, and about who I was as a woman in the world. I didn't know what that looked like, but I knew my feet were in the blocks.

．●．

LIFE HAS TWO KINDS of whiteouts. The first is often referred to as correctional fluid, and please, whatever you do don't get me started on the endless inappropriate tangents I could go on over a term like that. Most of us used this kind of whiteout in grade school, and by most of us I mean the really, really old people who went to school before the computers came along, you know, the before-computers-but-right-after-slate-tablets generation. Anyway, we brushed globs of whiteout over our spelling errors, and although it was supposed to hide our mistakes, it usually ended up looking more like a papier-mâché beacon for our eleventh-grade teachers to discover, once and for all, that we couldn't spell the word *garantee, guaruntea, guarantee.*

The second kind of whiteout is a weather system. It can happen in snow or sand, but I'm going to park the sand kind because, really, technically, that should be called a beigeout. A true white-out happens when the snow starts moving around like a cloud, either because there's so much of it or because wind, or fog, or both do some special dance with the snow that makes it move through the air. In essence, it means you can't see shit. For those of us sitting in some lodge, drinking steaming cups of hot chocolate with whipped cream, these types of whiteout are a beautiful, swirling image of winter just outside the window. "Quite a storm out there," we might say.

For those of us on a mountain, carving our second turn into a double black diamond, or, say, in our backyard, wondering where the door of our house went, a whiteout is something quite different. To be blunt, it's horrifying. All of a sudden you're like one of those characters living inside a snow globe, only you're not glued in place. So you start to feel queasy because you can't tell up from down and then, oh lord help you now, the three-year-old who is holding the snow globe starts shaking it around without any regard for the fact that you, the Mrs. Claus figurine inside, have vertigo. That's a whiteout.

It strips you of all reference points, and it makes you question where your friends went, the ones who were a pole length away just a few seconds ago. It turns terrain you said you could ski blind into a nauseating roller coaster of doubt. It makes you ask yourself if there is a possibility you didn't notice a rock face or some kind of giant gulley in the middle of Cougar Milk, a green run you have skied almost every Sunday for the past thirteen years. It makes you want to get on your hands and knees so you can confirm where the ground is, where your foundation went. You have no depth perception. It turns even the best of skiers into snowplowing toddlers who think that taking their goggles on and off a few times is going to help them see. It won't.

And of course, on the final day of my trip, perhaps as a clue it was over, the Universe plunked me smack-dab in the middle of this kind of whiteout. It was so thick I thought I was going to puke. To be honest, I'm not sure why I went up that day. I guess I wanted to make sure that the finish line really was behind me. I spent the first few runs blindly swimming, chewing through air in front of me as if it were a steak. I skied as close to the chair as I could, hoping each tower would provide a little contrast to orient me.

After a few runs, I decided to stop for a coffee.

Maybe the weather will shift.

I threw my gloves on the table in front of me and took off my helmet. I unzipped my jacket and hung it on the back of a chair. I took a seat, and for a moment I felt like I was on a plane, looking out the window as we soared through a thick bank of clouds. How is it possible to move so fluidly through something that looks so dense?

I looked around me, and other than a few staff members scattered around the lodge, it was empty. I looked at the huge stacks of forest-green food trays. Empty. I looked at the display cases, the ones typically stocked with banana bread and hearty-looking granola bars. Empty. I looked out the window in search of the mountains. A thick white mass stared back at me. My head fell into my hands.

"I'm done," I said. "It's over."

One hundred sixty-one days, and 4,161,823 vertical feet.

I stood up, put my jacket on, and slowly zipped it up.

Ten months. Five continents. Forty-five mountains.

I pulled my helmet over my head and clipped the chin strap closed.

Sixty-five beds, if you could call all of them beds.

I slid my hands into each of my gloves and walked down the stairs.

One pair of Tecnica boots.

I pushed the door open, and I walked out of the lodge. I looked at my skis, sitting lonely where I'd left them on the rack.

Four pairs of skis. Three and a half, if you're being technical about what happened in Japan.

I grabbed each ski, and one by one, I tossed them onto the snow.

They made a slapping noise as they landed. I grabbed my poles, the second pair of the trip, and wriggled each hand through the wrist straps.

I pushed my right boot down into its binding. All good. I pushed my left foot down, and I cringed.

Nine healers, including massage therapists, gong healers, chiropractors, and physios.

I took a deep breath, kicked the snow off the tops of my skis, and then finally, I skied off the mountain.

Well, I didn't really ski off the mountain. What happened was, the mountains picked me up and held me in their arms. Because you don't cross that kind of threshold on your own; you don't move through something that dense by yourself.

No, dear one, said the voice in my head, the one I'd realized had been mine all along. *No, my love, you'll be carried through that. You'll be carried right through to the end.*

The weather was still thick in the valley, and I couldn't see a thing past my very own hand. Perhaps that's all I needed to see. Perhaps that's what this whole trip was about—seeing myself, recognizing my very own hand as it fumbles around in the fog, searching calmly for the next door to open and then the door after that.

Looking back, I see just how perfect this ending was. Unable to see the past, not really sure about the future.

It was as if the mountains were reminding me that life itself was a whiteout. That the place we get lost is the very place that we're found, and all we need to do is put one foot in front of the other. Or, if you're so inclined, 4,161,823 of them.

POSTSCRIPT

An infallible method of conciliating a tiger is to allow oneself to be devoured.

—KONRAD ADENAUER

EPILOGUE: Rocky Mountain High

THERE ARE a lot of options when it comes to skiing in the mountains. The most obvious is resort-based skiing, which is the type I centered my trip around, but there's also cross-country skiing, park skiing, heli-skiing, cat-skiing, backcountry skiing, and more. This final story, coming almost five years after my trip concluded, takes us out of the world of resort-based skiing and into backcountry skiing.

There's a big difference between the two. Skiing at a resort involves things like lifts, runs that are groomed, and a ski patrol team that keeps you safe as you zigzag your way down the mountains. Additionally, resorts have washrooms, warming huts with large stone fireplaces, and restaurants that serve things like gourmet hamburgers, chocolate fondue, and dark frothy beer pulled fresh from the tap of your choice. Resort skiing is bliss, hideously expensive bliss.

Backcountry skiing is also bliss, but a markedly different kind. For starters, there are no lifts. It's sweat equity and topographical maps. It's skinning[1] uphill. It's sleeping in cramped, bare-bone huts

---

1   Skinning is a method of skiing whereby the skier attaches climbing skins

that smell of socks and damp merino wool. It's pockets full of granola and peeing in the snow. It's rugged, wild, and more physical than Olivia Newton-John could have dreamed. It's gladiator-style skiing, a Viking expedition on planks, and more than anything, it's cheap, thigh-grinding bliss.

In March 2016 I ventured out for my biggest backcountry adventure to date. The trip would have been considered a fairly simple outing for big-mountain pros and backcountry buffs, but for a gal used to racking vertical at ski resorts, this was a pretty big deal.

The trip was a multiday adventure in the Absarokas, a mountain range that runs from Montana through the northeast corner of Yellowstone National Park before crumpling to a close in northern Wyoming. We (being myself and a group of military vets) were set to ski to a hut located just above Cooke City, Montana, our base camp for five days and four nights as we explored the surrounding mountains. The trip was an initiative set up by the Sierra Club in an effort to get military veterans outdoors and more connected to the land they had fought so hard to protect. The goal was also to encourage more interaction between civilians and vets, and a handful of civilians, including myself, had been invited on the trip to share our love of the outdoors with the group.

I pounced on the opportunity as soon as it came my way, and because I was a little out of practice, I immediately stepped up my game on the fitness front to prepare. To be clear, what I mean when I say "stepped up my game" is that I moved from the occasional slow jog to slow jogging with a handful of squats thrown in.

About ten minutes into our first skin, I was struck with the fact that my handful of squats had not been enough to cover the required

---

to the bottom of their skis. The skin grips the snow, allowing the skier to travel uphill as opposed to sliding downhill. Nowadays, artificial skins, typically made of nylon, are used for this, but in the olden days skiers used animal skins, hence the name.

physical prep, not even close. It wasn't enough for a backcountry trip in general—five or six hours of ski touring a day. It wasn't enough for a backcountry trip at high altitude—five or six hours of touring at 10,000 feet. And it definitely wasn't enough to keep up with the group—otherwise known as a handful of ex–Navy Seals. There were two other civilians on the trip. One was a writer for *Backcountry Magazine* (in other words, the only difference between her and a pro skier was the fact that she carried a paper and pencil along with her), and the other . . . well, calling him a civilian is a joke, as he was a professional snowboarder, arguably the world's most recognized name in big-mountain riding. No biggie.

So there I was, me and my shaking quads, in the mountains for five days and four nights surrounded by a group of people so fit that I became convinced they were a rare breed of human mountain goats. Also of note? With the exception of the writer from *Backcountry*, I was the only woman on the expedition. I recognized the situation immediately. It was, to its core, the perfect trip for ramming all over the place. I felt as though I'd been handed a formal invitation, a tempting request that would require me to don my woolly cape and reprise the role I knew so well. I was the record breaker, right? I was the girl who had skied around the world, correct? The ram was being summoned.

Don't do it, I thought before I got on my flight.

This was more tempting than you might imagine. The months and years after my trip were some of the darkest of my life. Upon finishing, I struggled daily to find a way to bring my whole self to the table in "the real world." It's one thing to see and begin to understand the truth about yourself while on a year-long blitz around the world, but it's another thing entirely to actually live and breathe it. I knew this trip to Montana was an opportunity to stand tall within this truth, but I also knew there was a chance it could unravel everything I'd worked so hard to weave together.

Don't do it, I thought again as I stood in the parking lot that first day.

The group was standing in a small circle, making casual introductions to one another. I noticed an extraordinary amount of facial hair and waterproof fabric, the well-worn kind.

I took in the mountains behind us, the rugged, snaggletoothed chain-saw mountains, and I wondered what it was going to take to get to the top. I wondered what would be required on the second lap, and the third, and the ones that came after that. I wasn't convinced I could trust myself here, with these people, in this place.

We spent five days skinning up and skiing down every side of those mountains. And before we took off each morning, I took a few moments and stood on the small deck that had been built off the front of the hut. I watched my breath float through the air and I looked up at the mountains in holy communion, coffee in one hand and a sprinkling of faith in the other.

As it turns out, a sprinkling was all I needed.

In the early afternoon of the third day one of the guides, a guy named Wolfie on account of how much he looked like Teen Wolf, the Michael J. Fox version, asked if we wanted to go up for another lap. In true Viking style, most of the men simply grunted. They nodded their heads, and as they did, I noticed small clumps of snow flying from their beards, scattering in every direction. And then, as if in slow motion, they turned to me. They were looking for consensus. They wanted to know if I was going to man up.

"You guys go on without me," I said. I pointed to a patch of snow that was tucked behind a group of pine trees. "I'll wait over there."

"Are you sure?" one of them asked.

"Aw, come on," another goaded.

"Yep, I'm good," I said. "I've had a great day, and I want to quit while I'm ahead."

I clicked out of my skis, walked over to the patch of snow, and used my boots to stamp out a small platform. I sat down and watched as the group transitioned into their uphill gear. I noticed that a smile had spread across my face. They began their ascent, and as they did, I pulled a handful of gummy bears out of my pocket. I've never tasted gummy bears as delicious as the ones I ate that day, watching a group of people charge up the hill as I sat at the bottom, completely content, filled to the brim with happiness and a fresh hit of high-fructose corn syrup.

On the last night in the hut, I looked around the table, deep into the eyes of the weary men around me.

"I want to thank you," I said. "You've given me the ending to my story. I've spent a lot of time in the mountains trying to prove myself, trying to be someone or something I'm not, but this trip was different. I saw the mountains in a way I've never seen them before, and I want to thank you for sharing that with me."

The men grunted and nodded, and a few of them smiled.

∴

I GOT BACK TO Bozeman late the next day, and as soon as I arrived, I grabbed my phone.

He barely had a chance to answer before I was gushing.

"I had such a good time," I said quickly. "And I'm so proud of myself. So, so proud. There was no competition. No manning up. No shit-talking voice in my head. I was just me, and the mountains were different than before. It was calmer and more peaceful. I was so full of joy and ohmygodthemountainswerebeautiful . . . and my sleeping bag! My new sleeping bag was awesome."

"That sounds amazing, Bird," he replied. "I can't wait to hear more about it. My plane lands at nine, so I should be at the hotel around ten."

Our wedding anniversary wasn't for a couple of months, but Chris and I had planned an early celebration, a little getaway to mark four years together—just a couple of tigers wandering around in the mountains.

A Note about *Guinness*

IN APRIL 2011 I got an e-mail from *Guinness World Records* in regards to my application for "Most vertical feet skied in one calendar year." Their response included a list of everything required to prove I had broken the record.

The list was long.

I had to have photos, videos, and personal testaments from the various ski resorts visited. I had to have documentation about the vertical rise of lifts used, records of each run skied, as well as a handful of other pieces of evidence. While I had my daily, weekly, and monthly tallies of vertical feet skied, I had zero of the other elements Guinness was asking me for, and there was no way of gathering the required documents unless I did the trip again—and let me just tell you, there was no chance in hell.

What this means is that, regardless of my tallies and various other articles of "proof," I will never be considered the official record-breaker or -holder. The most unfortunate part about this is that my hopes and dreams of having my photo appear next to that of the Man with the Longest Fingernails are totally dashed.

On a positive note, I was contacted by a gentleman named Pierre Marc Jette in the fall of 2014. He reached out on Facebook and asked if I was "the girl who had broken the record." I told him yes, but, and explained the story. He went on to tell me he was thinking about going for the record that season.

I gave Pierre three pieces of advice, and they were (in no particular order):

1. Contact Guinness in advance.
2. To hell with records . . . ours or whoever's. The thing is, just doing it is what counts. Which, by the way, is exactly what Arnie Wilson told me.
3. *Allez, allez, allez, mon ami* (if you couldn't tell by his name, Pierre is French Canadian). I'll be cheering you on the whole time.

Pierre skied 6,060,000 vertical feet from November 2014 to May 2015. Pierre is a beast.

Acknowledgments

It takes a fucking village, a big one.

To Helen Chang at Author Bridge Media, who painted a picture of what this book could become. And to Jeraldene Lovell-Cole, who convinced me I wouldn't be doing it alone. To Danielle LaPorte and Linda Sivertsen for creating The Beautiful Writers Group. I cannonballed into that community with gusto and it changed my life. Linda . . . my dear sweet Linda, you turned closet doors into a magical portal, an entrance into literary Narnia. I am grateful for everything you've done for me, and I am grateful for everything you've done for so many women like me.

To the members of The Beautiful Writers Group past and present, you're the best cheerleaders a girl could ever ask for. Deep thanks to all of you, especially my Wolf Pack, Patti M. Hall and Carly Butler. You two poured your hearts into this book. You bore witness to a very shitty first draft and helped me through a truly mediocre second effort, making each version better than the last.

To Sandra O'Donnell, whom I met in the fall of 2014. We had coffee, I confessed that I knew nothing about anything, and she saved me. "Honey, sweetie, sugar," she said before grabbing my hand and telling me everything I needed to know. Sandra, you practically pulled doors right off their hinges on my behalf. Fuck me runnin' if I ever meet a champion as fierce and loyal as you.

To Sarah Hannah Woods, who I can only describe as an angel in human form . . . who is also hilarious. Sarah, I adore you. To Lauren Marie Fleming, who lent me an altar to kneel at. To Laura Rothschild, who has had my back from the get-go. To Amanda Thrower, whose deep love of Markhor rams and original art blows my mind. And to the one and only Janet Bertolus. I can't even. I literally cannot. The second you flew into my life on top of that broomstick, I knew we were sisters. Like actual, no-joke sisters from some past life, a pair of muse-channeling writing freaks who drink wine, and laugh, and dance with angels and fairies before turning into mist so they can eat Whoppers and Fritos by the pocketful. Oh wait, that's pretty much our life right now. Janet, I am eternally grateful, and I mean that in a cosmic sense—my appreciation for you will go on forever and ever, long past our slippery deaths. Also, I adore your husband, and although he has ruined steak for me, the fact that he allows me to take over your entire home for weeks at a time makes up for it. See you at the compound. #banetjertolus

To Ann Bosler, whose shoulder I have leaned on every single week for close to two years. To my clients, who have stood by me as I disappeared into the woods for weeks and sometimes months at a time, your support has meant the world to me. To Britt Chalmers and all of the staff at Middle Beach Lodge, who put up with the crazy lady in Room 35 for that month back in 2015, and to Jim Jameson (and the Jameson family), who allowed me to raid their white wine drawer and abuse their washing machine for that same month.

To all of my friends and all of my family—the people who have been cheering from the sidelines, as well as those who have come with me deep in the trenches. Thank you. Special thanks to my mother-in-law, who practically raised my puppy for me while I was swimming in a sea of words. And to my sister-in-law, Joanna, who sat through several days of me reading this book aloud. Your advice about what to leave in and what to take out was perfection. You've done this for me in writing and in life and I am indebted . . . it's kind of like I owe you a trip to Tofino or something.

To my high school English teachers, Patti Buchanan and Ms. Epp, who told me I had a strong voice, one that should be used. And to Nessa van Bergen, who was probably the first feminist to arrive at the scene. Ness, you taught me how to stir pots, take charge, and speak the hell up. You urged me to continue putting pen to paper, and your support (that has come in so many shapes and sizes over the last eighteen years) makes me want to throw my hands in the air and chant "I'm not worthy" à la Wayne and Garth. But I won't do that because I am worthy—we all are. You taught me that.

To my dearest Sefi, ten years in and you're still my one and only wizard. Thanks is not enough when it comes to you. Every time I've been fumbling in the dark, searching for a new route, a new way—boom, there you are. You've provided safe havens for me all over the world, and having you in my life makes me feel like I can breathe a sigh of relief, like everything's going to be okay when it's all said and done. That if we let it, life can be *shibumi*. And to all of the others who were a part of my trip: Ricardo, Pete Citrano, Veronika the Guanaca, Dave Gomez Johnson and everyone from Casa Tours, Theresa Clinton, Eve Hoter, Josh Comrie, his wife, Jodi, and their very clean carpets, Alix Rice, Whitney Stanford, Quentin Nolan and the whole gang at Liquid Tours, John Bunty Heraty, James McNeill, Kristin Gynnild and the staff at Principe delle Nevi, Pete Leathley, Helen Masding, Claire Thompson, Mike Smith, Joe Gaudet, and many more—you helped me sew the fabric of this story. Hell, you *are* the fabric of this story.

To my agent, Laura Yorke. You had me at hello. You are a literary mystic, and I adore you. I will never forget your generosity, how you and Harry opened your home to me, how you poured me champagne, how you stood by me over the last two years, and how you shot dart after dart into every single myth I've heard about the literary world being full of jaded people. And to my team at Harper Wave and HarperCollins. When I said the word *vagina* (with what some might call too much conviction) during our first meeting, not one of you flinched. Not one. Y'all just nodded and said, "Mm-hmm," like we were in the middle of a sermon, praisin' the Lord. I knew right then that you were my people. Karen, thank you for knowing that the world needs more stories about women who aren't broken. And Sarah J. Murphy, my Smurphasaurus Rex, thank you for helping me write one. You have made me a better writer and a better person, and you convinced me I could do finish lines with grace. More, please. I miss you already. To Hannah Robinson, I adore you. And to Jim Gifford for your deep voice and steady approach.

To my love . . . you saw the light of this book before I did, and you held on to it longer and more tightly than I ever could. The words on these pages would not be here if it weren't for you. I adore you, and on a side, I would marry you again tomorrow.

And last, to the whispers and callings, to spirit and muse: Papa, Sylvia, the Chief, White Buffalo Calf Woman, and to all of the others who helped along the way, including my beloved Ramsey—I didn't do this alone, and I know it. My little ego and I are sitting here in awe of what you've done, of what we've done together. I'm down on my knees. I'm yours. And I'm ready for more.

About the Author

STEPH JAGGER splits her time between Southern California and British Columbia, where she dreams big dreams, writes her heart out, and runs an executive and life-coaching practice. She holds a CEC (Certified Executive Coach) degree from Royal Roads University, and she believes courageous living doesn't happen with one toe dipping, but when we jump in, fully submerge, and sit in the juice. Think pickle, not cucumber. You can find her at www.stephjagger.com or on Instagram @stephjagger.